D1265587

SUN SIGNS AND HOROSCOPES

TERI KING

LONGMEADOW PRESS

CONTENTS

INTRODUCTION

Do you know what you want in life? Perhaps you dream of becoming a tycoon, a memorable lover or a great artist – or perhaps your ambitions are closer to home and you aspire to being a perfect provider for your family and a devoted parent. Whether you know what you want or not, there is a wealth of guidance here for you.

You will find that there is a pattern to the qualities you have – both the ones that make you attractive to others and the ones that tend to alienate them. What you discover may be a little painful, but finding out all there is to know about yourself is the first step to making the most of the abilities and opportunities you have.

In these pages you will learn a great deal about yourself – and also about your friends, relations and acquaintances. The sometimes perplexing ways in which others behave will start to make more sense. The outlines of well-known personalities that we give throw light on the qualities given by the Sun signs.

Here too is guidance for some of the everyday decisions you face – and for some of the more significant ones too – from what colour to wear and where to go on holiday to which partner to choose and what kind of work to look for.

What you will find in this book will help you to make the most of life and to face it hereafter with increased confidence and zest.

Teri King

ARIES

21 MARCH – 19 APRIL

OTHER signs strive to understand life, to explain it, experience and conserve it. But not the Ram. You are in this world for one reason and one reason only and that is – Adventure. You thrust into life and revel in new beginnings: most people born under this sign know little about constraints: throughout their lives, Aries subjects have to fight to overcome rashness, impulse and selfishness. At the same time, there is a certain resentment as to why you shouldn't be free to be yourself.

Other signs have built-in reserve inhibitions and because of this often they find it difficult to appreciate the Aries drive. You want what you want when you want it and that is always now. You have a hard time behaving yourself – like a child you grab at what or who you want and don't see any reason why you shouldn't. Regrettably this side to your character needs to be controlled so that you can exist alongside other people. However, at least Mother Nature has given you a good mind and it will help you to discriminate and mature up to a point.

Although it is true that you can be a little grabby, when you get what you want you are most likely to give it away. You are certainly not a saver or a miser.

Unlike other signs, you do not need a fan club or a following. It is enough for you to have the limelight and to be out there in front where everything is going on. If other people wish to follow you, you are quite happy: you will enjoy their company and they may be valuable in helping to clear up the mess and unfinished chores that you tend to leave behind you. Although you have plenty of energy, it comes in fits and starts. Endurance is not your strong point and sustained effort tends to exhaust you. You like to rush up to a challenge, fight with it and get it over and done with quickly. While the struggle is on you can show amazing strength and determination.

PERSO

FEMALE

Saint

- You are like a rocket on firework night: your wonderful energy hypnotizes and dazzles people. You are extremely enthusiastic, extroverted and the kind of person to whom other people cannot help but gravitate.

- You are a creative spark, you make things begin and get everyone around enthusiastic. Your courage and nerve take you everywhere, and those who know you well accept this. Of course it also helps that you are loaded with charisma.

- You need to have a cause in life and are often the spokeswoman in some area. You are honest, passionate, and filled with great personal power.

- You have a do-it-yourself attitude and what you can do is often more than a multitude of people put together.

- You are a leader and could end up doing anything from producing and directing a successful film to becoming a Nobel Peace Prize-winner. Once you get an idea there is no stopping you. You are so highly motivated that even if someone locked you up in a cupboard, you would discover a way of getting the job done.

- Chances are, you talk about your work over dinner, breakfast and even in bed. You will never allow yourself a moment when you can be just a woman with a woman's body and a woman's feelings. Instead, to keep yourself secure you strive to cultivate a successful image. The hardest lesson you will have to learn in this life is that not everybody wants to listen to you. Try to avoid crowding others with your career matters. The less self-conscious you become the more you will learn how to enjoy yourself. Be yourself, and forget the status symbols with which you identify too much. Remember that before you can become a public figure you first have to be a person.

Sinner

- You are like a storm in the night: you are pushy and impatient, oversensitive and arrogant. You are interested in a subject only if it relates to you. Otherwise, you rudely interrupt and let everyone know that you don't want to listen.

- You are also a fighter who doesn't understand defeat. That is mostly because you have a way of draining those around you until they give in to your demands just to shut you up. Your philosophy is 'What's yours is mine, but what's mine is my own.' With this in mind there is not much that you ever miss out on.

NALITY

Male

Saint

● You have a vitality that defies logic and confounds the medic. You are the sort of man who rushes in where angels fear to tread and you possess a toughness which can be truly intimidating.

● You have the spirit of a fighter and the wisdom of an elder statesman. Power is your password and positive thinking the light along your path. Part of your success in life is due to your high intelligence; part to your hard work. When truly devoted to a job, you are both inexhaustible and highly inspired.

● Defeat is something that has never been a consideration and certainly never a reality. Whether it is a woman, worldly success or the power to be free to try something new, you get it. You are a self-propelled person who attains the supremacy you seek and manages to keep it.

Sinner

● You are galvanized into action by self-interest, challenge and an unconscious desire to create bedlam. When you are after something you want, you are guiltless, ruthless and willing to sacrifice anything if it will help you to get ahead.

● You really want to be liked and can't understand why others dwell on the damage you do. You certainly don't.

● The lesson you need to learn in this life is to develop a sensitivity that goes beyond your own wants and needs. Often, though unintentionally, you are too self-involved. You have plenty of courage; use it to see yourself from the outside while you try to see others from the inside. If you can do this you will greatly expand yourself and your life. Stand back objectively from yourself and situations and give yourself room to look out. There is a big, wide world out there and although it was not created solely for you, certainly others want you around – however, they expect you to be a part of what is going on, not continually to insist in taking everything and everyone over. Remember, too, that other people's ideas and feelings are also valid and you will be on your way to bettering not only yourself but your life as well.

● On a personal level, you have a bubblegum attitude towards relationships: throw it away when the sweetness starts to wear off. It takes you little to no time to find someone else. Anyone who dedicates as much time as you do to his own self-satisfaction has to come out on top, regardless of his intelligence.

● ELTON JOHN BORN 25 MARCH 1947

ELTON HAS PROVED TO BE AS TOUGH AND ENDURING AS THE ARIES GEM, THE DIAMOND. HIS SHOWMANSHIP AND SPARKLE ORIGINATE FROM THE SAME STONE. ON HIS WAY TO SUCCESS HE USED GIMMICKS – INCLUDING OUTRAGEOUS GLASSES AND HEAD GEAR – THAT ACCENTUATED THE ARIES PART OF THE BODY, THE HEAD.

● BETTE DAVIS BORN ON 5 APRIL 1908

IRON IS THE ARIES METAL AND MANY ARIES WOMEN, INCLUDING BETTE DAVIS, DISPLAY AN IRON WILL. THIS IS THE SIGN OF THE WARRIOR AND FEW CAN DENY HER ABILITY TO TAKE ON THE BIG STUDIOS AND WIN THROUGH. SHE HAD AN EQUALLY FIRM GRIP ON LIFE. FINALLY IT WAS A STROKE (ARIES HEAD) WHICH OVERCAME HER.

● JOHN MAJOR BORN 28 MARCH 1943

JOHN POSSESSES OTHER INFLUENCES ON HIS CHART WHICH DIM HIS ARIES SUN. NEVERTHELESS HE DOES HAVE THE RAM'S MENTAL TENDENCY TO RUSH INTO DECISIONS WITHOUT GIVING THEM DUE THOUGHT AND CONSIDERATION, FOLLOWING WHICH IT BECOMES NECESSARY TO RE-THINK. THIS HAS LOST HIM MUCH PUBLIC CREDIBILITY.

ARIES in LIFE

AT WORK

Aries Boss Regardless of sex, when the boss is an Aries a rapid turnover in staff is inevitable, as this is the type who will arouse extreme feelings. Employees can certainly expect to earn their salaries, not because an Aries is a slave driver but because few people are fitted to withstand the pressure surrounding such a person. The mystery is how on earth Aries employers ever manage to complete a business transaction – they usually appear to be submerged in hundreds of simultaneous deals. Employees wonder whether they will be able to remember where their boss should be or what he or she should be doing – and in general the boss does not know either. Tactful reminders are needed from time to time.

The key word in dealing with the Aries boss is tact. Remember this particular boss has an ego and it needs stroking frequently.

Aries Employee The Aries is a valuable addition to any team, offering enthusiasm, zest and a head bursting with ideas. The ideal company for him or her is both fast moving and progressive, and a position held within it will need to be one where the Aries can enjoy maximum freedom of movement. Arians will probably avoid working for an organization where they believe they will be restricted or frustrated; the old established company where administration is conventional and paperwork abundant, holds no appeal for them.

Suitably placed, the Aries can ascend as dramatically as a rocket, leaving behind a trail of envious colleagues. Progress made is not always popular with others, as this type's drive inclines him or her to unscrupulous behaviour and achievements are sometimes accomplished at the expense of others. Somewhat arrogant and organizing manners do not make it easy for the Aries to win friends or influence people.

FAMILY MATTERS

ARIES MOTHER By no stretch of the imagination could you be described as 'the domesticated type'. You are hardly ever at home, to which you eventually return exhausted but happy from your multitude of interests. Motherhood does not come easy as it means the loss of your precious freedom. Furthermore, you have a tendency to become impatient with youngsters who are perhaps not as quick on the uptake as you are. Luckily you have a big warm heart and are certainly generous with your affections. You could never be described as a 'clinging mother'. From an early age you encourage your children to be independent. Others may think you somewhat harsh with your offspring, but you know that the weak have a hard time and so you encourage them to fight for what they want and not to dwell on failure or disappointment. You tend to get closer to your children as the years pass.

ARIES FATHER You like to think of your home as a place of relaxation where you can sit back, sip some wine in peace and entertain close friends or devote time to some ego-orientated project. The pitter-patter of tiny feet tends to interfere with your leisure time. Although initially you may be disgruntled by this, slowly you come to realize that perhaps there is more to life than throwing a smart dinner party. Because of your sporting tendencies you are much more likely to get on with male children, rather than female. The emotions of the fair sex tend to make you feel uncomfortable. However, once that bundle of contradictions blossoms into an attractive young female, you become fiercely protective and do your best to shield her from the harshness of the outside world.

To a son you become a friend, a tennis partner, and are an inspiration for him to be as successful as you. But bear it in mind that Aries finds parenthood difficult.

ARIES CHILD Aries children seem to attract little mishaps. If you are wise you will instil in your Aries child a healthy respect for sharp objects and fire, but you will have to resign yourself to a never-ending stream of injuries, especially to the face and the head. The young Ram displays many war-like traits. Although this can lead to physical violence, the Aries child will generally prefer to fight verbally. Conflict stimulates the Arian and arguments among friends will be the rule rather than the exception: a bloodied nose and a bruised lip can usually be traced back to a best friend, not to an enemy. Such a child is independent, original and sports-loving. He or she takes part in all school activities, the usual result of which is popularity. Loneliness in an Aries child is rare.

Nightmares are a problem to the Ram child and they can often be traced back to some sort of friction at school. It is important that you communicate and discover what is worrying them: Aries children do have a tendency to keep worries and problems to themselves. Gentle persuasion will help unlock any mental doors they may be attempting to keep shut. If you are a wise parent you will try to make them realize that they are being unreasonable on occasions and they cannot always expect to have their own way or come first. Failure to do this will leave the child to grow up into an unreasonable adult.

At play

Physically speaking you are strong, athletic and very restless and this energy needs burning off somehow. You are likely to play tennis, badminton or squash in the summer, and in the winter rugby, football or hockey.

Mentally you are fascinated by everything that is going on around you and this leads you to take part in local politics or head the nearest residents' association. Your great organizing skills are frequently called upon. Relaxation? For this particular sign, such a thing simply does not exist.

Money

When it comes to cash, you are someone who enjoys the game of making it and spending it. You are an impulsive shopper and once you are emotionally impassioned, you can say goodbye to any concept of economizing.

Some Aries collect heavy bills that bring creditors knocking at their door. When it gets really bad, they may refuse to confront the issues. You are quite likely to make paper aeroplanes from those unopened brown envelopes and send them flying swiftly into the rubbish bin.

Another sort of Aries has a strong survival instinct, pays bills on time and takes advantage of sound investments. Which type you are largely depends on the stage in life you have reached: this sign tends to be irresponsible when fancy free, but on acquiring responsibilities in the form of marriage turns towards security. However, you are not the type to derive a great deal of satisfaction from collecting possessions: you prefer to think that at any moment you could up and go if the mood struck you. This applies to everything – job, marriage, change of home, ability to take a trip. Money enables you to feel more in control. It also allows you those wonderful moments of self-indulgence.

Money in the bank is waiting to do whatever you want, and you have a way of commanding it to bring you magical moments of which you invariably make the most. You often think about collecting more possessions but this generally remains fairly theoretical. You are a pioneer who, fired up by ambition, will set out for the goldfields – but it is the excitement, the promise of further extravagances and the dangers involved that stir you, rather than lust for possessions.

Aries needs a sensible partner to apply a restraining arm when the Ram decides to go on the rampage.

It is rare to find an Aries who can resist a gamble. This may only occur occasionally, but there are some who simply cannot resist the dangers involved when it comes to putting their hard-earned cash at risk. Hopefully, there are benign influences at work on your particular birth chart which allow you to keep this side of your character well in check; otherwise you could very well become the bane of your loved one's life.

● TIMOTHY DALTON BORN 21 MARCH 1946

ALTHOUGH THIS TALENTED ACTOR IS A GOOD ALL-ROUND PERFORMER, IT IS INTERESTING THAT HE FINALLY GAINED FAME AND FORTUNE THROUGH JAMES BOND, A CHARACTER ASSOCIATED WITH GUNS AND EXPLOSIONS, BOTH THINGS RULED BY MARS THE ARIES PLANET.

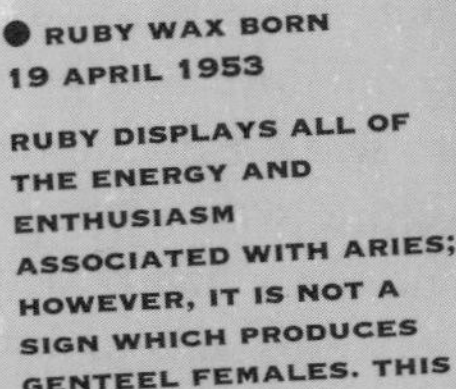

● RUBY WAX BORN 19 APRIL 1953

RUBY DISPLAYS ALL OF THE ENERGY AND ENTHUSIASM ASSOCIATED WITH ARIES; HOWEVER, IT IS NOT A SIGN WHICH PRODUCES GENTEEL FEMALES. THIS IS A GUTSY AND SOMETIMES CRUDE LADY. THOSE QUALITIES CAN BE TRACED TO THE NO-NONSENSE SIDE OF THE PLANET MARS, THE RULER OF HER SIGN.

● ANDREW LLOYD WEBBER BORN 22 MARCH 1948

ARIES DEVELOPS QUICKLY AND ANDREW WAS A CHILD PRODIGY. ALTHOUGH HE FOUND FAME IN PARTNERSHIP WITH TIM RICE, THIS SIGN DOES NOT CO-OPERATE WELL AND THEREFORE THEY SOON PARTED COMPANY. A LACK OF GIVE AND TAKE IS ALSO REFLECTED IN HIS PRIVATE LIFE; HE IS CURRENTLY ON HIS THIRD MARRIAGE.

ARIES *in* LOVE

Single

You are daring, dramatic and romantic. You are drawn to the drama of the first glance, the larger-than-life love, the smouldering flirtation. You want to be swept off your feet by a deliciously seductive bold soul who needs as much constant action as you do. You need somebody to build you up, strengthen your ego and flatter you like crazy. You also expect the opposite sex to appreciate you for your accomplishments.

You want to hear bells ring, cannons fire and be blinded by excitement. However, when you wake up and the bubbly has gone flat, then you quickly consider cutting out and finding some action elsewhere.

You are far more attracted to the superficial aspects of falling in love than you are to the commitment of 'for better or for worse'. You want a love life that is dreamy and never stagnant, with a constant array of new faces that appear on the scene to stop you admitting that, quite honestly, you are bored. You don't believe there is merely one love that proves itself to be perfection. Instead you like to live for the moment and leave yourself open for anyone exciting who may come tearing along to grab your attention. You are a highly sexual animal who strives for satisfaction of its needs and its needs are quite rapacious. You long for someone who is sexually uninhibited and as frank about their desires as you are. However, when you meet up with somebody to whom you are strongly drawn, who doesn't exactly beat a path to your door, you have not the slightest compunction in taking the initiative. This might mean grabbing their arm, knocking them down in the midst of your enthusiasm or simply staring at them relentlessly. You are not the most subtle of people. In your book, subtlety is simply a waste of time and time is of the essence.

You are the power house of the Zodiac, the giver of sexual energy. You are an action-packed dynamo, with great drive. However, in love you must learn to channel this vitality constructively and give pleasure to everyone. Sometimes you get burned, especially when you leap into love failing to be aware of the consequences. You are capable of meeting any challenge – when you have learned a bit of self-control, patience, and respect for the likes and dislikes of others. Any lover will appreciate your inventiveness, your vitality and your sunny disposition. Underneath that radiant self-confidence, however, there could be a tiny bit of insecurity. You might never admit it, but you long for a loyal, devoted mate who's going to put you first. Your ideal lover must also be a continual challenge (to earn your respect) and a safe harbour for your restless soul. Sounds impossible? Well, maybe that's why you fall in love too readily and with a resounding crash. You can expect an on-again, off-again love life, particularly in your early years.

Married

The difficulty here is that you are both freedom-loving and loving and this does not make for the most stable relationship. There is usually one special person to whom you devote your larger-than-life dramas. However, it is all those people on the side who usually pose the problems. You want to have your cheese soufflé and eat it too. Regardless of what you desire there are a lot of people who don't appreciate being shared. Occasionally you can be truly uncompromising and only for this reason do marital relationships bring problems. You need constant activity and excitement far more than you need a mate, but sometimes you take both just to try them out. Those little flirtations on the side which you need for your ego are really a constant interference with the feelings you express towards that married partner. And while, like a selfish child, you feel you must have both, the fact is that you really can't handle either. For your ideal is to have a little action in every corner. However, at a later date when the lights go out and you are left all alone, it is not exactly fun and games any more, is it? You have a strong tendency to marry late or not at all, but if you marry early you have an even stronger inclination to have affairs and to divorce.

Perfect Partners

When it comes to finding the perfect mate, the ideal is usually found amongst the other fire signs – if you are a typical Aries anyway. These are, of course, Aries, Leo and Sagittarius.

Aries with Aries This relationship holds a lot of promise, providing you can both decide that you don't have to be boss at the same time. You will woo each other with more aggressive enthusiasm than that seen during a general election. You are both passionate, energetic, full of new ideas and romantic in a flighty kind of way. Together you can stay up all night making your enthusiastic plans and hotly debating the current political situation. Between your minds there can be much sympathy, understanding and compassion, and between your bodies a tremendous amount of passion and sensuality. You will gravitate towards one another like two warships meeting during peacetime. After that the cannons just keep shooting off and so do your mouths. This relationship may be trying on the nerves, but it is certainly one to keep you fully occupied and stimulated.

Aries with Leo Aries's love of life will rejuvenate the Leo's brain cells and your passion will ignite the Lion's senses.

Together, you are the principle of passion personified, and when you sit side by side, the world seems to shrink away. When your egos are controlled, and this is important, the attraction is nothing short of alchemic. Your fights will make the neighbours blench but life will never be boring, and in your book that is very important.

Aries with Sagittarius This relationship is a definitely delightful adventure, although there will be times when Aries finds Sagittarius rather difficult to cope with. But at least the Archer is going to be a constant challenge and therefore will hold your attention far longer than most. The Sagittarian's charm is exciting and their sense of humour completely arrests your attention. This is one relationship which will never be boring. Sagittarius will present you with crazy schemes to make you laugh on some occasions and cry on others. The Ram is both charmed and challenged by the Archer. However, as both parties possess so many outside interests, it may be that they won't spend too much time together and this could be the very reason why they stay together.

ARE YOU A TYPICAL ARIES...

Answer honestly the questions below, using YES, NO or SOMETIMES; total up your score, allowing 3 for YES, 2 for SOMETIMES and 1 for NO.

...MAN?

1. Do you avoid thinking of your past?
2. Are you fussy about your clothes?
3. Do you think that greetings cards are a waste of money?
4. Do feminine moods baffle you?
5. Do you consciously try not to worry about your financial future?
6. Are orders hard for you to take?
7. Is it hard for you to delegate your work to others?
8. Do you consider yourself to be a good 'ideas man'?
9. Are you possessive?
10. Does motor racing appeal to you?
11. When your mate wants to make love after an exhausting day, do you refuse?
12. Do you often feel sadistic when making love?
13. Is it hard for you to express your thoughts when making love?
14. Do you believe that emotional men are weak men?
15. Do you get annoyed when other men stare at your mate?
16. Are the comforts of life important to you?
17. Do you enjoy the company of small children?
18. Is it hard for you to switch off business?
19. When your mate is on the phone and you don't know to whom she is speaking, does it bother you?
20. Is it difficult to accept No from a girl you really fancy?

ARE YOU A TYPICAL ARIES MAN ?

1–30 Although you may have some Aries tendencies they are certainly well hidden. I would suggest that you read some of the other signs for you will probably recognize yourself elsewhere, possibly under Cancer, Scorpio and Pisces.

31–50 This is the score of a 'saintly' Aries: you are lucky enough to have most of the virtues of this sign with few of the vices, and you can disregard the section about the 'sinner' type. You are a strong person, know exactly what you want from life and can obtain it without hurting other people, although perhaps you should focus a little more of your attention on the private side to life.

51–60 You are a true blue Aries for good and evil. It will be a good idea for you to read the section on the 'sinner' Aries several times for all your faults are written there in black and white and this may help you to recognize, accept and do something about them. Your strong 'Me first' attitude could lead eventually to loneliness.

...WOMAN?

1. Do you like expensive clothes?
2. Would you feel frustrated with a boyfriend who refused to argue?
3. Do you seem attracted to weaker men?
4. Are you impressed by extravagant presents?
5. Are you nauseated by women who have to talk to every baby they pass?
6. Do you enjoy organizing others?
7. If six friends arrived around dinner time, could you make a quick meal for them without getting flustered?
8. Do you believe a wife can advance her husband's career?
9. If you really fancied your newest boyfriend and he was a bit slow in making advances, would you drag him off to bed?
10. Do you believe that sentiment belongs to the mature?
11. Do you ring up men and ask them to take you out?
12. Are you interested in the Woman's Movement?
13. Do you feel inadequate or uncomfortable around small children?
14. Do you express your displeasure when physically frustrated?
15. Do you cherish old loves and mementoes?
16. For the majority of the time are you quickly aroused in a lengthy relationship?
17. Does the thought of a good steady job for security's sake depress you?
18. Is it difficult for you to express inner emotions?
19. Are you an aggressive lover?
20. Does the romantic approach amuse you?

ARE YOU A TYPICAL ARIES WOMAN ?

1–30 Your Aries characteristics are so well hidden they are almost non-existent. Look for yourself under a different sign, possibly one of the air signs – Gemini, Aquarius or Libra.

31–50 This is the score of a typical Aries. You are lucky because you have most of the good points connected with this sign and few of the bad. However, a selfish streak should be overcome as this will help to take the tension out of relationships.

51–60 For better or for worse you are a typical Aries. Pay attention to the section called the 'sinner' Aries as it is written especially for you. If you can learn to control these traits you will be a much more popular girl, but bossy and organizing behaviour will spoil many of your relationships.

LUCKY

	HOW LUCKY ARE YOU?	FOOTBALL POOLS	HORSES AND DOGS	OTHER FORMS OF GAMBLING
ARIES	The Ram is always ready to take a chance, although other people just think you are naturally lucky. You recover quickly from bad luck.	Keep to your usual pattern with the treble chance. New systems could be disappointing.	Stick to favourites for steady returns. The Grand National could be your lucky race.	You could have a big run of luck, so don't give up once you have picked a winning streak.
TAURUS	You prefer to minimize the risk and go for long-term investments, although occasionally you are a bit slow in snapping up opportunities.	Lucky numbers linked with family birthdays could work magic for you.	Stick to your favourite jockey, especially on big races and when he or she is on an outsider.	An occasional visit to the roulette table could swell the coffers.
GEMINI	You love to put money at risk, but you must keep within your means. You will always be lucky as long as you are not expecting too much.	Concentrate on symmetrical patterns, especially for games two and three.	Names always take your fancy. Any name linked with writing, travelling or teaching.	A fruit machine, especially when you are in unfamiliar places.
CANCER	You gamble for sentimental reasons, rarely sticking to a system. Try not to be too superstitious; it is your bugbear.	A system may suddenly pay off, but remember – it is sensible only to a degree.	Outsiders will be successful. Follow them.	Competitions could be lucky for you, particularly around your birthday month.
LEO	You love to win and generally do, but there is a tendency to gamble too much. Don't take speculations too seriously.	You will spot some lucky similarities to a previous season.	Second favourites and favourites will bring you in the best results.	You win at afternoon gambling which could be more profitable than the nightlife type.
VIRGO	You only take well-thought-out risks. You may think yourself unlucky but in fact your chances are fairly good.	An individually designed perm is likely to bring many gains.	Stick to form or follow a horse or dog in which you have a particular interest.	Give competitions in magazines or newspapers a whirl.
LIBRA	You like to spread your speculations over a wide front, so you may not win a big amount, just lots of little ones.	It is possible that changing your pools company could bring you a run of luck.	Lucky colours may be pink, blue and cream. A classic filly race could be lucky.	Take care not to become addicted to a harmless form of gambling.
SCORPIO	To you gambling is a battle to be fought and won. Once you have found a lucky streak, you will stick with it.	You may do better with results than with draws.	Pay particular attention to handicap races and trust a winning jockey.	You could do well betting on something outside sports.
SAGITTARIUS	You love to take risks and prefer lots of small bets. Yours is the luckiest sign of the Zodiac, but keep this to yourself.	Your own instincts are safer than the experts'. You often notice patterns and past form that they miss.	Antipost betting is likely to be more profitable than on-course punting.	You like cards, particularly bridge and poker. This could bring you steady gains over a long period.
CAPRICORN	You only gamble with small money. You are not the type to pop the family silver, or use your nest egg. Stay that way.	You must keep an optimistic frame of mind. Don't give up.	You are likely to be luckier with flat racing than over the jumps. Inside tips will help on dogs.	You constantly try to find a special system for roulette, but this invariably lets you down.
AQUARIUS	You approach gambling in a logical way – until you get that special feeling. You are probably luckier than you believe.	If anything, a system is likely to be ruinous. You would be better sticking in a pin.	Your luck is likely to increase if you follow a particular trainer.	Bet on tennis, cricket or even darts.
PISCES	You are always too willing to take other people's gambling suggestions when really you should be trusting to your own judgement and intuition.	Not your lucky area. All right though if you regard it as a bit of fun.	Sweepstakes could help to swell the family coffers, given the chance.	Premium bonds could provide you with a tidy little sum at some point.

YOU...

INVESTMENTS	COLLECTOR'S CORNER	LUCKY PERIODS	LUCKY COLOUR	
You generally get the best ideas from contacts.	Model soldiers, military medals and antique toys are fields where you can do well.	During the spring but also September.	Red.	ARIES
Stamp collecting and anything connected with property is usually lucky for you.	Glass, cutlery and porcelain. You are a great bargain hunter.	April to August are your best times, and then November and December.	Pink.	TAURUS
Gilt edge shares are a sensible investment and keep an eye on foreign stock.	You are good at picking up the unusual at car boot sales and auctions.	September and October, thanks to your opportunist streak.	Yellow.	GEMINI
Shares that have been depressed will start to show a healthy rise.	You could sell a family heirloom for more money than you expected.	Spring and mid-autumn are your lucky times, but quit while you are ahead.	All shades of purple.	CANCER
Move investments from one unit trust to another; it could be worth-while.	Old books and maps interest you and you might make a healthy profit.	August is a favourable time. You are frequently lucky when travelling.	Orange.	LEO
Shares in mineral companies and electrical firms.	Old machinery and gadgets fascinate you and could be profitable.	Late in the year is the best time. Expect a steady rise in fortunes.	Navy blue.	VIRGO
Part of your stockpile of cash could be positively shifted to equities.	Paintings, especially of the Victorian period, are good for you.	January, February and your birthday month.	Pale blue.	LIBRA
Take advice from an experienced person. They will put you on the right track.	Cigarette cards and military medals. Avoid selling family heirlooms.	Mid-April and mid-May. Also around your birthday.	Burgundy.	SCORPIO
Foreign investments are likely to be better than those at home.	Rare books, coins, movie memorabilia.	The Aries, Leo and Sagittarius parts of the year.	Turquoise.	SAGITTARIUS
You will do well by putting your money in a bright new firm that will soon go public.	Family jewellery which perhaps needs valuing. First editions. Important love letters.	Spring looks good, but October and December will be luckier.	Dark green.	CAPRICORN
Avoid taking the advice of friends before parting with hard-earned cash. Trust your own instincts.	Old surgical instruments. Books, sculptures and etchings are all good for you.	Spring, midsummer and November.	Electric blue.	AQUARIUS
Look at government saving schemes. Utilities.	Memorabilia from the pop and film world. Old maps and strange items with no practical use.	March, October and any Saturday could be lucky.	Sea green.	PISCES

TAURUS

20 APRIL – 20 MAY

THE Taurus period is the time when Mother Nature is reawakening. Taurus grabs the seeds of life in a firm, practical fist, gives them the chance to live and eventually reaps the rewards.

Taurus is certainly the warmest of the three air signs. Everything about the Bull is practical, although at the same time you are at one with nature and the Earth. The ruler of your sign is Venus, the planet of harmony, beauty and love. Even if a Bull doesn't actually work in the arts there is certainly likely to be some kind of creative hobby. At the same time you have a thirst for elegance, and are particularly susceptible to your surroundings. Not surprisingly then, you love to get away from towns and into the country; when this isn't possible, you are quite happy strolling in local parks and commons. This kind of gentle change of scene is what you need, you hate disruptive changes.

In truth, you don't really enjoy any change that means shifting your possessions or creates any kind of upheaval. Even when it is necessary to move into a better home or job, you are unsettled and nervous and it takes you quite a time to adapt. This isn't difficult to understand; your nature is based on the need for security. You want to be left to your own devices, to build your own world and – it has to be said – you are fairly materialistic. Security to you means possessions – objects you can touch, mortgage or sell if the need arises. You work hard for what you want; your endurance, determination and patience are quite astounding. When others have fallen by the wayside, you persevere. Even if your whole life pattern was suddenly destroyed, you would collect all the pieces and battle on.

You are sometimes emotionally rash, which may sound odd after describing you as methodical and conservative. Adaptability is something you need to work at.

PERSO

FEMALE

Saint

● You know how to get the most out of life: you encourage conditions which allow others to develop and flourish.

● Emotionally, you are more sensitive than you seem.Your reluctance to reveal your deep emotions can get in the way of your receiving the kind of attention you need.

● There are moments when your strength undermines you and to avoid the possibility of rejection you try to avoid recognizing your own needs. At this point, you play at being aloof and non-caring. You find it easier to walk away in intense pain, with overriding tact, rather than confront the fact that the hurt is killing you.

● You have a horror of being hurt which ties in with a deep-seated security need. Being abandoned by someone you trusted makes you believe you have lost everything: you feel as though the Earth were crumbling beneath your feet. One way to avoid this is to let other people know what you are feeling in the present and what you expect in the future.

● Those closest to you depend on you for your stability, stamina and your abilities in the face of problems. You are respected for your inclination to remain unruffled, regardless of the severity of any difficulty or storm, but at the same time you are very feminine with a quiet earthy kind of charm – a real earth mother in fact. You are a female of substance, who assesses the value of all experience. You see your relationships as durable investments that will bring you many rewards years into the future. You have a calm, determined approach to life and it gives you a great deal of control that many of your Zodiac sisters lack.

Sinner

● You are dogmatic and a faithful perpetuator of the status quo. You are not the type ever to shout 'Stop the world!' because it is unlikely that you are aware that it is even moving in the first place.

● You can be such a slave to your appetites that at times your body may resemble a Big Mac. You are probably one of the few people in the world who could consume a cold fried egg even when the fat has begun to congeal.

● You are about as emotionally sensitive as a traffic warden in the middle of the rush hour and as flexible as a slab of concrete. When it comes to love, your attitude is 'Take good care of yourself, you belong to me.' You are so possessive that you can be de-personalizing and often treat your mate as if he were your mattress.

NALITY

● If pushed past a certain point your anger has no limits. You bear a grudge past several human lifetimes and would never even think about giving anyone the benefit of the doubt.

MALE

Saint

● You are a cuddly toy with the traits of the chairman of the board. You know how to make cash – and having made it you know how to keep it.

● You are sincere, steadfast and strong, and practical in your approach to everything. You are stable and always examine the foundation of experience.

● You gain considerably from a deeply committed love relationship which is warm and secure. In love you tend to be romantic, but you are not one to hover in the clouds – you like to stay close to *terra firma*.

● You tend to see the world in black and white, and that is an attribute that can be very useful in business matters. Because your ideas are so well grounded, they easily take form in a practical fashion.

● Your talent with finance usually surpasses that of most professionals in the economic mainstream.

● Once you commit yourself to any situation, you tend to be persevering and determined. In moments of crisis you stand your ground solidly whilst your emotions remain unruffled. You utilize your talents in a steady solid way and in doing so have the kind of stamina that defies logic.

Sinner

● If you stand too long in one place you could start to take root. You suffer seriously from tunnel vision to the extent that you would miss a volcano erupting on either side of you.

● Your nature is earthy in the extreme and at times you have the charm of a caged gorilla. Your manners sometimes indicate that you belong in a zoo – you have been known to slurp soup conspicuously. You also have no reservations about tucking into a meal with both hands. Your love of food is obvious; you sometimes wear it on your tie and fingernails.

● Your body is likely to be beefy and your neck like a tree trunk.

● Money-wise you can be both greedy and selfish and you wouldn't lend your best friend the money for a bus fare.

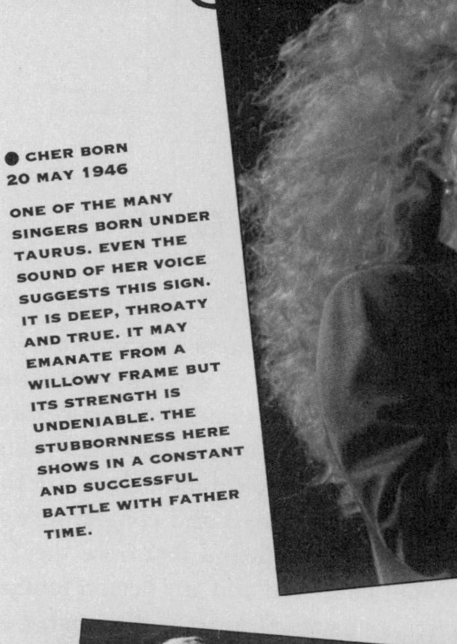

● CHER BORN 20 MAY 1946

ONE OF THE MANY SINGERS BORN UNDER TAURUS. EVEN THE SOUND OF HER VOICE SUGGESTS THIS SIGN. IT IS DEEP, THROATY AND TRUE. IT MAY EMANATE FROM A WILLOWY FRAME BUT ITS STRENGTH IS UNDENIABLE. THE STUBBORNNESS HERE SHOWS IN A CONSTANT AND SUCCESSFUL BATTLE WITH FATHER TIME.

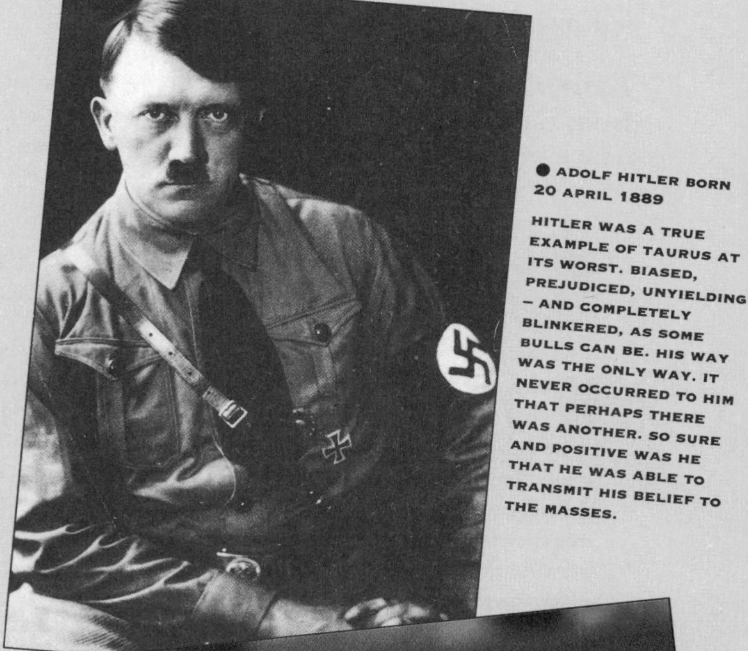

● ADOLF HITLER BORN 20 APRIL 1889

HITLER WAS A TRUE EXAMPLE OF TAURUS AT ITS WORST. BIASED, PREJUDICED, UNYIELDING – AND COMPLETELY BLINKERED, AS SOME BULLS CAN BE. HIS WAY WAS THE ONLY WAY. IT NEVER OCCURRED TO HIM THAT PERHAPS THERE WAS ANOTHER. SO SURE AND POSITIVE WAS HE THAT HE WAS ABLE TO TRANSMIT HIS BELIEF TO THE MASSES.

● GABRIELA SABATINI BORN 16 MAY 1970

GABRIELA'S STRENGTH, BOTH PHYSICAL AND MENTAL, CAN BE TRACED TO HER TAUREAN DETERMINATION TO BE THE BEST AND WIN. HER BULL-LIKE ENDURANCE HELPS HER TO WEAR DOWN HER OPPONENT AND HAS YET TO BE SEEN TO DESERT HER. A VENUS RULER AIDS HER TO RETAIN HER FEMININITY DESPITE THIS.

TAURUS in LIFE

AT WORK

Taurus Boss Taurus bosses are immediately either liked or disliked by those who work for them and any employee lasting more than six months is likely to stay for a good many years. They are averse to new things and should a respected member of staff try to leave them, they will do everything in their power to change the employee's mind. There are those who will find the Taurus stubbornness and conservative tendencies hard to take; they will soon find that once the Taurean's mind is set it cannot be moved and any person foolhardy enough to try and force a change of heart will probably soon be joining the ranks of the unemployed.

Taurus Employee As a rule young Taureans will decide early in life what their objectives are to be, and they are unlikely to drift for any length of time. Freelance work does not attract this type: the uncertainty of such a way of living would not appeal. Neither are they particularly suited for teamwork: the adaptability needed to work alongside others remains elusive to the Bull.

Ideally Bulls are at their best when doing their own thing with minimum interference and within the safety of an established company. Here their talent for order, method and routine can be self-generated and they are shown to their best advantage in such situations.

AT PLAY

Talented or not, most Taureans have an artistic streak. Many born under this sign struggle to cultivate a good singing voice; others repeatedly try to master the intricacies of a musical instrument.

Artistic flair is shown in the kitchen too – these are the

FAMILY MATTERS

TAURUS MOTHER As a parent you are protective, cherishing and nurturing. In this area of life you are almost unbeatable. The children instinctively know that you will always be 'there' for them, no matter what, and because of this they make allowances for the occasional burst of stubbornness. Your offspring are bound to be well fed and you may have to guard against turning them into fatties. You show your love freely and openly and you won't feel compelled to stuff your children full of goodies in order to compensate for what they are not receiving emotionally. Your ability to create a secure nest may mean that children will think twice before rushing into an early marriage.

Your home is your refuge from the world. You probably spend weekends building bookcases or cooking treats for the family. Your home is private turf, where you like to play and relax; that's why you prefer friends and relatives to telephone before they arrive – when they don't you can get a little frosty around the edges. Wherever you live, your surroundings evoke a lust for life and when you do have guests, the minute they walk in the door they are treated as though they were rescued from a storm. Your nurturing is more than welcoming – it's habit-forming. Mind you, when you decide that it is time they left, you may initially throw out some subtle hints, but if these are ignored then you can be quite blunt.

TAURUS FATHER The family is your bastion against the world. You are naturally domesticated and delight in creating a home with the most comfortable atmosphere. You are happy to spend your spare time making construction kits with your children, teaching your daughter to cook and allowing everyone to enjoy your culinary delights. Young children are a sheer delight to you and it is for them that you go out into the big wide world in order to do battle because you could not bear to think of your offspring going without. The children know that they can depend on you in a crisis and this makes them feel extremely secure. However, you very often find it difficult when your daughter starts dating. You are so fiercely protective that you will pick holes in anybody who shows even the slightest bit of attention. You will need to try hard to open up your mind to her various admirers, otherwise those strong opinions of yours could lead you to losing her.

TAURUS CHILD If the parents of a Taurus child are social butterflies they may be disappointed by their offspring for this type is selective and does not attempt to hide his or her disgust for people who do not come up to scratch. The young Taurean is a reserved and conservative individual, who is easily embarrassed and thinks twice before romping around the floor. Parties can be a real trial and the wise parent won't insist that the Taurus child should go or demand that he or she have fun.

If you feel you must coax your child out of a shell, then it would be a good idea to take both your child and a close friend to the party or gathering. This way, at least, there will be someone around to talk to. In fact, one close friend is all the Taurean child may have or desire to have, and parents will have to be able to provide a big shoulder when this special friendship is going through a negative phase.

gourmets of the Zodiac. You love to tuck into a large repast, probably one you have cooked yourself, and you make excellent hosts or hostesses. Friends are likely to vie for invitations to your home. Sometimes, the artistic streak is shown in a love of Mother Nature. Many Bulls are happiest pottering around the vegetable plot turning over the ground, reaping their reward at the end of the summer.

When it comes to sport, Bulls are either turned on or turned off. Physical contact sports such as rugger frequently appeal and you will support your team with a good deal of enthusiasm. The Bull, of course, likes to graze and some Taureans can be unbelievably sedentary. If this applies you plonk yourself down in front of the television and turn into a regular couch potato!

Money

Finance is probably your middle name and you are the sign who knows how to generate that nasty stuff called money. You never starve because however much money you have, you know how to make it work for you. Whenever you play Monopoly you like to play the banker because you enjoy fingering the notes. From the age of about 10 you probably had a secret savings account larger than your parents'. It was a rare occasion when your piggy bank was ever found empty, much to the envy of your friends. Since then you have probably managed to put away a tidy sum that gives you that special sense of security and safety. You like to feel you have something to fall back on for that proverbial rainy day that sometimes does crop up.

You have a horror of unpaid bills and are suspicious of charge accounts that make it all too easy to spend. You prefer, wherever possible, to buy with cash so that there is nothing hanging over your head, and you meticulously file away your receipts so that you can deduct as much as possible from the tax-man. However, you are sometimes so economical that you forget to live and enjoy the little luxuries that you are allowed. If this occurs you are letting your money victimize you. To save is being cautious but to hoard is to be foolhardy. When money preoccupies you to the detriment of all else it makes you a prisoner and inhibits your creativity and its expressions. Just occasionally remember to look up from your bank book and live.

The one area where you rarely stint yourself is on food. You prefer to buy the finest wines possible and the best cut of the meat, particularly if you are married, and you will not allow your family to go without even if it means giving up a summer holiday. However, those who try to part you from your hard-earned cash with anything as frivolous as a night out or a new outfit could be in for the razor-edge side of your tongue. One thing is for sure, if you are a typical Bull, then you are rarely caught with an empty bank account. Only occasionally do you 'splurge' – that's generally when you have been saving, and decide it's time to treat yourself.

● **PAULA YATES BORN 24 APRIL 1960**

SMALL, SLIGHT AND FEMININE – IT MAY BE HARD TO VISUALIZE PAULA AS A BULL. BUT THERE IS A STRONG EARTH MOTHER QUALITY ABOUT HER WHICH HAS PRODUCED HER FAMILY AND HELPED HER TO LEAD A SUCCESSFUL CAREER, AS WELL AS SUPPORT HER FAMOUS HUSBAND. ALL IS DONE IN A QUIET, EFFICIENT TAUREAN FASHION.

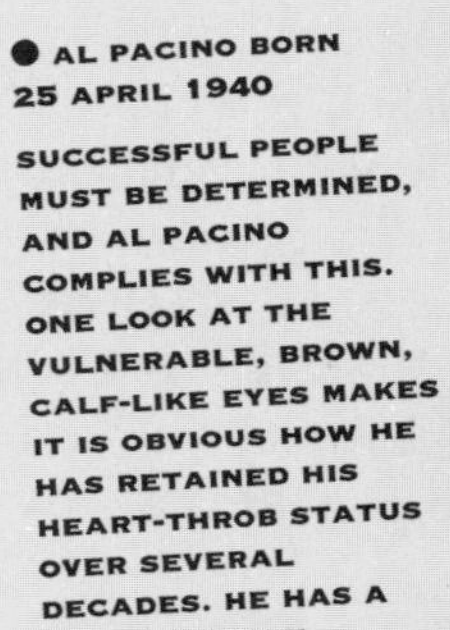

● **AL PACINO BORN 25 APRIL 1940**

SUCCESSFUL PEOPLE MUST BE DETERMINED, AND AL PACINO COMPLIES WITH THIS. ONE LOOK AT THE VULNERABLE, BROWN, CALF-LIKE EYES MAKES IT IS OBVIOUS HOW HE HAS RETAINED HIS HEART-THROB STATUS OVER SEVERAL DECADES. HE HAS A QUIET, MODEST TAUREAN QUALITY THAT APPEALS TO THE LADIES.

● **NAOMI CAMPBELL BORN 22 MAY 1970**

TAURUS ALWAYS HAS AN EYE FOR STYLE, ELEGANCE AND COLOUR, QUALITIES THAT ARE OBVIOUS WITH THIS PARTICULAR TAUREAN. SHE SHOWS THE BULL'S DETERMINATION TO ENDURE. THIS WAS CLEAR WHEN SHE TOTALLY CHANGED HER IMAGE IN AN EFFORT TO SUSTAIN HER SUCCESSFUL MODELLING CAREER.

in LOVE

SINGLE

When it comes to love you are an earthy romantic. You are sensual, emotional and never feel complete without a mate. At times you get yourself into a bad mood longing for the perfect love while you wait for the phone to ring.

Although you have a hard time showing it, you are highly vulnerable and sensitive and fear rejection to the point of obsession. In any relationship you have to know where you stand: being put in an insecure position that is neither one thing nor the other gives you a tremendous amount of pain. You are faithful to the point of tying yourself totally to one person. You find it easy to sacrifice your own interests for your mate's or to put your own growth and development in the background while you spend your vital energy hoping, waiting and wanting.

Because you are down-to-earth, you don't demand to be dazzled by a whirlwind romance. Instead, you opt for quiet evenings, homemade cooking and the flicker of candlelight.

In any love scene you are pleasure-loving, warm and cuddly. However, at times you have a way of wrapping your arms around another person which can break ribs. Let go of the jealous feelings you cling to. Potentially you will be a happier and more contented person and you are also likely to find yourself more loved.

Ruled by Venus, the planet of love and beauty, you are extremely sensual – all five senses are well developed. You know who you want, and are relentless in the chase. You are constant and loyal in your affections and guided more by emotions than reason. Determined and possessive once you have acquired what or who you want, be it a mate or precious jewel, you cannot be prised loose from what you deem to be rightfully, and sometimes wrongfully, yours.

You attract many admirers with your imaginative ideas and your earthy sensual charm. Romantically and sexually, you hate to be rushed and insist on being in control at all times. Although you rarely show violent emotion – you prefer to maintain a calm, peaceful, placid exterior – when you are pushed to extremes or feel you have been dealt with unfairly, others should watch out. That Taurean temper is famous for being the most devastating in the Zodiac.

One of your greatest assets is your staying power. You will chase a goal or person through thick or thin.

When you have problems of an emotional nature, they are usually caused by your possessiveness. You definitely like to have your own way and can't stand a hint of insecurity or indecision. You are a planner who knows exactly what and who you want and simply can't understand it when things do not go according to plan. You will do yourself a big favour if you avoid assuming that simply because you are moved by a member of the opposite sex, they feel the same way about you. Why not keep something in reserve until you have had time to check out the terrain? This way you will avoid much heartache.

MARRIED

Marriage for you is a definite: you want to be tucked in and cuddled at night. You find it difficult to feel complete without another person in your life. You desperately want emotional foundations and when they crumble, you will settle for even the skeletal structure they once were. You will hang on to a relationship long after it is over and with patience and a mystifying sense of perseverance you will struggle onward into an emotional mire. For a bad marriage to end, your spouse will have to leave you – and even then you may kill your ex-partner trying to get back together.

You are nurturing and possessive but often in a marriage you let yourself get into a deep rut. However, should your mate decide to seek excitement elsewhere, because living with you is like reading last year's news, you will suddenly develop the brute force of the Bull. When your prime possession is challenged, you can rouse yourself into a rage which would make anyone hide under the bed. Your solid character quickly dissolves into steam heat and you can be more dangerous than dynamite.

Basically what you seek in marriage are the more practical pleasures of earthly existence. You need emotional support and you certainly appreciate an array of creature comforts. In marriage you are extremely giving and committed – sometimes you even forget to take all that is due to you.

PERFECT PARTNERS

When finding the perfect mate, the Bull frequently turns to the other earth signs: Taurus, Virgo and Capricorn.

Taurus with Taurus For these two, life will either be full of trauma or full of boredom. A sensible attitude to the financial area of life applies to both and each approve. These two make splendid hosts and hostesses too and so their social life is going to be run efficiently and their home probably bustles with friends all tucking into the wonderful feasts that have been prepared. The need to express feelings is strong in both parties and they constantly strive to convey their emotions to each other. Where you find a Taurean relationship you find two happy, jolly and overweight people whose lives revolve around each other.

Due to the similarities in characteristics – both the vices and the virtues – this union is either excellent or a complete disaster.

Taurus with Virgo The Taurean will find the Virgoan honest, vulnerable, giving and loving. Both tend to enjoy quiet evenings at home and often they can be found revelling in a flickering fire, a chateaubriand and a bottle of fine burgundy. These two bring out the better sides of each other's character. They are considerate, warm and caring. Although Virgo is shy, the Bull can certainly melt that sign's inhibitions with animal sensuality.

This is a relationship based on deep rapport with a future of profound feelings.

Taurus with Capricorn Both parties show a sense of practicality and purpose and are truly drawn together. Capricorn is responsible, dutiful, loving and loyal, whilst Taurus is solid, stable, devoted and nurturing. Both have a shrewd sense of money, so there should be no disagreement in the financial area. Much mutual support, understanding and compatibility makes this combination one that is especially meaningful. Together they could move mountains or just keep pace with each other's hearts.

ARE YOU A TYPICAL TAURUS...

Answer honestly the questions below, using YES, NO or SOMETIMES; total up your score, allowing 3 for YES, 2 for SOMETIMES and 1 for NO.

...MAN?

1. Do you consider food to be one of life's great pleasures?
2. Is it hard to change your mind once it is made up?
3. Do you wrestle with the lazy streak in your personality?
4. Do you believe the romantic approach to sex pays off?
5. Are you hungry after making love?
6. When hung up on a girl do you long for her physical presence?
7. Are you persistent when refused sexually?
8. Do you hurt others with cruel words?
9. Do you regularly over-indulge in sex?
10. Can you become deeply engrossed in some art form?
11. Do you work harder when in debt?
12. Is your home all-important to you?
13. Does borrowing money worry you?
14. When a relationship begins to show disaster symptoms do you hang on and hope?
15. Do you prefer to watch sport rather than physically take part?
16. Do you prefer to be the one taking the lead when making love?
17. Does the idea of being in bed with two or more members of the opposite sex appeal to you?
18. Have you a strong jealous streak?
19. Do you eventually want a family?
20. Will your wife have to excel in bed?

...WOMAN?

1. Do you over-indulge in food when your sex or love life goes wrong?
2. Are you almost anybody's after good food, drink and a convincing romantic line?
3. Does financial security worry you?
4. Do you have strong ideas on what you want from life?
5. Does gardening interest you?
6. Is it hard for you to play it cool?
7. Do you take matters into your own hands when a relationship is progressing too slowly for you?
8. Do you have a weight problem?
9. Are you jealous?
10. Can you be revengeful?
11. Despite your feelings do you end a relationship if you suspect he is about to?
12. Do you like to lead in sex?
13. Are you thrown when faced with unforeseen changes?
14. Is laziness a problem for you?
15. Do you enjoy playing hostess?
16. Could cookery be described as an art form?
17. In health are your powers of recovery good?
18. Do throat problems plague you?
19. Do you believe that sex should be confined to two people only?
20. Do you over-indulge in sex?

ARE YOU A TYPICAL TAURUS MAN ?

1–30 Taurus seems to have passed over you pretty quickly leaving little trace of his influence. One or two things may sound like you but it is more likely that you will recognize yourself under a very different sign, possibly one of the fire signs: Leo, Aries or Sagittarius.

31–50 This score belongs to the 'saintly' Taurus and you should easily recognize yourself in that section of this chapter. Fortunately the nastier side of this sign will not apply and popularity and a contented life should be yours.

51–60 You are a true Taurean, good, bad and indifferent. Although you may get what you want from life, it is usually at the expense of someone else. Read the section on the 'sinner' Taurus, resisting all temptations to dismiss it as rubbish, for it may help you to overcome the more unpleasant aspects of your personality.

ARE YOU A TYPICAL TAURUS WOMAN ?

1–30 There may be a smattering of Taurus in you, but hardly enough to qualify you for this sign – you're far too adaptable and feminine. Search for yourself under Pisces, Sagittarius or Aries.

31–50 You are a typical Taurean and your life should be relatively uncomplicated, or this is the way you would like it. You may have one or two nastier characteristics, but for the most part you are a 'saint' Taurus rather than a 'sinner'.

51–60 The whole of the Taurus chapter should apply to you, including the 'sinner' Taurus. Try to control your stubborn streak long enough to read this several times as I'm sure you'd wish to improve yourself and lead a happier life.

CHINESE ASTROLOGY

Nobody can be sure how Chinese astrology developed: it has been in practice for thousands of years and all we are left with is the myth.

According to the myth Buddha extended an invitation to all the animals to join him on Chinese New Year. However, out of all those in the animal kingdom, only 12 arrived. They were the Rat, Ox, Tiger, Rabbit, Dragon, Snake, Horse, Goat, Monkey, Rooster, Dog, and lastly the Pig.

Because of his delight at their arrival Buddha decided to name a year after each one of these beloved animals and those born during a particular year would be endowed with some of the personalities of that animal. In order to find out which year applies to you, check the dates to the left of each section.

THE YEARS OF THE RAT

1924, 1936, 1948, 1960, 1972, 1984, 1996

The most obvious traits associated with Rat people are aggression and charm: it is very rare to meet an unattractive Rat. Neither will you find one who doesn't want to be a success and get as much power as possible. The Rat is power-driven, is a natural leader and has a hefty measure of deviousness. It is nearly always the case that the Rat's ends justify the means.

The Rat's gifts Sex appeal, influence, thrift, sociability, charisma, intellectual skills.

The Rat's sins Nervousness, acquisitiveness, thirst for power, deviousness, meddling.

The Rat's love-life Rats have many lovers in their lives and are particularly compatible with those born under their own sign and those of the Ox, Monkey and Dragon. The Rat gets on fairly well with the Tiger, Snake, Rooster, Pig and Dog but the rather sensitive Rabbit and Goat will find the Rat a bit too blunt and tactless for their liking. The Horse is also difficult to get along with because the Rat needs security and finds the Horse's changeability and self-sufficiency a little unsettling.

THE YEARS OF THE OX

1925, 1937, 1949, 1961, 1973, 1985, 1997

Ox people do not balk from hard work and have little patience with those who do. They have a fine imagination and can usually put new ideas into practice. They are gregarious creatures: they want approval and are not surprised when they are successful. This is because they walk towards their goal with diligence and perseverance. They invariably prove they are worthy when they begin to reap the rewards.

The Ox's gifts Strength of purpose, stability, integrity, diligence, eloquence, innovation.

The Ox's sins Bigotry, plodding, stubbornness, aloofness, vindictiveness, bias.

The Ox's love-life The Ox is guarded, taking a long time to establish relationships and feel relaxed with other people, but having become committed, remains faithful to a partner. The Ox is compatible with the Rat, Rabbit, Snake and Rooster. The Monkey, Dog or Pig, and perhaps another Ox, is usually a friend. There is little compatibility with the Goat, or with the Horse, Dragon and Tiger – the Ox wants serenity and those born under these signs tend to be too impulsive.

THE YEARS OF THE TIGER

1926, 1938, 1950, 1962, 1974, 1986, 1998

The Tiger's judgement isn't always perfect. This is because they can be irrational and passionate and they loathe rules they have not made themselves. Tigers need movement and change and often have many jobs as a result. They hate to feel confined or to stand still. They are rarely impressed by outward appearance and laugh at all forms of snobbery.

The Tiger's gifts Bravery, magnetism, authority, good luck, benevolence, fervour.

The Tiger's sins Hot-headedness, boastfulness, intemperance, rashness, changeability.

The Tiger's love-life The Tiger usually marries in youth and is best suited to the Dog, Pig, Goat and Horse. Friends are usually found amongst the Rats, Rabbits and Roosters. However, the Tiger finds the Ox and Snake a little too quiet and contemplative and is highly irritated by the Monkey's mischievousness. The Tiger finds it difficult, too, to get on with other Tigers, and with the Dragon, because both parties want to dominate the relationship and compromise is difficult.

THE YEARS OF THE RABBIT

1927, 1939, 1951, 1963, 1975, 1987, 1999

The Rabbit reeks of good taste and loathes ostentation in any form. This animal is drawn towards the artistic and the classical, and has an interest in art, history, music, the theatre, dance and cuisine. They are attracted by elegance. The Rabbit never borrows. They never tire of companionship or discussion. Their curiosity about the finer things in life is very real, and they are always tasteful and never ostentatious.

The Rabbit's gifts Tact, virtue, finesse, longevity, ambition, prudence.

The Rabbit's sins Squeamishness, pedantry, secretiveness, hypochondria, complexity, dilettantism.

The Rabbit's love-life The Rabbit is rarely short of admirers, often has many serious relationships before settling down, and is not the most faithful of people. This animal is extremely well mated with those born under the signs of the Snake, Pig, Ox and Goat. Due to their friendliness Rabbits can also get on with the Tiger, Dragon, Horse, Monkey, Dog and another Rabbit. The Rabbit feels uncomfortable with Roosters as they tend to be too frank and critical – Rabbits loathe any form of criticism.

THE YEARS OF THE DRAGON

1928, 1940, 1952, 1964, 1976, 1988, 2000

You cannot ignore a Dragon: they are almost always highly attractive and magnetic. To begin with they are really quiet, but there is something about them that cries out 'Listen to us and you won't go far wrong.' They have a natural authority, and command your attention even if you can't stand them.

The Dragon's gifts Success, good health, strength, pluck, sentimentality, enthusiasm.

The Dragon's sins Rigidity, infatuation, dissatisfaction, mistrust, craftiness, sometimes insensitivity.

The Dragon's love-life Dragons have many love affairs – they are flamboyant personalities. They are likely to marry young and are well mated to Rabbits, Snakes, Monkeys and Roosters. Friends are usually found amongst Rats, Pigs, Horses and Goats. Two Dragons can get on as they understand each other. Dragons will not find relationships with the Dog or the Ox easy, as both are critical of impulsiveness. It is also hard to form a relationship with a Tiger because, like the Dragon, this animal tends to speak its mind and is very strong willed. A power struggle could develop.

THE YEARS OF THE SNAKE
1929, 1941, 1953, 1965, 1977, 1989

The Snake is usually physically attractive: they have excellent taste, dress well and have natural elegance. The Snake thinks twice before giving advice and generally sits down, considers and ponders before replying. There is an inborn intuition about almost everything: they get a lot of hunches. Many are clairvoyant. Laziness seems to be the Snake's greatest pitfall.

The Snake's gifts Attractiveness, discretion, intuition, wisdom, clairvoyance, compassion.

The Snake's sins Extravagance, indolence, stupidity, presumption, dissimulation.

The Snake's love-life Romance is important to Snakes and there are many romances before they settle down. They are well mated to those born under the Dragon, Ox or Rooster, and provided they are allowed freedom, they can also build a relationship with the Rat, Goat, Monkey or Dog. However, they should definitely avoid another Snake as there is too much jealousy in this relationship. They have difficulty getting on with the down-to-earth Pig and the Tiger is too much of a disruption to their quiet ways.

THE YEARS OF THE HORSE
1930, 1942, 1954, 1966, 1978, 1990

Horses must express themselves freely and work in atmospheres that reflect them and only them: it is difficult for them to see other people's points of view. Horse people are generally rebels: they don't take kindly to advice or counsel. They like to strike out on their own wherever possible.

The Horse's gifts Persuasiveness, autonomy, popularity, dexterity, accomplishments, style.

The Horse's sins Haste, unscrupulousness, rebellion, selfishness, anxiety, pragmatism.

The Horse's love-life The Horse has much to offer and is extremely attractive to others. Because of this there will be many romances before they settle down. However, Snakes make protective partners, but despite family commitments they like to retain a certain amount of independence. The Horse is well mated to those born under the signs of the Tiger, Goat, Dog and Rooster. The Horse can make good friends with the Rabbit, Snake, Dragon, Pig and perhaps another Horse, but will find the Ox too serious and intolerant and the Monkey too inquisitive. There is not a great deal of compatibility with the Rat either.

THE YEARS OF THE GOAT
1931, 1943, 1955, 1967, 1979, 1991

Goats generally long for a secure situation, and they really don't know how to create it. They believe that whatever it takes to keep them happy is literally just around the corner. This animal lives in the present, and is capable of enormous effort towards the desired goal. The Goat is rarely happy when fancy free: either they remain part of a close family or else ensure that there is constantly a companion or mate by their side.

The Goat's gifts Sensitivity, perseverance, inventiveness, good manners, taste, whimsy.

The Goat's sins Lack of foresight, unpunctuality, parasiticality, morbidness, impracticality, fretfulness.

The Goat's love-life Romance is very important to Goats and there will be many romances before they give up their freedom. They want a secure background and are best mated to those born under the sign of the Horse, Tiger, Monkey, Pig and Rabbit. They will have a good relationship, perhaps, with the Dragon, Snake, Rooster and another Goat but will find the Dog and the Ox a little too serious. Neither are they drawn to the Rat's penny-pinching ways.

THE YEARS OF THE MONKEY
1932, 1944, 1956, 1968, 1980, 1992

Monkeys are lovable characters. They are stable, love children and animals, have an eye for detail and love to trail-blaze. The only problem is that Monkeys are a trifle childish and, like children, are often drawn to mischief. Those born under this sign can charm their worst enemy and this helps to make them popular and lovable.

The Monkey's gifts Cunning, stability, improvisation, leadership, wit, enthusiasm.

The Monkey's sins Deceit, self-obsession, silliness, opportunism, craftiness, over-indulgence.

The Monkey's love-life Monkeys marry young. Their mates will need to allow them to chase their many interests and indulge their love of travel. The Monkey is best suited to those born under the more gregarious signs of the Dragon, Rat, Pig and Goat. The Ox, Rabbit, Snake and Dog will also be enchanted by the Monkey. However, the Monkey is likely to be exasperated by the Rooster, the Horse and the Tiger, who have little patience with this mischievous character. A relationship between two Monkeys can work because they both understand each other.

THE YEARS OF THE ROOSTER
1933, 1945, 1957, 1969, 1981, 1993

Roosters are self-sufficient and burn with a need for novelty. They are fairly independent and don't need others around them for encouragement. They are resilient and strong: when life goes wrong, the Rooster people get up and fight back. Nothing fazes the Rooster: they are generators and energy oozes from every pore. They are perpetually on the move and ready for action.

The Rooster's gifts Conservatism, style, humour, candour, enthusiasm, resilience.

The Rooster's sins Bragging, blind faith, pedantry, dissipation, bossiness, over-confidence.

The Rooster's love-life Roosters generally have large families: they are loyal to their mates and well suited to those born under the sign of the Snake, Ox or Dragon. Provided they don't interfere too much in the Rooster's many interests the Rat, Tiger, Goat and Pig can also get close. However, two Roosters are likely to squabble and irritate each other and the rather sensitive Rabbit will find the Rooster a bit too blunt. Difficulties with the Dog are also likely.

THE YEARS OF THE DOG
1934, 1946, 1958, 1970, 1982, 1994

Give Dogs a crusade and they will be happy. This animal loves to see that justice is done. Even at their most bad-tempered, Dogs are lovable, if somewhat unyielding. They cannot be bothered with trifles. Dogs seek comfort and understanding, and like to spend their time with their companions. The problem often is that they are busy saving others and caring about causes that they forget to take care of themselves.

The Dog's gifts Constancy, heroism, duty, intelligence, morality, respectability.

The Dog's sins Criticism, self-righteousness, cynicism, unsociability, tactlessness, uneasiness.

The Dog's love-life Dogs have many admirers but aren't easy to live with. They are protective of their partners, and do everything to make them happy. They are well suited to the Horse, Pig, Tiger and Monkey and can establish a stable relationship with the Ox, Rabbit, Snake and Rat. It is likely that they will find the Dragon a little bit too much for their taste and they have difficulty in understanding the creative Goat and the highly critical Rooster.

THE YEARS OF THE PIG
1935, 1947, 1959, 1971, 1983, 1995

Pigs strive for security and are not afraid of hard toil. Despite their amazing naivety, they are quite shrewd. Pigs are ruled by their heart and are lacking in any kind of deviousness: even a hint that they might be guilty of something dishonest worries them enormously. Pigs are straightforward in everything. They crave culture and knowledge. However, they do over-indulge because of their love of good food.

The Pig's gifts Scrupulousness, sincerity, gallantry, good manners, culture, honesty.

The Pig's sins Naivety, wrath, materialism, hesitation, pig-headedness, self-indulgence.

The Pig's love-life Pigs have many romances before they think of settling down. However, when they do they are particularly well suited to those born under the signs of the Goat, Rabbit, Dog, Tiger and another Pig. Basically this open-hearted animal gets on with everybody with the possible exception of the Snake, who is too secretive.

GEMINI

21 MAY – 21 JUNE

NO other sign is quite as quick, bright and communicative as Gemini. Your mind reacts instantaneously to any given situation. You love to learn and you love to read – your understanding is as swift as your eyes. The subject that continually mystifies you is yourself.

It seems to you that those you know well are certain of who and what they are, where they are going and what they want. In spite of appearances to the contrary, you are quite honestly confused by your own nature: it is something you probably spend a good deal of time attempting to understand. Whether you succeed depends largely on other influences in your own individual birth chart.

Gemini produces inventiveness, versatility, high intelligence and the ability to talk yourself in and out of a situation in one second flat. You are cerebral rather than emotional. You express yourself swiftly, are sometimes gifted with languages, and can be quite excitable. You have a great ability to turn a phrase or tell a good story, usually embellishing as you go. It is hard for you to keep still.

You are drawn to speed, risks, mystery and above all novelty. One of your greatest horrors is the thought of boredom; regrettably this can descend quickly and so your pastimes and interests change with the weather. Your personality and lifestyle are an exercise in self-expression. You are a positive thinker and many other people respect and admire you for that.

You are magnetic and thoroughly enjoy meeting new people – and they are anxious to meet you, sensing your interest in them. Very few make as many acquaintances as a Geminian.

It goes without saying that when it comes to partying you are the life and soul. You are drawn to intellectual people because you want to pick their brains but rough types sometimes amuse you – especially if you can get a rise out of them.

PERSO

FEMALE

Saint

- You are an inquisitive type. Sometimes this drives other people crazy, but because of your intelligence others are generally willing to pay the price to take you on.
- You are clever, witty and quick. Your big dread is boredom and repetition.
- Your mind is restless, impatient, changeable and contradictory. You probably change your viewpoint every hour before you come to the final conclusion that you don't quite know what you think. You never really understand yourself, although you spend your life trying.
- You are a blithe spirit with a mischievous streak that others sometimes fail to appreciate. You have a sharp tongue and a sense of humour which some find scintillating, while others find you a little bit too cutting for their sensitivity.
- You are charming, verbal and spirited, but sometimes superficial in your assessment of other people.
- There is a general tendency for you to be more concerned with your mind than your body and you thrive on mental stimulation and challenge. However, you often get so lost in your own logic that you suffer from insomnia, a common Gemini ailment.
- You are energetic and have a mind like Mercury, a keen sense of order and a need for a firm structure to support your experience. You may stay in a job that is not satisfying if the rest of your life is unstable. You may even get locked into a relationship in which very few of your needs are met either because you fear intimacy or because you lack faith in your own ability to create greater happiness.
- Men find you both maddening and emotionally detached. Quite often you are. They want, of course, to get your total attention. Your greatest attributes are your love of laughter and your ability to see life as comical.

Sinner

- You are a party girl who wants to be everywhere at the same time. You hate to be alone because you are bored with your own company: you would rather hang out in a supermarket than discipline yourself to read a book.
- There is no doubt that you are clever, but you are compulsively shallow, capricious and superficial. You can be a dispassionate people-user and an exploiter of a generous person. Since you are changeable your needs vary from

NALITY

minute to minute, and you never hang around long enough either to return a favour or to offer a helping hand.

● Although your mind is quick, it is lacking in depth – it is difficult to spend time around you without donning ear plugs. You love to gossip and you rely on mind games to give you a sense of personal power. However, you are open to the fact that you are out for yourself – your actions speak even louder than your words.

MALE

Saint

● You have a stimulating personality that can charm snakes and a versatile mind that is equal to anything.

● Mentally smoke comes out of your ears and you enjoy a great deal of success in the intellectual sphere.

● Your personality is adaptable and you are interested in a multitude of subjects. Your spontaneous enthusiasm and way with words are the hallmark of your success.

● You are an original thinker who is logical and reflective, analytical and objective.

● Generally you are extremely popular with a large crowd of friends and acquaintances. You have a keen sense of humour which often makes you the centre of attention.

● Women love to be around you because you are so fun-loving. Children like you because you make them laugh.

Sinner

● You can be inconsiderate, lacking in compassion and detached. Too often you make promises that you do not keep and you repeatedly prove yourself to be undependable.

● You have the attention span of a 1-year old and the memory of an amoeba. Your behaviour is erratic and your feelings very flighty: being around you is exhausting. Feeling distresses you. You change your mind every minute of the day and then forget what it was you finally wanted. You can be cruel, callous, conniving and calculating and your pithy comments have an acidity which can kill. In the area of love you are an enthusiastic game player who is seriously committed to non-commitment. You will stand a person up without batting an eyelash and if you are married you will probably have more affairs than someone who is single.

● Basically you love the challenge and a chase, but when it comes to winning the prize, you really don't know what to do with it.

● J.F. KENNEDY BORN 29 MAY 1917

LIKE MARILYN J.F.K. HAD THE ABILITY TO BE EVERYTHING TO EVERYBODY. HE ALSO POSSESSED THE GEMINIAN ELOQUENCE AND WAS A TALENTED SPEAKER AND WRITER. HIS TALENT FOR SPEED READING IS A TYPICAL GEMINIAN TRAIT. GEMINI'S MIND AND BODY WORK FAST.

● MARILYN MONROE BORN 1 JUNE 1926

GEMINI HAS THE ABILITY TO BE ETHEREAL – LIKE ITS ELEMENT OF AIR, IT CAN STORM IN LIKE A GALE OR WAFT IN LIKE A BREEZE – MARILYN DID BOTH. HER GEMINIAN MYSTIQUE MADE IT EASY FOR HER TO BE ALL THINGS TO ALL PEOPLE; SADLY, THE PRICE SHE PAID IN THE END WAS THAT SHE LOST HERSELF.

● JASON DONOVAN BORN 1 JUNE 1968

GEMINI IS THE SIGN OF TWINS – NOTE THAT HE AND KYLIE MINOGUE, BOTH GEMINIS, ROSE TO FAME IN THE SAME TV PROGRAMME. JASON HAS THIS SIGN'S ADAPTABILITY TOO AND LOVES TO TAKE ON NEW CHALLENGES. TO REMAIN THE SAME WOULD BE BORING, SOMETHING LOATHED BY ANY TRUE GEMINIAN.

in LIFE

AT WORK

Gemini Boss At first Gemini employers will give the impression of being easy people to work with: friendly, humorous and casual, and displaying great interest in all those who work for them. Indeed, they will rarely go out of their way to be difficult as they prefer to be liked by all. But they can be a sore trial.

Chaos is the most apt word to describe the confusion surrounding Geminians. They have 101 matters in hand, all demanding immediate attention, and will generally proceed as if it were possible to be in two places at once. Their office routine is practically non-existent – this type will tackle their business affairs in a way understood only by themselves. But Geminians possess a quick intelligence, knowing exactly what is happening or where they should be, and cannot understand other people's puzzled faces.

Gemini Employee Gemini employees are often observed by others with amusement, rushing around the office or factory, attempting to tackle at least two things at the same time with a sense of urgency which may lead onlookers to suppose the world is about to end. And indeed the well-integrated Geminian can accomplish more in just one day than the majority of their fellow workers will in a week.

The 'sinner' type, however, may give the impression of being a veritable tornado but rarely executes anything efficiently and will leave others to clear up the confusion and uncompleted jobs left in their wake.

The odd thing about Geminians is that although they are generally filled with enthusiasm, energy and drive, all three can instantly desert them in the face of pressure, and those who wish to obtain the best from them should leave them undisturbed to progress in their own chaotic, but often brilliant, way.

FAMILY MATTERS

GEMINI MOTHER Motherhood doesn't come naturally to the Gemini female basically because it means being 'grown up', something that no matter how hard you try, you never quite manage. Nevertheless you have a lot going for you as a mother. Because your brain is constantly in a whirl, you are able to stimulate your children and they invariably come to you with their questions because of your knowledge. However, whilst the children will adore you while they are young, when they get into their teens they may find you something of an embarrassment. A Gemini parent may be a mother but she is also a woman. You will flirt with your son's friends and your daughter's boyfriends. However, if your children are born under the air signs, namely Gemini, Libra or Aquarius, then they are quite likely to understand you and realize that you mean no harm.

The Cancer or Scorpio child may find Gemini behaviour all a little bit too much. On the credit side, the Gemini mother is always willing to learn and immerses herself in her children's interests. You always seem to have the answer to any problem.

GEMINI FATHER Like the Gemini woman, the Gemini man is no natural father. Luckily, though, this is a sign that likes to learn, and parenthood is viewed as simply another learning process. This father crawls around the floor playing with the children's toys, perhaps even more than they do. You tell a mean bedtime story and usually leave the children so excited that they are unable to sleep. Once you have got the hang of this 'father thing' you follow your children's interests and progress with a great deal of fascination and sincerely try to learn from the mistakes your parents made in the past.

The Gemini father can be quite ambitious for his offspring and must try to avoid the pitfall of comparing his children with those of his friends.

GEMINI CHILD The Gemini child has no trouble in mixing with other people. True Geminians are fickle and forever involved in petty squabbles, so best friends are changed within an hour – it may be wise to make attempts at instilling some kind of loyalty.

At some point parents will notice that the Gemini child has little trouble with reading. No Geminian will object when called upon to recite, for they all delight in communicating with others and showing their knowledge, whether verbally or on paper. As to other interests, if one attempted to list a Gemini child's passions and interests, it would fill the remainder of this book, so varied are they. Because of this an attempt should be made to encourage specific activities.

Parents need not worry about a physical hobby for fear of insufficient exercise for this type's everyday rush through life keeps him or her fit. Besides, any sports the Gemini child may be interested in will change daily, although sprinting will appeal and the child could go far in this direction.

Mentally, however, there may be one or two problems. In early life, Geminians find concentration very difficult. A book, however, filled with facts and information will fascinate this particular child. The Gemini sense of humour is well developed so the more ridiculous the facts the better!

At Play

Basically other people love you because you love people. Enthusiastic, curious and comfortable with all types, you have a myriad leisure-time activities: you are the type who invariably has some current 'fad'. You may become an enthusiastic gardener, in the summer time anyway. You may join the local dramatic society for a couple of weeks then shelve it in favour of joining the tennis club. Then you meet somebody else who is off pony trekking and you ask them if you can accompany them. You even play at playing.

In your lifetime you will get through hundreds of interests and pastimes, never knowing which is your favourite. That is because you go with the moment and what appeals today may very well not appeal tomorrow. One thing is for sure: you find it hard to sit still.

Writing is therapeutic, whether you are successful at it or not. Sports and athletics are frequently enjoyed. Dancing, too, is considered to be fun: after all it affords you opportunities to flirt with the opposite sex.

Money

When it comes to shopping, you should be locked up every time you get out your credit card. It really doesn't seem to matter how much you earn, you never have the remotest idea where it went and sometimes wonder if it simply walked away on its own. Of course you never think to check out your wardrobe which is so jam-packed that your clothes get wrinkled just hanging there. You forget that you just bought some latest gadget for your car or kitchen, or picked up a first edition which you simply couldn't resist (all that happened last week and therefore now it seems a bit old). And I shouldn't think you have ever considered checking your purse for the six lipsticks you bought on the spur of the moment at lunchtime.

Although there are always exceptions, generally when it comes to managing cash you are a bit of a fiend. You have more credit cards than a tycoon and you regard them with the same kind of fondness as a pig does its trough. You are madly impulsive when spending and tend to grab at whatever catches your fancy on the spur of the moment, and have the ability to conveniently forget when you have made a mistake or wasted some cash. The chances are that whatever you buy will bore you after a few minutes and so you travel onwards, looking for something else to purchase in order to stimulate that overactive head of yours. It is doubtful whether you will ever save very much unless you acquire considerable responsibility in which case you are capable of seeing the error of your ways. Fortunately you are unlikely to get hooked on gambling, but you do like a little flutter from time to time, although it is the risk that excites you rather than the prospect of winning any further money.

● PRINCE BORN 7 JUNE 1958

PRINCE, LIKE HIS SUN SIGN, IS A CHAMELEON. HE CAN TAKE ON THE INFLUENCES AND COLOURS OF ANY BACKGROUND AND USE THEM CREATIVELY. HIS MOVEMENTS ARE QUICK, JUST LIKE THE METAL QUICKSILVER, WHICH IS ASSOCIATED WITH THIS SIGN. NERVOUS ENERGY IS COMMON TO THE TWINS AND HELPS TO KEEP THEM SLIM.

● JOAN COLLINS BORN 24 MAY 1942

JOAN COLLINS IS A TRUE GEMINIAN. SHE POSSESSES THE YOUTHFUL LOOKS, THE WICKED SENSE OF HUMOUR AND THE ABILITY TO BOUNCE BACK IN THE FACE OF ADVERSITY SO TYPICAL OF HER SIGN. SHE HAS RECENTLY TURNED HER HAND TO THE GEMINIAN TALENT OF WRITING. A TRUE CHILD OF MERCURY.

● PAUL GASCOIGNE BORN 25 MAY 1967

WHEN THIS FAMOUS FOOTBALLER BURST INTO TEARS LIKE A LITTLE BOY ON TV SCREENS HE GRABBED THE NATION'S HEART. IT WAS THE GEMINIAN CHILD-LIKE BEHAVIOUR, SO VULNERABLE AND NATURAL, THAT WE FOUND SO APPEALING (BIG MEN DO CRY); IT WAS HARD TO RESIST.

Gemini in LOVE

Single

In love you are a crazy madcap and an emotional puzzle. You either want everything at once, or you think you want nothing at all. Sometimes others think that the most you give to anyone is audition privileges. And if you feel that you are getting bored during the first couple of minutes or so, you are quite likely to wave the person away with the question 'Who's next?' Too often in relationships you worry more about being entertained than you do about loving. You are looking for a perfect partner who carries the guarantee that they can satisfy your every whim.

You are highly stimulated by a good intellect and if someone asks what qualities made you fall crazily in love, your almost certain response will be 'the mind'. Whilst a great body also helps, no doubt you are far more pleased and titillated by a witty retort than by a little stroke on an erogenous zone.

For the Gemini mind love is a dangerous thing. When you finally get your hands on someone you have analysed too much you behave like a fussy gourmet if the steak is too well done and from that point on there is nothing you can do but send it back where it belongs.

Love for you is like a spoonful of sugar: too little leaves you wanting, too much makes you sick. It takes your mind a long time to understand your feelings. Some Geminians never find out at all.

Jealousy, possessiveness and too much staying at home don't work for you. Your quicksilver mind needs stimulation. You have a hunger for human interchange and are geared to flirting and having fun. It is not easy to persuade you into entering a relationship – especially a binding one; generally, the more freedom you have, the more likely you are to stick around. You can't help yourself; you are easily tempted by new experience, but will stay around someone who intrigues you. Anyone who tries to mould you to their pattern, tie you to tradition, or fence you in with domesticity had better think more than twice before getting involved with you. Variety is truly your 'spice of life'. At the first sign of boredom you are off. Hardly surprisingly then, yours is frequently a much married sign and often associated with scandal. But it all keeps you on your toes, doesn't it? And that is exactly what you need.

Married

Since you treasure your freedom, are critical and something of a flirt, marriage is not exactly top of your list of priorities. Of all the activities that life has to hold out to you there are many other things which you will prefer to do rather than to commit yourself to the matrimonial stakes. Basically you like a lot of variety in your love life and are not that inclined to settle down of your own accord. Until you are thirty-something you still get your thrills more from shifting relationships than a stable situation. Fundamentally you prefer a playmate to a marriage partner.

It is extremely important that you feel respect for the person you marry. You actually find it preferable to be intellectually overshadowed than to have to re-educate someone. You need a highly adaptable situation which offers you a great deal of freedom – not one where you feel chained to the bed. You also appreciate a dynamic personality that can keep up with your pace and has the patience to cope with some of your inconsistent moods. The fact is, you are possibly waiting for your mind – not your heart – to be swept off your feet and the longer you spend flirting around, the less time there will be for real loving.

Perfect Partners

When it comes to finding the perfect partner, it is likely that you will be drawn to the other air signs, namely Gemini, Libra and Aquarius.

Gemini with Gemini He will appear to her to be the ideal man, for he seems to understand her need for partnership at a high level. He agrees with her ideas on individual growth, and in intellectual matters, they are in accord. He is able to be her companion, lover and husband whenever necessary but unfortunately he will also rely on her maternal instincts – which may not be well developed – to indulge his child-like manner. These two are able to quarrel without bitterness developing afterwards. Their relationship can be most satisfactory unless one of the partners is of the 'sinner' type – then, it takes a strong down-to-earth personality to cope with the other person's perception, irresponsibility and aptitude for twisting the truth.

Sexually they are very much in tune and able to achieve great closeness because needs are shared and thus they have a mutual understanding. Awareness of the desire for mental stimulation in one another means they each fulfil their search for novelty, leading in many cases to participation in elaborate sex games.

Gemini with Libra Both love people, parties, the idea of a midnight rendez-vous and the kinds of amusement that have that incomparable lustre of the 'first time'. The Libran wants a mate who will be a soul mate. Geminians never really consider such a thing but are always willing to try something new. Both subjects are born under an air sign and so they should have similar attitudes to feelings and intellect. A need for personal freedom is shared, as is a need for enjoyment and constant change. An ideal situation should exist in their home when both partners are an equal force. The Libran is a highly sexed romantic and can provide much mental stimulation for the Gemini's active head. Life could very well be one long ride on the merry-go-round and it should never be dull.

Gemini with Aquarius These two are likely to stay up all night long discovering the secrets of the universe. Both are on a perpetual quest of 'Why?' and never cease searching – even in the middle of making love. Both parties are willing to share their ideas, their interests and their friends, and senses of humour should be compatible. This airy combination enjoy meeting new people, going to parties, and discussing the personal habits of the hostess for hours. While the sexual passion here is not likely to make either partner pass out, the ideas that are mutually inspired are enough to steam up the windows. This could either be a match made in heaven or a platonic love with the luminescence of the stars.

ARE YOU A TYPICAL GEMINI...

Answer honestly the questions below, using YES, NO or SOMETIMES; total up your score, allowing 3 for YES, 2 for SOMETIMES and 1 for NO.

...MAN?

1. Are married or attached women irresistible to you?
2. Do you believe that you can make it with any woman if you really put your mind to it?
3. Are you attracted to a woman's mind in a lengthy relationship?
4. Are you a talkative man?
5. Do you loathe possessive women?
6. Could you be faithful to any one woman for life?
7. Can you be pretty crude in sex quite naturally?
8. Despite your trendy image do you harbour what may be considered some old-fashioned ideas?
9. Are you a jack-of-all-trades?
10. Are your moods changeable?
11. Are you self-critical?
12. Do you enjoy travel?
13. Is your curiosity insatiable?
14. Are you aroused sexually through your mind rather than through your body?
15. Do you discuss your sex life with male friends?
16. Are you totally free of inhibitions?
17. Do you find it difficult to persevere?
18. Does it make you feel good to have several women in love with you?
19. Do you prefer a stimulating conversation to a mediocre romp in bed?
20. Do you enjoy subjugating your women?

...WOMAN?

1. Is mental stimulation important to you before sex?
2. When writing do your thoughts run ahead of your pen?
3. Do you suffer from extreme moods?
4. Are you talkative?
5. Do you have a quick nervous mannerism?
6. Does fantasy play an important role in your sex life?
7. Do you use the words 'I love you' a little too readily?
8. Would it really put you off to make love in silence?
9. Does the chase and challenge of a relationship stimulate you more than the actual sexual act?
10. Do you ever rebel against routine?
11. Do you think you should feel more maternal than you do?
12. Do you believe that mental compatibility is the most important thing in a relationship?
13. Are you always attracted to the wrong people?
14. Do you feel claustrophobic when a man tries to possess you?
15. Are pretty speeches important to you when making love?
16. Do you take great delight in trying to shock?
17. Do you spend hours trying to dissect yourself?
18. Does insomnia plague you due to an overactive mind?
19. When making love does the use of four-letter words stimulate you?
20. Do you believe that making love is an art form?

ARE YOU A TYPICAL GEMINI MAN ?

1–30 You are not a true Geminian for another sign would appear to loom large on your personality; if one could delve into your birth chart it would probably be discovered that an earth sign is your true influence. Search for yourself under Virgo, Taurus or Capricorn.

31–50 This is the score of the 'saintly' Geminian. You are probably a great success with women and in much demand socially. However, consideration and a little more patience with your slower fellow creatures will quickly develop.

51–60 If the section on the 'sinner' Geminian fits you, as it probably does, then you could be the kind of man to cause a great deal of trouble for other people by your flighty behaviour. You may consider yourself to be quite a lad with the ladies, but if you ever looked back over your shoulder you would discover a trail of frustrated women. Try to be more thorough in everything you tackle.

ARE YOU A TYPICAL GEMINI WOMAN ?

1–30 Gemini has left no visible trace on you. Your conservative and practical outlook would seem to indicate the presence of an earth sign in you. Try reading another sign, possibly Taurus, Capricorn or Virgo, but don't try to make it fit – when you have discovered your correct influence it will be quite obvious.

31–50 You are a typical 'saintly' Gemini, which means that although you may consider yourself to be neurotic, in fact you are well-balanced, versatile and adaptable. You could possibly improve yourself if you could conquer your weak concentration and delve a little deeper into those things that come under your wandering eye.

51–60 Jack-of-all-trades will be a phrase constantly used when referring to you. You are a typical Gemini for good and evil, and although it might help you to read the section on the 'sinner' Gemini, it is unlikely that you will truly read and digest the information seriously or properly. That's the way you are.

HOL

	WHAT YOU WANT FROM A HOLIDAY	YOUR TYPE OF HOLIDAY	WHERE TO GO	WHEN TO GO
ARIES	Fresh air, excitement, the chance to tackle new activities, meet new people. You need something very different from your usual routine.	The experimental, perhaps a self-catering or camping holiday.	The Costa Brava, Sardinia, East Africa, Cornwall.	Midsummer onwards – but shorter trips should be taken in October.
TAURUS	Serenity, contact with nature, a return to familiar places. Locations with a cultural background.	Go somewhere which evokes memories, especially somewhere you loved as a child.	Eastern Europe, Greek Islands, English South Coast resorts.	Springtime is ideal – but plan a further holiday in September.
GEMINI	New acquaintances, mental stimulation, something new to learn. You need a holiday that will keep your grey matter whirling.	A city holiday. This allows you to see the sights, go to plays, drink and eat well.	Bonn, Paris, Italian Riviera, Israel, London, Brighton, Blackpool.	May, July or November are your best months.
CANCER	Chances to dream, and act out fantasies. Visit places which are romantic, with traditions stretching way back.	Preferably by the sea, or on a canal. A homely place where people are friendly.	West Indies, New York, North Africa, Bournemouth, Scotland.	During your birthday month of July.
LEO	Funny times with close friends. Sunshine is important as is food, as you will need to store up a lot of energy for the winter.	As luxurious as possible. Spoil yourself.	The Alps, Lebanon, France, Thailand, the West Country, Bath.	Winter holidays: February. Summer holidays: late June.
VIRGO	The chance to be made whole again – invigorated, refreshed, cleansed – and to be really yourself. Let worries disappear.	You need sea, mountains and perhaps a health farm away from the crowds.	Paris in springtime, Switzerland, Jerusalem, the English canals, Norfolk.	Spring or early autumn are the best times.
LIBRA	Friendly faces and the chance to see new sights, especially those steeped in history – you need to feel cultured.	Get off the beaten track but avoid hot countries. Mix self-catering with hotels.	Austria, the Netherlands, Scandinavia, Ireland, the Lake District, Devon.	During the summer school holidays if need be, but also at Easter.
SCORPIO	Dramatic sights, the chance to lead a super-charmed life. Also to concentrate on one person and improve that relationship.	Choose a touring holiday with spectacular landscapes.	North Africa, the USA, Rhine Valley, Snowdonia, Scarborough.	May and July are the choicest months, but a short November trip will be restful.
SAGITTARIUS	Bracing air, the chance to be free, to throw everyday life to one side and show off your adventurous spirit.	Go for wild unspoilt country or you could try a city of learning.	Portugal, Sicily, Majorca, West Wales, Oxford, Cambridge.	June and September are the best times.
CAPRICORN	Contact with another age, another people. Good service, good food, all with excellent entertainment at hand.	Somewhere you can meet new people and widen your vision and knowledge.	Ski resorts, health farms, first-class hotels, French Riviera, Edinburgh.	August or October. Earlier in the year you could need to be close at home.
AQUARIUS	A different scene as well as a holiday for the mind, some lively place with a fine community spirit.	A gracious city with lovely countryside nearby: inland waterways maybe.	Amsterdam, Italy, Denmark. At home enjoy local festivals and traditions.	March, July and November are good times for you.
PISCES	You want to be wafted away on a sea of fantasy. Ideally you would like to live in a holiday resort all the time.	Go where you can get away from the modern world.	Disneyland, Channel Isles, Germany, Brittany, Dover, South Coast resorts.	April or school summer holidays. Try to avoid travel at weekends.

IDAY

HOW TO TRAVEL	WHO TO GO WITH	WHAT TO DO ON HOLIDAY	COMPLAINTS	
Own transport – but car hire is a good idea. Younger people can hitch-hike.	Family members may be difficult at times. Best to go with younger people.	Swimming and other outdoor sports. Mix with the local community.	Kick yourself for taking the wrong wardrobe. Moan to hotelier about soiled linen. Check these out.	ARIES
Rail or air. Once you arrive, use local methods of getting about.	Friends, family or a childhood companion.	Visit museums, art galleries, stately homes. Sunbathe. Visit local industries.	Kick yourself for not taking travellers' cheques. Easily avoidable.	TAURUS
A mixture of air, rail, road and walking.	Friends at work, neighbours or brothers and sisters.	Try to learn a foreign language. Listen to local music. Find really unusual presents.	Blame yourself for leaving a useful gadget at home. Blame the local shopkeepers for bad manners. Easily avoidable.	GEMINI
By sea if possible – so why not a cruise? This would really relax you.	Parents, your own family or a platonic friend.	Try a new sport even if you make a fool of yourself. Read while you sit on the beach.	Blame yourself for getting a date wrong. This gets a relationship off to a dodgy start.	CANCER
By unusual forms of transport: hovercraft, a brand-new car, or even Concorde if you can afford it.	Your lover. Take nobody who will cramp your style.	Dress elegantly and beautifully. Cultivate glamorous new friends.	Blame yourself for trusting a cheap-skate travel firm. Be irritated by strikes.	LEO
By cable car, boat, plane or coach. Best of all in your own caravan.	Like-minded people: you don't want friction on holiday. A new companion.	Get close to nature. Study local craft industries.	Blame yourself for not doublechecking documents. Easily avoidable.	VIRGO
Sometimes on water, but a package holiday will be reliable.	Your mate, sweetheart or school friends.	Do some painting or sketching. Revive memories. See live shows.	Blame yourself for mislaying a possession. Moan about local traders ripping you off.	LIBRA
Coach or car. If using public transport book your seats well in advance.	Family or friends – but you can escape with your own mates.	Keep a photographic record of your activities. Join in the local fun.	Blame yourself for getting lost. Doublecheck maps.	SCORPIO
Horseriding is a favourite Sagittarian means of transport.	Go with fun people, but you also need one older and more experienced companion.	Roam around. Try some fishing or sailing. But do keep in touch with folks at home.	Blame yourself for being impatient with locals.	SAGITTARIUS
Air or car. If buying a new car then make sure it is running properly before you go.	Familiar friends – but allow yourself the freedom to meet new faces.	Shop for bargains and household goods. Walk. Swim. Go to the races.	Blame yourself for leaving things to the last moment.	CAPRICORN
You love flying. You may even take up gliding whilst on holiday.	You could go with a close friend – or relatives if the children aren't too boisterous.	Enjoy unusual galleries, museums, safari parks and zoos.	Blame yourself for not being fussy enough in the first place.	AQUARIUS
Ship or rail. A new service will be best, giving comfort and saving cash.	Go with the family or friends but expect to meet new faces when you get there.	See plenty of local sport. Be daring with nightlife. Hear some serious local music.	Blame yourself for leaving holiday gear behind when it is time to return home.	PISCES

CANCER

22 JUNE – 23 JULY

MOST Cancerians feel misunderstood. This is because although you have a great sense of humour and are a good listener, an open-hearted friend and a sympathetic person all round, you suffer from melancholia which can give you an awful and somewhat unjust reputation.

Crabs protect everything that they consider their own. Peace of mind is extremely important and you do everything you can to keep trouble at a distance. Your way of dealing with problems is to bide your time in the hope that the difficulties seen in advance may never occur; when forced into action, you circle around hesitantly, rarely considering a full frontal attack. Like the Crab, your symbol, you prefer to move backwards and sideways, pausing and considering, before darting in for whatever it is you want.

You are very security conscious too. You hold on to everything you have with that Cancer claw, whether it be ideas, loved ones, a job or your possessions. This is why many Crabs find it extremely difficult to throw away all those little mementoes they have gathered over the years.

You are capable of giving a tremendous amount of time and nurturing to other people and are the first to offer assistance when you notice suffering. You simply can't bear to witness anything or anyone suffering needlessly.

You have tremendous powers of perseverance, once a commitment has been made. It may be difficult for you to get off the launching pad but when you are on your way you seem psychologically oblivious to setbacks. You do not expect to achieve your goals overnight. If difficulties mean you have to start all over again, then you are quite ready to do just that. While others grind their teeth down to the gums, you just chew away at the opposition and obstacles until they are worn down completely and you triumph.

Finally, then, despite your low and high moods, underneath you are always lovable, gentle and sincere to those who understand you.

PERSO

FEMALE

Saint

● You have more desires, cravings and wishes than you or anyone else knows what to do with. You are a moon child who wears her moods on her sleeve along with a lot of wishful thinking but basically you are the kind of person whom everyone needs to know and experience.

● You have a delightful way of anticipating somebody else's needs before they happen and of offering your help.

● Because of your super-sensitive nature, you are a lot more vulnerable than the average person. Be careful where you place your sympathies – it doesn't take much for others to begin to take you for granted.

● You need a lot of love to keep you happy and are prepared to give back more than your share in return. You are a highly sentimental woman who is happiest when being sought after and catered for. In turn, you love to nurture – you have probably never had a plant that drooped, died or contracted a strange disease. You crave constant reassurance that you are loved, wanted and appreciated. In general, you are a romantic who cries at weddings, late-night movies and memorable moments.

● The problems in your life often assume the proportions you have witnessed on the screen or stage.

● You spend a great deal of time seeking roots in places and people outside yourself. Likewise you give others far more power than you would ever allow for yourself. Despite your fears, you can endure any storm. When responsible for anyone else you can be a formidable attention-getter and will fight hard for what you want.

Sinner

● You are your own worst enemy, always at the mercy of your moods. You are filled with insecurities and live your life on the defensive. You overcompensate with masochistic fantasies and throw yourself into self-created dramas which pit you against the world. Surprisingly enough, on the days when you feel more irritable than melancholic, you may massacre somebody else's feelings with a savage remark. This is displaced anger at work. It is quite likely that you are repressing the anger you feel because somebody told you last week that your new hairstyle didn't suit you. When really provoked, your temper tantrums tempt others to give you anything just to get some peace and quiet.

● Too often you become enslaved in situations in which the human warmth and compassion barely live up to that of a prison. When you tenaciously clutch at what is worth something to you without considering what you are really doing to yourself, you create an unfortunate personal situation that it may take years to rectify. Try to remember that it is important to learn to stand on your own two feet.

MALE

Saint

● You are a warm, vital and sentimental man who lives through his intuitions despite his vulnerable emotions. You are thoughtful and shrewd and have a bright intelligence which makes a quick assessment of any situation.

● You have a highly creative imagination which could bring you recognition in the arts or a great deal of pleasure in your leisure time.

● You get a great deal of pleasure out of giving: you probably inundate your loved ones with presents.

● Although you are shy and modest, you are also sensual and affectionate and sensitive to those little romantic touches that make the opposite sex's hearts flutter.

● You are a proverbial family man who knows how to make the most out of the domestic scene and you enjoy giving your children more attention than you probably got from your own parents.

Sinner

● Regardless of any matter at hand, your emotions make you suspicious, moody and super-sensitive. You yearn for love but when you get it you usually exercise some kind of mind control in relation to it. Those that love you have to constantly prove it – in your own subtle way you are so demanding that you can drown a person in your personal needs, even when you are being cool and aloof.

● One of the greatest offences committed against you is that of omission – you live in fear of the idea that you have been overlooked, or, worse, that nobody has even noticed.

● Another high-ranking sin on your list is that of indiscretion. On occasions you may be more secretive than a Scorpion who has lost his voice and cringe at the thought of someone letting your secrets loose on the world. Unfortunately almost everything in your life is a secret that will violate you if it ever gets out. You lie about your favourite food and drink, fib about your personal preferences and refuse to talk about your emotional makeup with anyone.

● In matters of love you can be as possessive as a king cobra but sulk rather than hiss.

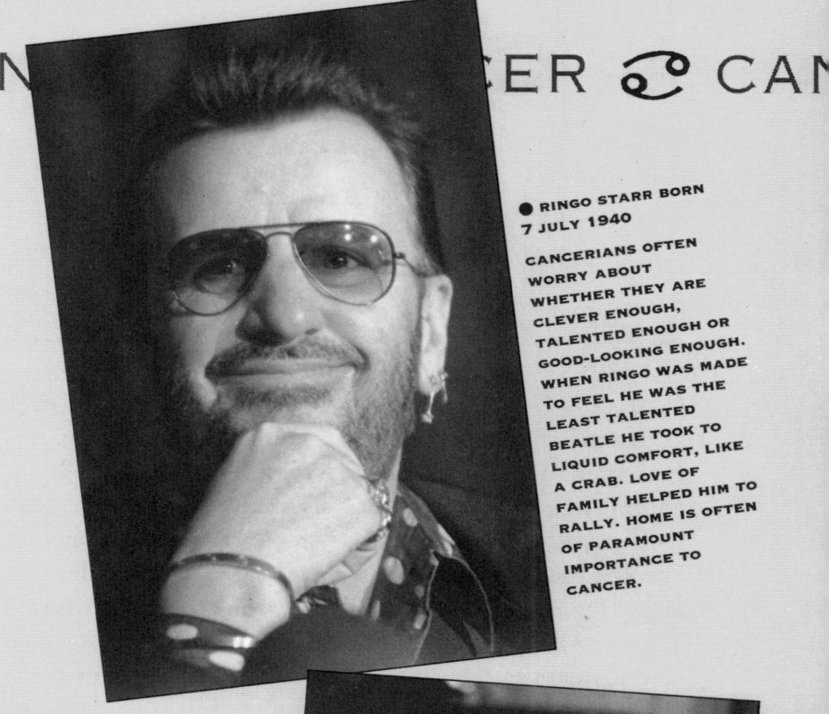

● RINGO STARR BORN 7 JULY 1940

CANCERIANS OFTEN WORRY ABOUT WHETHER THEY ARE CLEVER ENOUGH, TALENTED ENOUGH OR GOOD-LOOKING ENOUGH. WHEN RINGO WAS MADE TO FEEL HE WAS THE LEAST TALENTED BEATLE HE TOOK TO LIQUID COMFORT, LIKE A CRAB. LOVE OF FAMILY HELPED HIM TO RALLY. HOME IS OFTEN OF PARAMOUNT IMPORTANCE TO CANCER.

● PRINCESS DIANA BORN 1 JULY 1961

THE PRINCESS OF WALES SHOWED HERSELF TO BE A TRUE CANCERIAN WHEN SHE FELT SLIGHTED BY HER HUSBAND AND RESORTED TO DRASTIC MEASURES IN ORDER TO DRAW ATTENTION TO HERSELF. NOBODY SHOULD FREEZE OUT THE SENSITIVE CRAB. IT SIMPLY ISN'T EQUIPPED TO COPE AND CAN REACT IN THE MOST SURPRISING WAY.

● HARRISON FORD BORN 13 JULY 1943

EVEN THE MOST SUCCESSFUL CRAB IS DEVOTED TO HOME LIFE. HARRISON WENT A STEP FURTHER AND BUILT HIS OWN NEST, TIMBER BY TIMBER, AND HE ESCAPES TO IT WHENEVER THE CHANCE ARISES. THERE IS ALSO A STRONG THEME OF FANTASY IN HIS FILMS, AND FANTASY IS A STRONG PART OF THE CANCERIAN PERSONA.

CANCER in LIFE

AT WORK

Cancer Boss When the boss is a Cancerian, one either settles into his or her closely knit clan or moves on. This character values loyalty above all else and expects it as a natural right. Cancerians are instinctive individuals, and if their instincts tell them that a person will not or cannot slip into the routine, then the employee concerned will be given marching orders without further ado and will probably leave in a state of confusion. If, on the other hand, one is able to adapt to this complex individual the rewards can be great for Cancerians are generous to a fault with those they trust and respect.

This boss approves of strong domestic impulses in those who are for him or her, and is most sympathetic when problems arise in that area.

Cancer Employee Although adaptable, Cancerians do not always comfortably slip into a vacant place. Others may mistake their sensitivity and adaptability for weakness and it is only with the passing of time that the tenacity and determination lurking beneath the surface are discovered. But once happily situated, Cancerians can enjoy considerable popularity. Others will recognize the sympathy and compassion in their character and soon they will find themselves involved in all their problems. However, should the subject's boss be unfortunate enough to feel the Cancerian gaze boring into the back of their head, it will be because this individual has decided that it would be rather nice if he or she could attain their job – and sooner or later, that ambition is sure to be fulfilled.

This is a hard-working, highly organized person who knows how to make his or her shrewd sensibilities work best. That Cancer tenacity usually wins through in the end.

FAMILY MATTERS

CANCER MOTHER If you are a true Cancer then you were born with a strong maternal streak which showed itself when you were a child when you constantly liked to play house with the boy next door. You cluck around your brood like the proverbial 'mother hen'. Some children may appreciate all the attention which is showered upon them, realizing that it is only your concern that leads you to behave in such a fashion, whilst others, the more freedom-loving members of your family, may find your attentions stifling and could later grow to rebel against you, resenting the stranglehold they may accuse you of exercising over their life. The important thing is not to go to extremes. Care by all means but try to do so at a distance. If you monitor your children's every move from birth to the first date, they could grow to resent you. You are an intuitive person and know when you are going over the top.

CANCER FATHER You are a loyal and devoted father who gets a great deal of pleasure out of providing for your family. You are the proverbial family man and have no ego problems when it comes to sharing out the chores. You are fiercely protective of your family and heaven help anyone who does them any harm. When they do, you don your suit of armour and prepare for battle without giving quarter. Your children will grow up in a secure home and in the full knowledge of how much you care for them.

Your big problem occurs when it is time to let go. The Crab would rather lose a claw than let anything or anyone out of its grasp. Take care, then, when your children reach their teen years. By refusing to admit to yourself that your children no longer need you in the same way as they once did, you could lose them. When this time comes, avoid the temptation of forcing your offspring back into being your little boy or little girl. Refusal to accept this could lead to a lot of heartache on your part.

CANCER CHILD The Cancer child is mother's natural little helper, trailing behind her, sweeping, cleaning and dusting. Baking time is seventh heaven. Give the little Crab a few scraps of pastry, a rolling pin and peace will reign for hours. Any kind of toy which will encourage this domestic interest will be most acceptable – toy vacuum cleaners, teasets, ironing boards – don't be put off if your Crab is a boy.

Should your Cancerian be one of the overweight variety, then he or she could be in for a tough time where friends are concerned. Bullies invariably pick on the more vulnerable and the Cancerian sensitivity makes an ideal victim for jokes. Eventually the little Crab will develop a tough outer shell but inside he or she will be lonely and miserable. Remember this type is not naturally gregarious and usually prefers to locate a kindred spirit and stick like glue with true Cancerian tenacity. Naturally when this precious bond is threatened in any way the bottom will fall out of the little Crab's world. Then he or she will need all the love you can muster to act as a buffer.

Never tell a Cancerian who is down to pull themselves together or apply pressure when party invitations are extended. Your Crab will know if a bully will be present although he or she may not wish to tell you so.

At play

Your friends are an important part of your life and you live in service to them. You have no idea how to say no when asked for aid, regardless of the difficult situations this may place you in. Much of your spare time will be spent running around offering help and assistance wherever you believe it to be necessary. Because of the nurturing nature of the Crab, cooking and gardening are usually high on the list of recreations. You can spot a Crab in midsummer, mouth bulging with raspberries, cream dripping down his or her chin – Cancerians have a wonderful knack for growing luscious crops.

Although domesticated, those born under this sign often suffer from itchy feet and look forward to any kind of trip that is in the offing. On the first sunny day during the summer, you pack your loved ones into a car and head for the sea. It doesn't matter if it is just above freezing: you feel summer is approaching and that is all that counts.

On the sporting front the Crab is naturally attracted to watersports. Whether it is surfing, diving, yachting or sailing, you are happy in the water, on the water or simply close to it. Simply sitting by a fishpond can restore the Crab's equilibrium! The cinema is a favourite sedentary hobby as it allows members of this sign to become lost in a romantic fantasy: you will be the first one to whip out a tearstained hanky when the emotional action becomes unbearable.

Money

You tend to cling to money when everything else in your life seems unsettled. You are a formidable saver even if you make barely enough to pay the rent. Plenty of money is a means to greater independence since you hate borrowing and any indebtedness. You are shrewd enough to be a financial wizard and are the kind of person most likely to get rich quick. You have a highly organized mind that thrives on economic details, combined with a tenacity to sacrifice a little of the present for those blue chip investments that will pay off later on. You love little luxuries, without being self-indulgent. Good food, good wine, a beautiful home and the pleasure of occasional outside entertainments appeal highly to you. You spend money readily on fine possessions that will last you a lifetime, but you are never tempted to spend your last penny on rubbish or a shopping spree that takes you by storm. You know how to put your mind where your money is and you always come out making more.

You are far too emotional for cash to ever bring you happiness or satisfaction. What it will bring is a good deal of security and creature comforts, which, of course, it can supply. When all goes well, you'll give away your last penny; when depressed, you can be downright mean.

● MERYL STREEP BORN 22 JUNE 1949

THE CANCERIAN CAN RUN THROUGH THE GAMUT OF EMOTION, FROM A–Z. MOST OF MERYL'S FILMS HAVE DEMANDED A STRONG EMOTIONAL INPUT AND HER ABILITY TO FEEL HER ROLES HAS LARGELY CONTRIBUTED TO HER TREMENDOUS SUCCESS. SHE IS ABLE TO MAKE US EXPERIENCE THE HURT ALONG WITH HER.

● GEORGE MICHAEL BORN 25 JUNE 1963

IN TRUE CANCERIAN STYLE GEORGE MICHAEL PULLS AT OUR EMOTIONS THROUGH HIS SONGS. HE TOO, LIKE ANY TRUE CRAB, IS DEVOTED TO HIS FAMILY AND THEIR BACKING HAS GIVEN HIM THE FAITH HE HAS IN HIMSELF. HIS CONCERN FOR OTHERS EXTENDS TO THE WIDER WORLD THROUGH HIS PART IN LIVE AID.

● JERRY HALL BORN 2 JULY 1955

JERRY USED HER CHARMS AS WELL AS HER INSTINCTIVE DOMESTIC ABILITIES IN HANGING ON TO HER ELUSIVE ROLLING STONE. SHE CLEVERLY MADE THEIR HOME SO WELCOMING THAT MICK USED TO FIND IT HARD TO STRAY FOR ANY LENGTH OF TIME.

CANCER *in* LOVE

SINGLE

Romance can be a shifty business for the Crab: one step forward, two steps back. Pop out and see what reaction this gets and then start the whole procedure all over again. However, once a relationship looks like a long-term proposition, you begin to put aside your ring-of-roses technique and attach yourself like a limpet to the object of your desire. You believe in sticking by your loved ones and protecting their interests come what may, yet your security needs often prevent you from exploring your full and diverse emotional range. You are not the type that enjoys brief encounters: you much prefer to move cautiously from one relationship to the next.

Above all else, you want to establish a close and loving bond with somebody, even though your practically impregnable self-defence frequently prevents a smooth emotional exchange and makes you extremely evasive to the people you deal with. This leads to your feeling misunderstood, rejected and even neglected. However, once you have found that special someone, then emotionally you feel whole and you are able to fulfil your relationship and express love, tenderness and affection to your heart's content.

MARRIED

Marriage means a lot to you, since you crave the kind of emotional security that lasts for ever. One-night stands are not your idea of emotional satisfaction, even if you had a whole line of lovers waiting for your attention. You heartily believe in 'happily ever after' and want to see if it can work for you. However, sometimes you try too hard and have difficulty admitting that a bad relationship is definitely a failure. If it finally breaks apart, despite your tears and dramas, you often become bitter and disillusioned.

Fundamentally you want someone to come home to and to wake up with and this means more to you than a castle in Spain or a diamond from Tiffany's. You find your greatest excitement in people and have a sentimental nature that longs for situations to bring out your deepest emotions. You want intimacy and sensual contact, based on trust and communication. However, your defencelessness often proves to be an obstacle to what you want most and people have a hard time getting through to you. Consequently you suffer deeply. As you stumble through the anger that seems to imprison you, your aloof behaviour can blight your marriage.

Because the conditions of marriage satisfy so many of your urges, it is highly unlikely that you will remain single. However, it is imperative that you give relationships time to develop and grow before making any final decisions.

PERFECT PARTNERS

When it comes to finding that special someone, frequently the Crab turns to the other water signs, namely Cancer, Scorpio and Pisces. These three signs are best suited to understanding your complex nature.

Cancer with Cancer Two domestic, romantic and sensitive people should be able to use these mutual characteristics as a good base for a happy relationship. Excess sensitivity, however, can lead to trouble. Every word and action taken so literally can mean constant hurt for one or both of them and a serious problem could completely flaw them. The Cancer possesses a retentive memory and the causes of quarrels are brought up again and again. Much time is wasted in petty bickering, dredging up the past. However, if they can detach themselves emotionally from their relationship and look at what is bothering them, then they will discover that they have much to be grateful for. When arguments do occur, they will both be quick to offer a reconciliation. Both personalities are highly complex and emotional and should try to view life with a more realistic eye. Sexually the intricate feelings of both can cause trouble, for the occasions when desires coincide may be all too rare. This, coupled with a tendency for each partner to expect the other to adapt, makes for plenty of drama. Not too good you might think – but you are wrong. If there is one thing that the Crab loves it is plenty of drama, lots of reconciliations and kissings and making-ups. Therefore this could be a perfect partnership for this particular combination of signs.

Cancer with Scorpio Both of these signs are motivated by emotion and intuition. The bond they share will usually be an exceptionally strong one. They know how to love wholeheartedly, insist on fidelity and keep a jealous eye on their relationships. Sexually, the chemistry is unmistakable and inescapable. These two know how to possess each other completely and make each other feel precious and wanted. The Cancerian's usual loving approach to sex is widened in this relationship. He or she is able to express themselves more freely and become much more passionate. This is a relationship which often produces gifted children. Regardless of which sign is the female, she will give him lots of praise and moral support, never criticizing in public and even thinking twice about doing it in private. She will be able to create a relaxing and tranquil atmosphere which he will never want to leave, with good food, good wine and good company. He in turn will realize that she is at her best at night and will take her out for moonlight strolls and a dip in a pool. He will pay her compliments which she will soak up like a sponge and he will reap the fringe benefits. Once these two are possessed and obsessed with each other, neither will ever want to leave.

Cancer with Pisces The psychic rapport here will leave both parties starry-eyed. They will sympathize with one another's mood swings, share a box of tissues during weepy movies and each will remember what the other wore on the day they first met. They are hyper-sensitive to one another and they will know not only what each other thinks but why. They will both find themselves saying the same things simultaneously, finishing up each other's sentences and respecting each other's ideas. This relationship is made up of lazy weekends by the sea, evenings of champagne and candlelight, and winter afternoons in front of the fire with tea and muffins or perhaps a glass of wine each. They will confide their favourite fantasies to each other and then make them come true. They will set the scene with dreamy mood music and try some x-rated pillow talk. Bearing in mind that this is a water combination, they will make love in the bath, under a waterfall or in a shower. There will be oceans of affection and the bond between them could last well past anyone's lifetime and perhaps two lifetimes.

ARE YOU A TYPICAL CANCER...

Answer honestly the questions below, using YES, NO or SOMETIMES; total up your score, allowing 3 for YES, 2 for SOMETIMES and 1 for NO.

...MAN?

1. Are you protective of those you love?
2. Does the sea attract you?
3. Do you long for a large family?
4. Is a drink with the boys important to you?
5. Does the idea of being in bed with two women appeal?
6. Do you place women on pedestals?
7. Do you keep letters from old lovers?
8. Is your memory retentive?
9. Do you work slowly and carefully?
10. Do you secretly enjoy having dependants?
11. Is it hard for you to suggest new ideas or new ways of making love?
12. Do you believe in one affair at a time?
13. Do you participate in some kind of sport?
14. Does travel attract you?
15. Do you care how others see you?
16. Do you think that the permissive society has gone too far?
17. Do you enjoy being in the limelight?
18. Is it hard for you to recover when a deep relationship ends?
19. When others smirk at sentiment or romance are you annoyed?
20. Do you expect your woman to revolve her life around you?

...WOMAN?

1. When watching a film or reading a book are the impressions you receive from them hard to shake off afterwards?
2. Does the romantic side of history appeal to you?
3. Do you think marriage is incomplete without children?
4. Is it difficult for you to stay with an unfaithful man?
5. Are you self-protective?
6. Do you feel uncomfortable at the thought of taking the lead in bed?
7. Is a martyr complex part of your personality?
8. Do you enjoy the limelight in any form?
9. Are you easily hurt?
10. Does the sea attract you?
11. Do you take your sexual affairs seriously?
12. Have you a weight problem?
13. Are you influenced greatly by those around?
14. Is it hard for you to have more than one sexual affair in progress at a time?
15. Do you suffer from morbid thoughts and moods?
16. Do you lose those you love because of your tendency to cling?
17. Are you good with money?
18. Do you dread being alone?
19. Do antiques interest you?
20. Are your sex fantasies mostly romantic?

ARE YOU A TYPICAL CANCER MAN ?

1–30 Your love of personal freedom is far too strong for a Cancer, although you may possess one or two of this sign's characteristics. Such an independent outlook must belong to Gemini, Aquarius, Sagittarius or even Libra. Try reading these chapters for one will be you down to the last detail.

31–50 You are probably an excellent husband or provider and therefore typically Cancer but some women may be bored by such a domestically inclined man; do try hard to widen your horizon and become more extrovert.

51–60 This score belongs to the 'sinner' Cancer. Read this section carefully and attempt to make some changes. Life can be tough for a man with your sign but self-pity is not an attractive asset and it can only do you harm; put morbid thoughts from your mind and keep busy when you feel this mood threatening.

ARE YOU A TYPICAL CANCER WOMAN ?

1–30 You are much too independent, resilient and uninhibited to be a true Cancer; no doubt one or two characteristics may sound like you but you seem to be ruled by a far tougher sign. You may find yourself under one of the air signs: Gemini, Libra or Aquarius.

31–50 You have answered your questions as any typical 'saintly' Cancer would. Unfortunately, this sign is a sensitive one and life must seem quite hard for you at times, but a woman as feminine as yourself will find no trouble in attracting a big, strong man to protect her. But do try to be a little more resilient.

51–60 This is the score of the 'sinner' Cancer and belongs to a woman similar to the one above; the main differences are the reactions to disappointments, for this type can develop unhealthy mental attitudes: martyr and persecution complexes are easily assumed and need to be controlled. Read the 'sinner' section carefully for it may help you to overcome your weaknesses.

PASSION

	ARIES MAN	TAURUS MAN	GEMINI MAN	CANCER MAN	LEO MAN	VIRGO MAN
ARIES WOMAN	Both parties must understand they can't be boss at the same time. Passionate but short-lived relationship.	They are heading in different directions, but only she is going anywhere. His lack of adventure will bore her to death.	She has a temper that will shake him out of his senses and if he begins to play games he will end up on her cold doorstep.	He is lovable but his affections are not for her. The Aries outbursts send him into sudden withdrawal. Fire and water equals steam.	Passion personified. When they sit together the world shrinks away. She may get more than she bargained for.	He is cautious; she compulsively throws caution to the winds. He is frugal, she spends. A relationship only for the sadomasochistic.
TAURUS WOMAN	For a Taurus to fall for an Aries, is like an orphan in a storm watching a rich family celebrate Christmas. If you like fight, go ahead.	The longer these two stick together the longer they stay in one place. This seems secure, but it's the worst kind of stagnation.	She needs stability; he can't live without change. She worries about security while he can't think past the present. Fun sexually.	If these two can pass through the communication gap, they will realize there is a lot of feeling there. A relationship which could work.	Sexually she spells animal but can exhaust him if he is the ambitious type. Usually a relationship based on blind infatuation.	Both enjoy a quiet stay-at-home evening together. There is much deep rapport and strong feeling here. The relationship could work.
GEMINI WOMAN	Here the challenge never stops. They get to each other but neither wants to be the one to say it. Complex relationship.	At best this relationship should be confined to the bank where he gets paid for telling her how to run her life. Not a good idea.	With two split personalities, activity is stimulating. These two just have fun. A great sexual experience and can be a good relationship.	Her only hope is to stop talking and start listening. Both need to travel, put away emotional masks and try leaning on one another.	She is fickle and he will struggle to get her attention. At the same time he will find her very funny. Very exciting relationship.	He thinks she is too crazy to be responsible. She thinks he is too cautious. They like to talk, so sex won't get a look in.
CANCER WOMAN	Her cooking and sexual expertise will send him into ecstasy. She will stick with him; whether he will stick by her is another story.	These two find their security fantasies fulfilled and for both this is a lot. She has finally got someone to lean on.	She fattens him up, nags him about his untidiness and sulks when he leaves her alone at a party. But a pleasing sexual experience.	This is a relationship of deep understanding with a degree of compatibility and passion.	When she can't get her own way she is weepy. At first this is effective, but after a while he begins to feel claustrophobic.	He doesn't understand her need for attention and she doesn't understand the discipline that he puts on his mind.
LEO WOMAN	Between these two there is warmth, passion and admiration. He is one of the few who can get away with telling her what to do.	Not a match made in heaven as both have wills to topple the highest oaks. Purely a sexual affair.	Gemini man gets bored unless she beats him at being amusing, which can be exhausting. Good sexual affair.	A last resort. His supersensitivity will strangle her nerve endings. He finds her cold and bossy, one to be avoided.	These two together spell either love or hate. Sexually they are compatible, as is their love of luxury.	This lady is not good for his mental health. Her temper makes his stomach twinge and his nerves shudder.
VIRGO WOMAN	He wants immediate gratification while she will wait for something meaningful. Hardly a recipe for success.	In terms of a serious relationship, this is a team to marvel at. This union has stability that makes it look too good to be true.	He can't help but like her, she is so kind, warm and caring. She would have to be a committed masochist to take him on.	She loves the way he courts her, and he is thankful for the way her affection makes him feel appreciated. This relationship could work.	He is at the mercy of his heart; she is ruled by her head. If she is masochistic, it might just work.	They agree on everyday things, but when it comes to being spontaneous and fun loving they look at each other and mutter 'Boring!'
LIBRA WOMAN	Sexually he takes her by storm, but there is a price to be paid: she will need to put up with his temper and his selfishness.	He will give her so much attention that she will stop whining. If they spend all their time in bed, good – but if not, watch out.	She is beguiled by his humour; he finds her gracious and charming. Commonsense is lacking but it could turn into a fun partnership.	He will give her the attention she needs. When she wants to go partying, he will make excuses. An uneasy, difficult partnership.	She is frightened of his anger and will watch for early signals. Running away from him will keep her in good shape.	He enjoys her vivacity, and appreciation of beautiful things, but he could start to nag her. Good sexual relationship.
SCORPIO WOMAN	Sexually things look good and she loves it, but once they get out of bed the passion and starry-eyedness could fade.	He is sensitive, domesticated and often a good cook. Ms Scorpio looks for passionate intensity and she is not going to find it here.	He goes in every direction but never gets anywhere, while she stays in one place. A relationship for friendship.	If she respects his feelings he will allow himself to be controlled by her femininity. The relationship could be satifying.	She makes him wonder if he is listening to a foreign language. He simply can't understand her. A hopeless relationship.	The basic difference between these two is that she feels the world through emotions and he sees it through logic. Something has got to give.
SAGITTARIUS WOMAN	These two are freedom loving, friendly and optimistic. His active competitiveness will spur her on. A good partnership.	Her idea of fun is lots of physical activity. His idea of physical activity is sex or eating. This isn't going to work.	Both are adaptable, adventurous and a little crazy. Life together will not acknowledge any limits. A good attraction of opposites.	He needs her beside him: she needs space. She finds his dependency hard to accept. He would have to be masochistic to take her on.	Like never before she will feel fantastically full of love. She has plenty of vitality to capture him and seduce his senses. A great relationship.	She lives her life without any idea of limits but he lives through restrictions which he struggles to rise above. Very little in common here.
CAPRICORN WOMAN	She is ambitious so that he feels inferior. A good working relationship but precious little else.	She is strong and dignified and has a lot of feeling. He is warm, with an earthiness to make her feel at ease. Great relationship.	Not a match made in heaven, but possibly hell. Neither can understand the other. Friendship may work.	She is touched by the way he seems to care about her but has a hard time taking his moods. A game of Monopoly might be more fun.	She is charmed but he will need to cut out the flirtatious behaviour: for her nothing is casual. They have very little in common.	These two will indulge each other's workaholicism. He will applaud her tenacity and drive. This relationship can work.
AQUARIUS WOMAN	She awes him with her humanitarian impulses. He overpowers her with his list of achievements. A pretty good relationship all round.	These two characters eat different things, see different things and want different things. Anything shared will be pure coincidence.	He has never found a woman so easy to get along with and she has never met a man quite so crazy. A very good relationship.	He craves closeness; she is happier at a distance. He enjoys quiet evenings; she prefers crowds. The differences are mind-boggling.	He shouldn't try to understand her, just experience her. Through her patience and understanding he will learn to love.	He has a way of taking up space that makes it seem cluttered and confining. She can make him feel like a third sock. Best to stay as friends.
PISCES WOMAN	Shegets her feelings hurt at inconvenient moments and he has a way of treading on them without noticing. Friendship only please.	Both tend to be enslaved by sensual pleasures – adore a marathon of sex until dawn. A truly wonderful relationship.	Both parties are mysterious; however she has depth and emotion, while he is a thinker. The confusion may hold them for a while.	He sympathizes with her mood swings, cries with her and remembers important dates. She is impressed and this is a great relationship.	For a while these two feed on dreams and the air reeks of romance. But once reality intervenes, there is very little to keep them together.	She finds comfort in chaos while he prefers the kind of order found from control. Friendship maybe, but romance unlikely.

MATCHER

	LIBRA MAN	SCORPIO MAN	SAGITTARIUS MAN	CAPRICORN MAN	AQUARIUS MAN	PISCES MAN
ARIES WOMAN	This combination could produce a strong blistering romance – for about a week. What happens after is truly sobering.	Egos clash and bruise. He will get miffed if she speaks about herself or mildly outraged when she ignores him. Love–hate relationship.	She is charmed and challenged by him. Every time she screams and points he disappears. It can work if she can subdue her ego.	He is exciting, provocative and a bit crazy. He admires her drive and ambition. He may attract her if she has a father complex.	When she loses her temper, he will walk away and when she threatens to leave him he will calmly say 'Go ahead'. Not a good idea.	She needs a man strong enough to stick up for himself. The Aries lady is the main force but with compromise it could work.
TAURUS WOMAN	He is a romantic and wants to hear bells ring; she prefers silence and solid ground. Unforgettable experience but short lived.	Fatal attraction. Her heart will get caught up in his contradictions and he will enjoy watching her trying to get out. Best avoided.	He is the tough man of adventure while she much prefers to lounge about watching the world go by. Not a lot in common here.	She admires his ambitions and hard-working nature. He respects her resources and her security needs. A very compatible union.	This man's deepest desire is to have wings; hers is to have an anchor. Difficult to see what they could possibly have in common.	This man will lead on her so hard she won't be able to stand up. But when she needs him – he's missing.
GEMINI WOMAN	These two think of each other as fun and laughter, and share the urge to conquer the world. Highly compatible.	No way can he control the Gemini woman because she is a law unto herself. This causes savage sarcasm – they won't last a week.	He likes her best as a constant amusement, but when he has to consider her emotions the lively moments start to drag.	She lives for now while he plans his life past the point of old age. He conserves money; she has a great enthusiasm for spending it.	She is impressed by his ingenuity and ability to make simple things interesting. He is curious about how she can make complex things simple.	A totally incongruous relationship. In time she is turned off by his emotions; he finds her a chatterbox. Could be highly sexual.
CANCER WOMAN	She needs to be smothered in love while he needs to sit back and think about it. Sexually she could be in for an education.	She is born to love and care, but standoffish Scorpio prizes his independence.	She needs a romance with someone who will provide her creature comforts, he seeks a short fling.	Here is the security she needs while she is a woman who can give him the warmth he needs. A good relationship.	He is good hearted, but if she wants a man to hug and make passionate love to, she had better look elsewhere.	Sexually, these two send up smoke signals and make bells ring. Both will fall deeply in love.
LEO WOMAN	If she behaves and he is the mature type this could last. This lady's pride doesn't take kindly to competition.	Exciting, but as emotions condense into steam heat she will stand back and watch her sanity go up in smoke.	He is a traveller and an adventurer. With him, she is delighted beyond any of her wildest dreams. A compatible relationship.	She won't want this man unless he treads lightly. He is the original male chauvinist – his price for fidelity is control.	She is impressed by his logic and eccentricity; he is dazzled by her beauty and poise. But will he have the stamina to tame the lion?	Initially he vows undying love but next week she may catch him kissing the girl next door.
VIRGO WOMAN	She needs to be needed, but he has too many needs. It could be quite an experience sexually and romantically but she will get disillusioned.	Here is a lot of talk but little action – passion does not reign supreme. She will probably be prepared to pass by this relationship.	He wants excitement; she wants earthbound love. She needs to be needed; he is self-sufficient.Not a marriage partnership.	He seems ambition itself but inside he's a little boy. He needs appreciation and applause and she is just the woman to give it.	He has a hard time working out how they can be so detached. He finds her obsessions make him impatient.	She is quiet, shy and sensitive; he is chaotic and dreamy eyed. The difference here can be awesome.
LIBRA WOMAN	There are no limits on romanticism with these two. They have the ticket to the stars which reach out to them as they make love.	She is reliant; he is too independent to understand her dependency and is simply not interested in all she wants to share. A disaster.	He will give her full attention while the relationship is fun, but if she needs a man to be responsible then she may as well forget this one.	The Libra woman likes to lean but when she does so on Mr Capricorn, there is a price to be paid. They bring out the worst in each other.	He will be her best friend and help with her problems, but when she treats him like a pillow all the fun ends.	Emotionally these two are similar. She wants a man to lean on and he wants a woman to lean on. At some point both will topple over.
SCORPIO WOMAN	Mr Libra is in love with love while Ms Scorpio is out looking for devotion and sometimes enslavement, and she won't find it here.	Both are intense, jealous and possessive. She is warm sensual and self-critical. Unless they agree, hostilities may run under the surface.	She is jealous and possessive while he is always coming and going and often does not know in which direction. Not a good idea.	She admires his ambition but gets lonely when she never sees him. This relationship could turn into a bitter emotional battle.	He loves her mind and sexuality but her emotions are another matter. He has a lot of theories but little else.	Mr Pisces sees himself as mysterious but she can see right through him. This can work out but Mr Pisces has got an awful lot to learn.
SAGITTARIUS WOMAN	She is adventurous and constantly on the move and he shouldn't be surprised if he has to buy a sturdy pair of hiking boots to keep up.	She finds him charming and sexually powerful, but she does have a hard time undertanding his emotions. A temporary attraction.	An enviable couple who typify the romanticism of the good life because they know how to make the best out of every situation.	He is extremely dutiful but terribly intolerant of her. Furthermore he has a will which could make her easily forget she is a free person.	These two can enjoy a future full of travel. Whether they go in reality or only in their minds, every day will be a great adventure.	He is sentimental and divorced from reality. She is impulsive and chaotic. There is plenty missing from this relationship.
CAPRICORN WOMAN	While she sits back and smoulders, he analyses what he should be feeling. When she wants him to grab her, he will remain cool.	His mysterious behaviour brings out her insecurities: at one point she is swimming with head above water, the next she is drowning.	His basic attitude is don't worry: hers is that she has to worry because nobody else is going to. Not a good idea.	This is more of a primitive power struggle than a starry eyed romance. Tolerance is totally lacking in this partnership.	She is independent and freedom-loving; he is pragmatic and a little insecure.The differences go on and on.	This man floats somewhere above the clouds while she is rooted firmly on the Earth. More a case of leave me than take me.
AQUARIUS WOMAN	He has never had such undivided attention. She can make him feel like he has never felt before. A great relationship.	When he is making love, she will be regretting the fact that she missed the news. These two are completely incompatible.	He is riveted by her many interests while she enjoys his overwhelming enthusiasm. A fun loving and most compatible combination.	She is a dreamer; he is a man of the world. She is fascinated by people but he is concerned with himself. Both should look elsewhere.	This relationship is one of mental stimulation and devotion, always changing but never confining. Both love being together.	She lives in the future; he gets stuck in the past. She is friendly and detached; he is aloof and sentimental. A world of difference here.
PISCES WOMAN	She fears her feelings while he enjoys his. He relies on reason; her intuition will get her anywhere. Sexually things are good, but unlikely to last.	Her controlled desire and his devouring control are both so powerful that they may finish up on the floor. What a way to go.	She will love his boyish charm. He will be seduced by her steamy sensuality. But deeper differences will drive them apart.	He will be the father figure she has been searching for and she will be his romantic woman. Fantastic relationship.	He looks at the world through his mind and she sees it through her emotions. The attraction was unlikely in the first place.	This starts off as poetry in motion but after they land, then what? Good sexual relationship.

LEO

24 JULY – 23 AUGUST

THE symbol for your sign is the Lion and justly so, because you are commanding and certainly hard to overlook. Like the Sun, your planet, you pour out your golden rays and influence but you are only human and your lack of restraint is often your undoing. Many of the problems in your life are because you are too well meaning. You want everyone to share in what you feel you have got to give them. Problems come when others resent you telling them what you think is good for them. Still, once you turn on that wonderful charming smile of yours, you are probably the easiest person in the world.

There is a sparkle about you. You have an irrepressible faith in yourself and life. Strangely enough you also possess a strong self-sacrificing quality. Your whole life is a search for a cause, a special person to devote all your time and energy to. You are an excellent leader and take command easily in any situation or crisis that crops up. Power, in fact, falls about your shoulders like a royal mantle. You can certainly be counted on when life goes wrong. You frequently regard problems as a challenge and usually have little difficulty in overcoming them.

The Lion, of course, is a proud and self-sufficient animal and you need very seldom ask for assistance. If it does become necessary your request is made in such a way that some sort of exchange is implied – your unsubtle attempts at subtlety are often the source of amusement to those who know you well. You always repay favours at the first opportunity, for you hate to think you need to rely on anybody.

When it comes to expressing gratitude you can be enthusiastic, even fulsome with your thanks. You can even manage the odd tear if the occasion warrants it. People who are close to you will notice that you are really just going through the motions, and that underneath you believe that when someone does you a good turn, it is only what you deserve.

You know you are the life of any party, but despite this you feel the need to demonstrate it to others repeatedly. There is no doubt about it – you are a lot of fun.

PERSO

FEMALE

Saint

● You exude glamour and can outdo anybody even in a pair of overalls. You love parties and people, and usually see the world like a highly coloured epic film.

● Because of your objective awareness of yourself, you have a fine sense of humour and laugh the hardest when the many dramas in your life turn into a complete fiasco. You never have to go looking for excitement because you find it happening at the greengrocer's or in the checkout at the supermarket.

● Your constant enthusiasm dazzles those who enter your life. Men often confuse the strength of character they see with the strength of your passion, as well as misinterpreting your own personal warmth for seduction tactics. However, what you enjoy most is dramatic game playing.

● You possess a great love of life but expect it to reek of glamour and romance.

● You are independent and ambitious as well as highly motivated: your objective is leadership on a major scale. Your difficulty is that you can't appreciate your achievements on a more modest level.

Sinner

● Quite frankly you are a snob who likes to wear her designer labels for all to see. Your desire is for the appearance of success and power – if a substance is found wanting then the façade will often do. This also applies to the men who move through your life.

● Men are never quite certain what it is you really want, although sometimes they get the idea that it might have something to do with manipulation as you leap across the room shouting your orders. Your rage can break glass and the gleam in your eye seems to threaten the normally self-confident person. They tend to be intimidated by you. However, you really want to be treated like a little girl: you cry as that lover makes a beeline to the nearest door. As far as love goes, you gravitate towards men who make you look good. Because appearances must always be kept up at all costs, you have no time for anyone who is minus money, power, status and good looks.

● You want a lover to adore and adorn you, not to love you. Life is much safer when softness comes in the form of furs, or brightness in the gleam of a diamond. Yes, you've got it in one. You are a gold-digger.

NALITY

MALE

Saint

● Inside you are a really lovable kitten but you would rather roar than let others know it. You are proud, ambitious and driven and view your achievements only as an extension of your personal power.

● Your overwhelming ego is a façade that protects your tender emotions. Your needs for self-glorification are so compelling that you are easily taken in by sincere flattery and feigned helplessness and sensitivity.

● To you life is only a collection of the very, very best. Why drink a lager when for a little extra you can have the finest burgundy? Why settle for a Fiesta when you can have a Mercedes? Of course, you may have to use your food money for the next year for the downpayment.

● Tenderness, warmth and passion flow from you freely along with advice on how to do everything better. You may appear to be shy and reserved, but the chances are that at home you are more overbearing than a bull who has someone cornered. Other people will bear witness to your daily suggestions and demands for self-improvement.

Sinner

● You like people to move at the reasonable pace of immediately, if not before, but if you are a lazy Lion, you sink into a nice comfy armchair and daydream about how your energies will easily consume the world once you stir yourself.

● You can be bossy, boastful and bombastic. Not only were you made for the good life, you created it. Your wife, as well as your dog, calls you master.

● It is obvious that you are compulsively unfaithful: you need intense action from every angle, marriage could never be enough for a person as active romantically as you. Your favourite type is the more flashy female – the ladies must look good, your reputation is at stake.

● Diplomacy and concern for the dignity of others are not your strong points: nor is concern for the dignity of others. Strange how someone so in love with the truth builds his life on lies and is intimidating to those who venture to be honest.

● You have egotistical rages, but they are nothing more than a put-up job to prove to yourself that you really have some kind of power. However, in truth, it is only a matter of time until those around you get exhausted with your competitive performances. In the end your emotional immaturity will always betray you and those who will remain in your life will be the ones that you need but never really want.

● NAPOLEON BONAPARTE BORN 15 AUGUST 1769

THERE IS INVARIABLY A DICTATOR, OR AT THE VERY LEAST A LEADER, LURKING WITHIN ALL LEOS; THAT NAPOLEON AND MUSSOLINI WERE BOTH LIONS IS NO SURPRISE. LEO MUST BE IN FRONT AND ON TOP. HOWEVER, THERE IS SATURN ON NAPOLEON'S CHART, AND THIS BROUGHT ABOUT HIS EVENTUAL DOWNFALL.

● MADONNA BORN 16 AUGUST 1958

IN HER OWN WAY, MADONNA IS SOMETHING OF A DICTATOR AS WELL – A DICTATOR OF FASHION AND SEXUAL BEHAVIOUR. SHE IS MOTIVATED BY LEO'S NEED TO BE NOTICED AND WORSHIPPED AND WILL GO TO ANY LENGTHS TO FULFIL THOSE INNER URGES.

● ROBERT DE NIRO BORN 17 AUGUST 1943

HERE IS YET ANOTHER STRONG LION WHO LIKES TO BE OBEYED – HENCE HIS REPUTATION OF BEING DIFFICULT TO WORK WITH. THE LION'S EGO NEEDS ARE STRONG AND DEMANDING AND ANYONE WHO IGNORES THEM DOES SO AT THEIR PERIL.

in LIFE

At work

Leo Boss Leos make ideal heads of any enterprise. They understand and appreciate the different qualities of others, and rarely waste time or energy asking from people what it is not in their power to give. Commands, to be effective, must be easily understood and therefore the Lion's style is simple and straightforward. Approval is definite and unmistakable; displeasure intimated without hesitation. Leo bosses are capable of enjoying hard work but their efforts can be erratic and exasperating to those around. They will toil without rest and then quite suddenly lapse into an utterly lazy phase during which they will be immovable, stirring only when they deem themselves ready to carry on. Everything about this type is concerned with the big and ambitious: Leos have no time for petty or small ideas and those who wish to work for them will either fit in with their rather set ways or move on.

Leo Employee It is rather difficult to imagine Leos working for somebody else, for they generally try to work for themselves. This can lead to interesting freelance work or the formation of one company after another, although failure often ensues due to insufficient planning. When employed by others, Leos are ambitious individuals and will rise through the ranks as quickly as possible. Initially their outward arrogance can lead to resentment amongst colleagues who will soon come to realize that this is a façade used to cover their generous and warm hearts.

They possess depth of vision and will at once see the general shape of a scheme or project, but sometimes they may lack an eye for detail and others will find themselves covering up their mistakes. When suffering from gloom, flattery and encouragement from others will greatly assist Leos to pull themselves back. The Lion usually gets what he or she wants. The only thing you reflect on is time. Where does it all go?

FAMILY MATTERS

LEO MOTHER Although the Leo mother is full of warmth, love and compassion, nevertheless you can be a sore trial to your children. You are fiercely ambitious not only for yourself but also for your loved ones, and offspring are expected to shine not only at school but also socially – after all they are your ambassadors in the big wide world no matter where they may go.

When children play up and get themselves into trouble, you tend to care more what other people will think about you rather than your children's misdemeanours. Luckily because of the abundant love you give, your children do their best to please you most of the time and when they do let you down, there is no need for harsh punishment. One look at your woebegone face is enough to make them feel guilty for the rest of their lives. However, when in the bosom of your family, it is difficult to find a warmer or more loving parent.

LEO FATHER Like his counterpart, the Leo father has high hopes for his children. Sometimes too high. This man needs to guard himself from expecting from his children what they are incapable of either being or achieving. You must learn to accept and encourage the talents they have, even if they are not the ones you were expecting. You are full to bursting with love and pride for your offspring but need to try hard to find out what is best for them, and not you, and then act accordingly.

At times your home is something of a circus when you invite people home and then forget about it. This can cause embarrassment when they arrive – at some point you have to enquire where you met and where they are from. However, rarely are you covered in confusion, this being reserved for your family and the newfound stranger. Such a situation usually stems from the fact that you are so proud of your home and family that you want to share them with others. When overtaken with such generosity it might be a good idea to make some notes in your diary. This could save red faces and swell your friendship circle – as if it needs enlarging; you probably have enough friends to last you a lifetime.

LEO CHILD It is group activities which will appeal to the Leo cub. You can be sure that they will always have their own little gang of which – it goes without saying – they will be in total command. Therefore any trouble the little angels get themselves into is sure to have been conceived by your little kitten. You can ignore that dazzling smile and the protest of innocence. Generally speaking, your Leo will be an extremely popular child and will cause you few problems. However, if for some reason they are spending most of the time sitting in front of the television, you can bet that the reason for the neglect by their contemporaries will be due to boastful arrogance and an exaggerative nature.

Young Leos have a habit of bossing other children around which, if it doesn't annoy the children, will infuriate other parents. Because of this parents need to apply a restraining hand. Don't scold the child harshly in front of friends, but try to instil a sense of justice: the Lion cub can take the lead today, but tomorrow it must be the turn of a friend. Young Leos must be taught to respect this.

At Play

There is nothing a Leo likes better than showing off and therefore you are quite likely to be drawn into the local amateur dramatic society and will possibly be either its leading light or a dictatorial producer of one ambitious production after another.

When it comes to the open air, Leos occasionally like to potter around in the garden, but tend to expect an instant display. You bring that touch of boldness to bedding out schemes, mixing exotic plants with English country garden flowers and are a dab hand at roses too. The Lion is sociable and artistic, often found amongst the crowds at an exhibition in an art gallery, always hoping to meet the artist or some famous celebrity. However, on hot sunny days there is nothing you like better than to loll around in the garden on a comfortable sunbed with a large exotic drink. In this instance you are the picture of contentment and the neighbours can hear the purr even several blocks away.

Money

Where money is concerned, Leo has the fastest credit card in the west. No one can spend quite so lavishly or as quickly as the king or queen of the jungle. You definitely prefer convenience buying which means not knowing how much you have spent before you get the stamina to check your chequebook at a later date.

As a child your first words were probably 'I want it'; since then they have changed to 'I'll have it now'. Spending is a cure for any ailment. Flu calls for a new gadget for the car. The bad cough can be cured by purchasing a fine bottle of wine. Exhaustion is tossed to one side with a pair of new boots. Anxiety and depression can be too costly even to mention.

There is one thing to be said for the Leo – you will never be one of those people who wonder where their money has gone. With you it is not hard to guess: it's on your back (just read the labels) or in your home (how could you miss the leather settee or the fur rug?). Money to you is merely a means to an end. Sitting by itself in a savings account it is simply not taking you anywhere and when there is never any time, how can you possibly be expected to wait for interest?

When it comes to spending, nobody does it better than the Lion. You are an expensive dresser, and look good in original styles and off-beat colour schemes. There is an elegance and distinction in your taste. Everything about you reeks of class. You would rather go without than settle for anything cheap or of poor quality. The image you present to the world is all-important to you. Both sexes spend quite a lot of time in front of the mirror, ensuring that they look just right.

● WHITNEY HOUSTON BORN 9 AUGUST 1964

UNLIKE OTHER LEOS, WHITNEY DOES NOT WANT TO DOMINATE THE WORLD, BUT DOES WANT A COMFY COSY CORNER. LOADS OF ATTENTION IS ALSO NEEDED; THIS IS WHY UNTIL HER MARRIAGE, SHE WAS SO OFTEN SEEN AS DESOLATE AND SAD. LOVE IS ALL IMPORTANT TO THE PUSSY CAT LEOS, THEY GROW AND DEVELOP WHEN GIVEN A DAILY DOSE.

● BILL CLINTON BORN 19 AUGUST 1946

IT IS QUITE OBVIOUS THAT THE UNITED STATES PRESIDENT POSITIVELY WALLOWS IN HIS POSITION AS THE MOST POWERFUL PERSON ON THE PLANET. HE HAS LOADS OF LEO CONFIDENCE, BUT IT IS DOUBTFUL THAT THIS WILL IMPRESS THE AMERICAN PEOPLE FOR LONG. A CASE OF LEO PROMISING MORE THAN IT CAN COMFORTABLY FULFIL?

● SEAN PENN BORN 17 AUGUST 1960

SEAN IS DEFINITELY AN ALLEY CAT RATHER THAN A LION, ALTHOUGH HE DOES TRY TO BE THE LATTER. HE TENDS TO KICK AND SPIT AT ALL AND SUNDRY WHEN HE FEELS IGNORED. THIS WAS PARTICULARLY TRUE WHEN HE WAS MARRIED TO MADONNA, WHO CLEARLY THREATENED HIS OWN HIGHLY SENSITIVE EGO.

LEO *in* LOVE

Single

What you want is passionate glances, those feelings of a first love and those feelings of a last love. Yes, you definitely love love even more than you go for romance. Even for the most ambitious Lion, life really isn't worth living without love. This isn't simply a matter of being lonely: it is because whilst Virgos believe they are what they eat, you believe that what you are is tied in with who you attract, and if this isn't happening you are miserable. You are extremely idealistic, and are able to create a fantasy world that can protect you from what you don't want to see – often the truth of the situation. When you are finally disillusioned you retire wounded. You are left aloof and unhappy, channelling your energies into the professional side of your life. But the pain doesn't disappear.

Where your emotions are concerned, you are extremely vulnerable. This is because you have tremendous ego needs.

Although you are creative, you also know how to use the talents of others. You inspire them to achieve more than they thought possible. This characteristic is especially appreciated by your sexual partners! You rarely waste time – your methods are simple and to the point. As a Lion you want to be adored – and to be in love. You are greatly disappointed when things don't work out according to plan, often putting up with a less than ideal relationship because your great pride hates to admit defeat in anything. You love passion and intrigue and usually have no difficulty finding either. You can create enough drama to satisfy your theatrical style. However, when you finally give your heart to someone, you are loyal and faithful. What do you like most? Recognition and romance. But sometimes you get that mane tangled up; flattery can send that common sense straight out of the window.

You can sell anything, including yourself, to anyone – especially if you believe in what you are doing. Yes, you can always tell a Leo – but you can't tell him or her much. That's because you expect your loved ones to revolve their lives around you and don't take kindly to sharing the limelight. Clearly, it is important that you use some sense before dashing up the aisle, otherwise this will be an experience you will repeat again and again – but then possibly you might just like life this way. After all you would probably enjoy all of the drama that this would entail; however, it could prove tough on that poor Leo heart of yours.

Married

The Leo's need for affection, approval and love will push you in the direction of marriage at some point. However, what happens after the pronouncement of vows can be quite another matter. If you are a 'sinner' Leo at some point you will yearn for greater freedom. If you are a 'saintly' Leo your goal will be self-expansion and the right relationship will be a continuing source of inspiration. In general your need for partnership is far more urgent than most people realize because there is a profound desire to refine the ego of another person.

The mind is clearly in your concept of love: marriage can be a merry meeting of the mind and the heart, but if you enter into it only because you are lovelorn, seeking gratification rather than growth, marriage can be a terrible mistake. Sit back and consider your goals: the life you may save might just be your own.

Perfect Partners

When it comes to finding ideal mates, frequently the Lion finds happiness with a fire sign such as Leo, Sagittarius and Aries.

Leo with Leo No sign is more generous or warm: the Leo's ability to love is great and this combination can ease any threatening problem. Both share a love of ostentation, and derive much pleasure from making their home a showplace for all to admire. When in the hands of a Leo man, financial affairs are generally unsettled for he is inclined to gamble with life using all or nothing. But with two Leos contributing, when one of his gigantic enterprises fails hopelessly, then maybe one of hers will be paying off. As a rule Leo confers on its subjects a strong sex drive, therefore in this relationship much time may be spent in bed and many a domestic quarrel solved there. The physical attraction could be inescapable, and the wants, needs and desires shared. This can lead to an overactive sex life which may develop in various directions as sex can be separated totally from love. Infidelity may be tolerated provided honesty is preserved. This is an intensely passionate union.

Leo with Sagittarius In this relationship both parties will have found the right person to give them all the warmth and generosity they so desperately need. However, Sagittarius gives to everybody and Leo will need to recognize this fact, otherwise that big heart could be badly bruised. Finance promises to be a little bit chaotic as both harbour a tendency for crazy gambles, but somehow somebody's luck always seems to be in and this saves them from the poorhouse. Both parties believe in a certain amount of freedom to go out into the big world and conquer it and they will back each other to the hilt in all their crazy schemes and ideas. This can be an extremely promising relationship providing they can learn a few lessons. Initially they must learn to tell the difference between praise and flattery. Realistically neither needs to keep being told every single day that they are the greatest, the best, the handsomest or the most charming. Also they need to listen to other people and not insist on making all major decisions. If they can observe these few simple rules, then this relationship can be made in heaven.

Leo with Aries The confidence of Aries could hold great attractions for the Leo: the Ram's constant involvement in life earns respect. But both Leos and Arians have sensitive egos and must avoid trying to jostle for the position of power. Luckily with all the warmth that is likely to permeate this relationship it is quite likely that they will work out some sort of rota where they can take it in turns to be boss. On a cash level life may be a bit difficult because each party here has a well-developed sense of the full comforts of life and can suffer considerably when forced to go without. Sexually this pair are hot stuff: there is likely to be smoke emanating from the bedroom. Each party is fiercely energetic and likes to experiment so it is not difficult to work out what these two will be doing in their spare time.

ARE YOU A TYPICAL LEO...

Answer honestly the questions below, using YES, NO or SOMETIMES; total up your score, allowing 3 for YES, 2 for SOMETIMES and 1 for NO.

...MAN?

1. Are you accused of taking your woman for granted?
2. Can flattery impair your judgement of character?
3. Can you gracefully accept 'No' from your date?
4. Are you strongly attracted to the best material things in life?
5. Are you fiercely proud?
6. Do you frown upon lovemaking in cinemas?
7. Would you complain if your date looked untidy?
8. Is it hard for you to apologize?
9. Sexually would you try anything once just to see what it is like?
10. Do you gamble with life?
11. Are you over-generous with your affection?
12. Does wealth impress you?
13. Do you regard sport as a waste of energy?
14. Do you think that every woman has her price?
15. After a week of sexual abstinence are you bad-tempered?
16. Is it hard for you to sacrifice yourself for others?
17. Do you believe that the man should be the boss in the home?
18. Are you extravagant?
19. Do you forgive easily?
20. Do you think the man should lead in bed?

...WOMAN?

1. Does the idea of back-of-the-car sex appal you?
2. Are you impressed by the appearance of wealth?
3. Do you need regular sex?
4. If your man arrives looking like an unmade bed to take you to the cinema are you annoyed?
5. When sexually frustrated are you likely to go to bed with someone you would not normally find attractive?
6. Do you value and look after your possessions?
7. Do you write to somebody when it isn't your turn?
8. Does dancing appeal to you?
9. Can pride make it difficult for you to apologize when you are in the wrong?
10. Are you too often fooled by appearances?
11. Are you a fool for flattery?
12. Do you always put makeup on before going out to the shops?
13. Do you long secretly for a life of ease?
14. Do you hate cheap clothes?
15. Would you feel justified in dropping your boyfriend if he didn't quite come up to your standard in bed?
16. Are you a gambler?
17. Are you attracted to traditional furniture rather than contemporary?
18. Can you forgive and forget?
19. Do you feel a good argument clears the air?
20. Does the idea of a rich husband appeal as long as you could have a good lover discreetly?

ARE YOU A TYPICAL LEO MAN ?

1–30 Your intuition and powers of perception rule out Leo as your birth sign. It is more likely that you will recognize yourself in the chapters on Pisces, Scorpio or Cancer – read these first before searching elsewhere.

31–50 Apart from some pride and a streak of laziness, you are a warm, generous and nice person, a typical 'saintly' Leo and so that section will be of particular interest to you. A man with this sign usually goes far in his career and is always the leader rather than the follower.

51–60 You possess many of the good qualities associated with this sign but an overbearing and arrogant attitude can at times lead to trouble; your tendency to value all from a financial standpoint also needs to be controlled. Read the section on the 'sinner' Leo and digest the faults listed there.

ARE YOU A TYPICAL LEO WOMAN ?

1–30 This is not the score of a Leo: your priorities in life are all wrong, although you would be well advised to cultivate some of this sign's warmth and generosity. You will probably find yourself under Aquarius, Capricorn or possibly Virgo.

31–50 You are a true Leo with all the warmth, generosity and depth of feeling of this sign. Your weak point will be careless judgement which can lead to many unhappy affairs. Try to look a little deeper than the surface and read the section on the 'saintly' Leo for this should be you.

51–60 This score belongs to the 'sinner' Leo which means the big heart of this sign is mostly interested in its own desires. Your materialistic side should be controlled for this would make life a lot easier for you; try valuing people for their worth as human beings rather than for their bank balances or usefulness. However, not even a bad Leo can be all bad as this is the warmest of signs.

HEALTH

ARIES

Healthwise a magnificent sign, although excess vitality can be a danger and self-control is needed: Aries is accident-prone, especially where hot or sharp objects are concerned. Eye problems, migraines and general headaches are a possibility. Health is usually impaired when too much is taken on – Arians should learn to delegate instead of wearing themselves out.

TAURUS

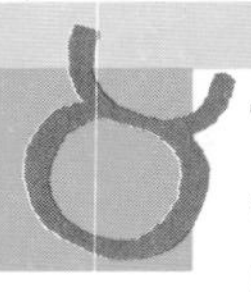

The Taurean's natural vitality is often excessive and should be used constructively, otherwise it may consume itself and develop into morbidity. Dangers to health are laziness and self-indulgence, and even sensuality, gluttony and drunkenness. Throat problems and glandular disorders are very common, and probably strike when Taureans are run down.

GEMINI

Geminians are live wires but most of their vitality comes from nervous energy which can suddenly desert them when a job becomes irksome. Nervous exhaustion frequently follows their tremendous outbursts of activity, and Geminians need plenty of sleep, fresh air and a sensible diet. Accidents to hands are likely and, as this sign rules the lungs, smoking should be discouraged.

CANCER

The stomach and the breasts are ruled by this sign and much attention needs to be paid to dieting if irritations are to be avoided. Worry can result in indigestion which may in turn produce defective circulation, and a tendency always to fear the worst does not help the subject. An overactive imagination inclines Cancerians to vivid nightmares.

LEO

Leos are either exceptionally strong and radiating vitality or forever sick. Discordant environments, hurt pride and unrequited love can all react on their health. The best medicine is peace, love and harmony. Leo rules the back – subjects need to guard against accidents to this area; and the heart – foods low in cholesterol will help quite considerably.

VIRGO

The typical Virgo is very wiry and capable of enduring long hours of work and physical fatigue. Healthwise this is a very strong sign and illness, when it occurs, is brought on mostly by overwork and too much absorption in practical matters. Serious illness is rare because of the Virgoan's enthusiasm for physical activity, and care with food and diet.

HEALTH

LIBRA

Librans are strong as long as their sense of balance remains undisturbed, but when upset their nerves and constitution will suffer indirectly. When run down, Librans should rest, watch their diet and develop appreciative qualities through music, poetry and art. This sign rules the kidneys too so it is best not to over-imbibe and to drink plenty of water.

SCORPIO

Healthwise Scorpios have tremendous endurance and great powers of recovery. They take pride in the length of time they can work without sleep and mostly get away with it. When they do fall ill, no patient is more trying, for they put no faith in anyone other than themselves. The genital area is ruled by Scorpio and infections in this area are usually above average; occasionally the bladder gives trouble too.

SAGITTARIUS

Because Sagittarians are so sports-loving, they are generally in good shape but their over-activity can react on the nerves and periods of relaxation are necessary. This is the most accident-prone sign in the Zodiac – hardly a day goes by without Sagittarians acquiring a fresh bruise, scratch or cut. Fevers are another hazard but in general Sagittarians are hale and hearty.

CAPRICORN

In health matters the black moods and depression experienced by Capricorns can prove to be the most detrimental hazard, directly reacting onto their physical wellbeing and, in particular, the stomach. Capricorns should adopt some method that will allow them to step outside their problems in an effort to curb this weakness. A confidante would be most helpful.

AQUARIUS

This sign rules the blood. Sluggish circulation manifests itself with cold feet and hands. Any weakness is likely to be in this area and should be watched in order to avoid more serious trouble. Fresh air seems to be congenial to this type when under par. Calves are prone to mishap.

PISCES

Pisces rules the feet and this area of the body is very vulnerable. There may be accidents to them and this consideration is all important when choosing shoes. The alternate Pisces exaltation and depression can also have an effect on the physical wellbeing. Pisceans need to fight strenuously to retain a sense of perspective, so that they can remain healthy.

VIRGO

24 AUGUST – 23 SEPTEMBER

VIRGO is often misrepresented. You are practical and cautious, yet adaptable and busy; modest, straightforward, loyal and very trustworthy.

The Sun passes through your sign at harvest time, when prudence suggests that all that is worth keeping should be put in its proper place. You are strong on conservation, be it the planet, your resources or your money. You discriminate through your intellect too, rarely rejecting anything or anyone through habit or instinct.

You are a great observer of people, and are frequently found standing in a corner, watching and listening while you decide who would be the most interesting person to talk to. This is because you are greatly concerned with improving your own mind and knowledge and really can't be bothered wasting time talking to frivolous chatterboxes.

You have a tremendous eye for detail and an instinct for analysis. You will sift through the smallest of details to find out what is going on underneath. And because of this you listen and remain quiet until you are sure of your audience. You don't have any real desire to make waves.

If you look closely at your life it is likely that you will notice that although you say you want meaningful relationships, somehow you deliberately avoid them. This is a basic conflict usually caused by the way you naturally insulate yourself against the emotional imperfections of the world. However, you should realize that nobody is perfect and that includes you. Once you have accepted this, your attitude will become more positive and your life less complicated.

One of your most admirable traits is your lack of egotistical behaviour. Neither do you cloud issues with your own intolerance or prejudices. You see things clearly and are able to discard all that is really not essential.

You have an active imagination that is only likely to get out of hand in romantic affairs. You use it to try to improve conditions and circumstances around you.

PERSO

FEMALE

Saint

● Fundamentally you are an old-fashioned girl who believes in morals and privacy. You despise public displays of affection, people who talk while they are eating and people who never know when to shut up. You are intelligent, cautious, analytical, prudent and very understanding.

● Your mind is so organized you could probably run a large corporation from behind the scenes. However, your emotions are so vulnerable that at times you feel like a teenager with acne. Given a chance, you are capable of finding fault with every aspect of yourself and of wishing you could trade identities with any random passerby.

● Your feelings are very delicate and so are your emotional demands. You will probably be the last person to give an ultimatum and the first to try to accept something even if you can't understand it. Believe it or not, you are highly sensual but discriminating. A man's mind may be the first thing to attract you, but you would never say that it is the sexiest part of his body. You have a certain earthiness and no man who really knows you can deny it.

● When you are feeling doubtful or mentally anxious or insecure, immersing yourself in nature seems to have a protective and purifying effect on you. You are not the type to cry on other people's shoulders but you have to let your anguish out somehow and physical activity is often your most inconspicuous form of relief.

● Although you probably do not realize it, you are viewed with the highest respect in your circle. You are a woman who has her life so much under control that at times you take it for granted. What other people consider to be gigantic tasks, you attack with calm and composure.

Sinner

● You tend to be a creature of routine and habit. Imagination is non-existent and you have the kind of intellect that wears other people to a frazzle. Your thought process operates on preconceived facts and narrow opinions, which seldom have anything to do with insight. Your mind is mechanical, your attitudes computer-like.

● Passing time in your company is extremely tedious. You are a worrier who always looks for something to complain about. You are compulsive, talk too much, eat too much, think too much and sadly never come to any happy conclusions. Your rigid thinking and restricted opinions depress you so much that you overcompensate with self-indulgence.

NALITY

Male

Saint

● There is no denying you are an industrious person. You probably get up at dawn to begin work and finish in the wee small hours. You frequently hear people muttering about recreation, and you decide that this must be an enjoyable kind of work. Work is your source of excitement; however, even more exhilarating than work is the feeling of accomplishment you get from doing it. Only rarely do you give your body a rest. When you are not working, you can be found batting tennis balls and when you are not batting tennis balls you can be caught thinking about some new kind of work. The most exciting moment in your life, next to falling in love, was probably the day when your new computer arrived. Naturally, it and you went straight into the bedroom where you worked on it instead of on your partner.

● Fortunately there is more to your life than non-stop work. There is also love, and that is quite important. In general, you want to get married so that you no longer have to take the time away from work to worry about your love life. Obviously the most efficient way of doing this is to have it waiting for you at home.

● You are loyal, honest, caring and consumed with the idea of being a good husband. Even if you run to the bathroom to brush your teeth before you kiss that mate of yours, this is only an example of your consideration.

Sinner

● You are a relentless workaholic. Your attitude to the world is eccentric: you make a tremendous fuss about how much you help other people but the fact is that you could give a lecture on how to be self-serving. You are the most deadly kind of chauvinist, for you disregard what you don't believe and you believe in only that which you want to. You are small-minded, totally subjective and destructively critical. However, when you tear down anything or anyone, interestingly enough it is never work of your own.

● Because you are petty, argumentative and at the same time desperate for approval, you are as irritating as a persistent fly who keeps eluding its demise. You have an extremely swift tongue and a sharp mind which you waste on sarcastic remarks and meaningless chatter. When you speak your listeners should feel grateful to get your criticism about what is wrong with them and why – at least in your book. Yes, you are a person who always has an eye for improvement, except when it comes to your own conduct.

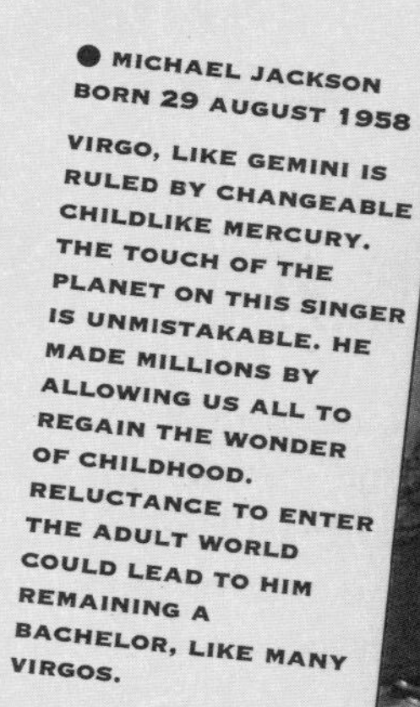

● MICHAEL JACKSON BORN 29 AUGUST 1958

VIRGO, LIKE GEMINI IS RULED BY CHANGEABLE CHILDLIKE MERCURY. THE TOUCH OF THE PLANET ON THIS SINGER IS UNMISTAKABLE. HE MADE MILLIONS BY ALLOWING US ALL TO REGAIN THE WONDER OF CHILDHOOD. RELUCTANCE TO ENTER THE ADULT WORLD COULD LEAD TO HIM REMAINING A BACHELOR, LIKE MANY VIRGOS.

● LAUREN BACALL BORN 16 SEPTEMBER 1924

EVEN AS A YOUNG GIRL OF 18, LAUREN HAD THE GRITTY NO-NONSENSE SIDE TO HER CHARACTER WHICH BELIED HER THEN WILLOWY FRAME. HER TOUGHNESS ATTRACTED HUMPHREY BOGART BUT CAUSED MANY OTHER LEADING MEN AND PRODUCERS A FEW HEADACHES. VIRGO KNOWS WHAT IT WANTS – IT IS AS SIMPLE AS THAT.

● RICHARD GERE BORN 31 AUGUST 1949

RICHARD GERE HAS THE VIRGO ABILITY TO WALLOW IN THE MUD, FIGHT OFF ADVERSARIES AND STILL SEEM CLEAN AND UNRUFFLED. VIRGO IS A VERY PARTICULAR AND FUSSY SIGN, AND HE WILL NEVER PERMIT HIMSELF TO BE DISCOVERED LOOKING SOMETHING OF A MESS. HIS QUIET DEMEANOUR IS ALSO GIVEN TO HIM BY HIS SUN SIGN.

VIRGO in LIFE

At work

Virgo Boss Their love of perfection can make Virgos particularly difficult bosses. Accuracy and method are very important to them and on occasions staff will find themselves completely bogged down by petty details or minutiae. However much one may try to please these characters they are rarely lavish with affection or praise and seldom popular. Others may regard the Virgo as fussy and even old womanish, but if they are employed by a Virgo, they will either have to accept their boss for what he or she is or move on.

Luckily when some major crisis arises within the office or factory, the Virgo calmly seeks out the source of irritation and decides which is the best way to act. Strangely enough, although excellent in emergencies, the Virgo can be thrown by something quite trivial. This usually occurs during periods of nervous tension when the Virgo sees everything out of proportion. A high standard is expected of those who work for the Virgo boss and those with no vocation for work may be dealt with quite unmercifully.

Virgo Employee Virgo workers apply themselves efficiently but quietly to taking in even the smallest detail. They are, sadly, passed over when praise and appreciation are handed out to more extrovert workmates, who may have stolen the credit. In fact, Virgos may appear forever doomed to work without sufficient reward or recognition. They give of their best and are extremely practical; Virgos are both careful and eager to help their colleagues. Their constant need to be occupied often stems from their nervous energy, but the trouble is that they find it very difficult to let up and their ideas on relaxation can seem like hard work to others. To be happy in any situation, Virgos will need to come to terms with themselves, try to relax more and understand that others do not have their sense of vocation.

FAMILY MATTERS

VIRGO MOTHER It is not easy being a Virgo mother because, let's face it, you believe in everything in its place and a place for everything, and when children come along this simply is not possible. Certainly with time you begin to adapt to this and then you turn your critical eye on your child's progress or personality and attempt to polish them up as one would a gemstone.

The important thing to remember for you is to show your child how you feel. There is plenty of softness inside, so why keep it to yourself? And for every negative remark that is made you should make at least two positive ones. In this way you will not cause any complexes or hangups in your offspring.

As a typical Virgo mother, you like a clean home, and no matter what the temperament of your children is, eventually you will expect them to toe the line. Concessions are made in the early days, but not when the dreaded teens strike. However, to be fair, you are certainly a caring mother – the question is, do you convey this fully to your children? Certainly this is easy to do when they are young and cuddly, but it will be during their adolescent years that your patience will be tested to the fullest.

Hopefully you have a gentle, kind husband to lend you support. You are going to need it. Your success as a mother depends on the amount of love you receive from your mate.

VIRGO FATHER The Virgo father is rather similar to his female counterpart although he is unlikely to be around quite as much, because he is a workaholic. It may take a couple of years before offspring actually work out who this strange man is who occasionally pops into their life. If you are determined to spend so much time away, at least give your full attention to your children when you are at home. Avoid berating them over small things and listen to their problems. They will be glad of your advice, providing you can resist the temptation to nag. Do not expect standards of hygiene from a 10-year-old that you might from a 20-year-old. It takes time to learn how to be perfect. Something you should be able to appreciate.

VIRGO CHILD The Virgo child is a discriminating individual so don't expect him or her to be surrounded by thousands of friends. They are selective and know who and what they like. This, together with a tendency to criticize others, can make this child feel lonely at times. However, when young Virgos do find a friend, help to keep the relationship going by extending invitations. If they finally take to someone, they will stick to that friend through thick and thin.

Parties are, not surprisingly, agony for this type. Being self-conscious the Virgo is not a good mixer. Never force a Virgo into party going if it is quite obvious that it is bound to upset him or her. This child does not belong to the funny hat, whistle-blowing and jokey fraternity. Left to develop in their own good time, they can emerge as self-confident, selective and sophisticated individuals so don't push them into being something they can never be.

At play

Virgos sometimes think the word 'recreation' is just another way of saying time for extra work. Despite this, there are times when even you realize that it is essential to get a little break. This may only be pottering around in the garden, trying to perfect details around your alpines: Virgos delight in rock gardens and enjoy making miniature landscapes with dainty plants, waterfalls and dwarf conifers. You are also keen on entertaining and showing off your hard work – Virgos are frequently found dragging out the barbeque. Mind you, guests may be kept waiting a long time until everything is perfect.

This sign has a keen eye, therefore when it comes to games, snooker, darts or billiards may appeal. Although you are quite interested in watching physical contact sports, you are not too keen on getting yourself all dirty. Tennis is much more your thing, possibly due to the nice white outfit which, of course, must be immaculately clean. Sporting activities allow the Virgo to work off considerable nervous energy.

Money

You are conservative with cash and would never be the kind of person who likes to own too many credit cards. Because you keep neat records you are rarely left stranded by lack of cashflow. Every 50p spent is very soon replaced by another 50p.

You cannot understand others who are victimized by their own money and whose chequebooks are in a complete mess. Basically you believe in budgeted, controlled spending and view money as a sound security. Holidays are saved for, as are those various other little luxuries which someone else might buy on credit in one of their more impulsive moments.

When your hard labours result in some spare finance, you are more than likely to sink it into a wise investment than to squander it on a new car. Wealth is not the overriding desire in your life – security is. Your prudent ways pay off when you can comfortably pay your bills and then make the most of the money left over. One thing you hate to worry about is basics and money is about as basic as you can get.

One thing you will never stint on is health matters. When you can afford it, you are quick to spend on a health plan which will guarantee you peace of mind. Furthermore, you can usually be found haunting the health food shops, looking for tempting titbits to gratify your taste buds. While you are there you will stock up on a million vitamin pills you believe you need – and you are probably right. Just the act of buying them is in itself usually enough to make you feel healthy.

● JASON PRIESTLEY BORN 28 AUGUST 1966

JASON FOUND FAME IN THAT POPULAR TV SERIES, *BEVERLY HILLS 90210*, AND AS A VIRGO, WHAT ELSE WOULD HE BE PLAYING BUT A CLEAN-CUT, CLEAN-LIVING YOUTH? VIRGO'S RULER MERCURY, THE PLANET OF YOUTH, WAS OBVIOUSLY TWINKLING WHEN HE JOINED THE CAST ON THIS YOUTH CULT PROGRAMME.

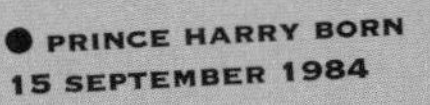

● PRINCE HARRY BORN 15 SEPTEMBER 1984

VIRGO IS OFTEN THE SIGN WHICH, BECAUSE OF ITS NATURAL MODESTY, OFTEN SPENDS ITS LIFE SERVING. THIS WILL BE ESPECIALLY TRUE WITH THIS YOUNG PRINCE, FOR BEING THIRD IN LINE OF SUCCESSION TO THE THRONE, HE WILL ALWAYS BE IN HIS FATHER'S OR HIS BROTHER'S SHADOW.

● KEANU REEVES BORN 2 SEPTEMBER 1965

ALTHOUGH KEANU MAY BE QUITE AT HOME IN UNUSUAL ROLES ON THE SCREEN, IN HIS PRIVATE LIFE HE IS A TYPICAL VIRGO, RETICENT ABOUT PUBLICITY AND OFTEN RUDE WHEN OTHERS PUSH THEMSELVES ONTO HIM. NATURALLY, HIS PRESS HAS NOT ALWAYS BEEN GOOD. VIRGO'S SHARP TONGUE CAN TAKE OVER THIS STAR ON OCCASIONS.

in LOVE

Single

Fundamentally you want love more than anything you can think of, but, and it is a big but, there are a lot of things you don't want along with it. Because of this, first impressions are crucial. Immature and crude behaviour can prevent you granting somebody a second chance. Although you can appear cold, aloof and unduly critical, you are in fact shy and supersensitive.

A fine mind is the first thing to attract you and after that, warmth and human consideration rate very high on your list of priorities. What you desire is to feel needed and cherished. In return you are willing to devote yourself to the welfare of the one you love. When there is little action on the romantic front you tend to overcompensate through work. However, there is no denying that although an intellectual accomplishment can pick up your spirits like a double vodka, there is nothing like coming home to someone you love to give your life that extra lustre. You want to expand yourself through love and strangely enough you find it when you least expect it, since it is one area in your life that you simply can't organize, order and plan.

If you look closely at your life, you will probably notice that although you state that you want meaningful relationships, you often deliberately avoid them. This is because of a conflict between your character and Mother Nature. Bear in mind that you tend to insulate yourself from others for fear of discovering their emotional imperfections. However, if you do this then you will end up alone, and you will be surprised to find that people may just care enough for you to make some concessions. However, remember that give and take is a two-way street, and you may have to do a little rearranging of yourself and your priorities too (unless, of course, you are already perfect – which, let's face it, is extremely unlikely). Your nature, as a Virgo, does not relish involvement with others because of the possibility of personal hurt. And yet deep inside you really long to give yourself completely. All this complication is part of the price of being a Virgo. Remember, 'nothing ventured nothing gained'. And if you are feeling lonely, remember this is the natural outcome of your failure to reach out to others. You can be so critical and clear about work matters, and it is a pity that you find it so hard to use the same clarity in the more intimate side to life. This can be more meaningful, more intimate and worthwhile than work and certainly deserves equal time and energy. You seldom give in to an emotional impulse. Certainly you experiment with love, but it's usually no more than that – the expression of an inquisitive need to find out what you're missing rather than giving in to an insane, irresistible attraction. Don't miss out on love through too much calculation or analysis.

Married

You definitely do expect to get married at some point, basically because you find superficial encounters rather unsatisfying. To your mind, marriage is the symbol of the emotional security that you desire. Within this relationship you look forward to deep intellectual and emotional rapport as well as calm and order. Shared interests and a high degree of emotional compatibility are in the long run more important to you than physical passion. Nevertheless, there is a strong likelihood that your heart was once broken by a romance with someone who took you by storm, leaving little time for you to think, prepare or plan for what happened next.

Faced with a mate's infidelity you may experience feelings of bitterness so intense as to haunt you for years afterwards. Rejection in any form is a horror to your psyche which often prolongs emotional pain by getting obsessed by it. On the other hand, should you yourself decide that a relationship is over, then you can be remarkably cool about the entire matter. Virgo, as a sign, has a fairly high divorce rate but only because these types are often too set in their ways to make the necessary adjustments required in marriage.

Perfect Partners

When looking for Virgo's perfect partner it is often found among the earth signs, Virgo, Capricorn and Taurus.

Virgo with Virgo A mutual outlook on life provides the reason why this relationship starts up and if both are idealistic, it seems they will work very hard at it. Attitudes to money are shared: both are ruled by commonsense, practicality and a need to save for unforeseen events. As long as they have separate careers then all may be well, but both possess a critical eye which will be turned on one another and the less time they have to think about each other the better. Everything is participated in jointly from cooking their food to writing the laundry list and all is executed in detail – it is impossible for the Virgo to be slapdash. Outside interests need to be encouraged for these two perfectionists have a lot to offer the world.

Sexually, they could initially be strongly attracted, but if one or other makes a mistake in bed, then with no hesitation a criticism will be made. Sex, though, is unlikely to be the basis of this relationship as too much time will be spent improving matters elsewhere.

Virgo with Capricorn A strong physical attraction could exist between these two and similar attitudes to financial matters could deepen a bond. Ambitious Capricorn will go far with Virgo's encouragement. These two are a well-matched pair on the sexual level but neither revolves their world around this side of life. The experience should be a close and mutual expression of love though, strengthening and not ruling the relationship. Each will help the other make things grow, whether it be plants, flowers, bank accounts or the affection between them. Both, too, can be rather old-fashioned and romantic and so supply the needs of others without any friction or difficulty whatsoever.

Virgo with Taurus The Bull is friendly, patient and honest with his or her feelings – far more on Virgo's wavelength than almost anyone else. Their outlook on life and attitudes to money are identical. And both enjoy planning for the future. Each has a deep-rooted fear of debt, and all of this supplies them with a firm foundation for a relationship. The Taurus is the more intense of the two and this should help Virgo to shed some of those inhibitions. The only cause for friction is the Bull's occasional laziness; if concessions are made life can work out perfectly for these two.

They will have an active sexual life, although it should be conservative, lusty and straightforward.

ARE YOU A TYPICAL **VIRGO...**

Answer honestly the questions below, using YES, NO or SOMETIMES; total up your score, allowing 3 for YES, 2 for SOMETIMES and 1 for NO.

...MAN?

1. Do you feel unappreciated at work?
2. Do you take any physical exercise to keep yourself fit?
3. Do you admire men like James Bond?
4. Do you prefer your sexual affairs one at a time?
5. Are you critical?
6. Do you think that routine is important?
7. Are you fussy with your food?
8. Do you long to be more extrovert in bed?
9. Do you take time over everything you do?
10. Can you be faithful in a lengthy relationship?
11. Does sexual deviation embarrass you?
12. Are you shocked by other people's sexual habits and behaviour?
13. Would being in debt worry you?
14. Are you turned off easily over some small matter?
15. Would you notice if your woman was wearing a new sweater?
16. Do you lose respect for women whose sexual appetites can equal men's?
17. Are you conscientious?
18. Do you think the family should be limited to two children?
19. Do you always make certain someone has taken precautions before making love?
20. Can you do without much sleep?

...WOMAN?

1. Do you think the importance of motherhood is over-emphasized?
2. Are you fussy about your food?
3. Do you think that financial security is more important than sex in marriage?
4. Would dirty fingernails put you off making love to their owner?
5. Are you critical?
6. Is it hard for you to make new suggestions in bed?
7. Do you think that others may consider your sexual morals old-fashioned?
8. Can you abstain from sex for a week with ease?
9. Are you happy to be financially independent of your man?
10. Do you enjoy looking after others?
11. Would you be horrified if your unmarried daughter became pregnant?
12. Do you believe in method and order?
13. Does your taste in clothes centre on simplicity?
14. Can you work hard on little sleep?
15. Does waste of any description worry you?
16. Would you make an excuse if you were not feeling like sex and your man was getting amorous?
17. Do you think that permissiveness has gone too far?
18. Do you have neat handwriting?
19. Does your mind work quickly?
20. Do you think men have an easier life?

ARE YOU A TYPICAL VIRGO MAN ?

1–30 Your Virgo characteristics are almost non-existent. The softer personality you would seem to possess suggests Pisces, Scorpio or Cancer so look at these chapters next.
31–50 You are a 'saintly' Virgo and so with luck you may have missed out on the more unpleasant aspects of this sign, although the critical eye would still be a part of your personality; this is fine as long as you keep it under control.
51–60 Yours is the score of the 'sinner' Virgo which can have unfortunate effects. You may be almost impossible to please and the way you expect everyone to conform to your strict code of behaviour can make you a sore trial to your admirers. Read the appropriate section using your critical faculty on yourself.

ARE YOU A TYPICAL VIRGO WOMAN ?

1–30 You are definitely not a typical Virgo. Your mind is too broad and versatile: look for yourself under Sagittarius, Gemini or Libra but don't try to fit yourself into those signs if they are not appropriate.
31–50 You are a true Virgo woman and although you may have many fine qualities, it is possible that you may miss out on an awful lot of fun. If you could try to accept people for what they are without making attempts to change them, then life would be much happier for you. Your career is likely to be very important to you.
51–60 This is the score of the 'sinner' Virgo and it makes you very difficult to live with. You will lose many friends and lovers if you cannot learn to shut your critical eye on occasions. Read the 'sinner' section carefully and try to accept the relevant points and then change.

LIBRA

24 SEPTEMBER – 22 OCTOBER

YOU are gracious, intelligent, charming, friendly, sympathetic and a wonderful friend. Therefore it is always a surprise when you suddenly spoil yourself by turning your character upsidedown and become critical, moody, fiery, jealous and unyielding. Being a Libra isn't that easy, because your symbol is the scales and although you fight hard to balance them, you rarely manage to get it right but veer from one extreme to the other.

You are renowned for your sense of harmony but at the same time you do manage to stir up an amazing amount of strife and discord in your life. You may consciously begin an argument if you are talking to someone you feel is making too many generalizations or being too dogmatic and who seems to suggest that all other opinions are wrong. You might not give a stuff about the subject of the argument but you are not going to just stand there without putting the other side of the question. It's all down to balance in those scales.

In your personal life it is extremely difficult for you to make decisions. You may be good at manipulating other people when necessary, but when it comes to making up your own mind, you consider and reconsider so many different possibilities that in the end everything seems impossibly confused and no one could sort out the tangle. This indecision can be extremely annoying to lovers as well as friends. Still at least those who are closest to you know better than to try and rush you because one impatient word or gesture makes you dig in your heels with amazing stubbornness – you feel it is your right to be indefinite if that is how you choose to be.

PERSO

FEMALE

Saint

- You love old movies and love songs, and most of all you love romance. Your favourite days are St Valentine's Day and your birthday.

- You hate being taken for granted, begging for affection and anybody with bad manners. You come alive when you get plenty of loving attention and positively thrive on being appreciated. You are the kind of female men like to be around because you are warm and womanly.

- The world often benefits from your creative efforts, whether it is some wonderful dish you have invented in the kitchen, a writing project or a piece of music. Giving parties is one of your favourite pastimes and attending them a particular treat for your guests. You are a classic sensualist and a pleasure seeker but at the same time have the kind of perseverance to fulfil anything you put your mind to. You can accomplish a multitude of far-reaching objectives in your career and each of them has to be a labour of love.

- While you have no problem making major decisions, the little day-to-day ones drive you potty. You agonize over whether to have coffee or tea, to wear pink or blue, or to tell your lover to take a long walk over a short cliff or just ask him to pick the spring beans.

Sinner

- Should a man stop you to ask the way you are likely to see a possible affair. You are a lady with a lot of needs and your motto tends to be 'let no man go to waste'.

- As soon as you began to talk you wanted to get married. Because you are passive, unassertive and ineffectual, you decided that maybe a man was what you needed. You are the type that brings out the worst in men – they love to boss you around. Before long you usually find yourself a secure place as half of a couple.

- Next to being totally taken care of, security is probably your favourite thing. Once you find even the mildest excuse for a man, you hang on like a limpet. To get rid of you a man has to come close to having you killed off, or he could fix you up with one of his enemies. No one has ever told you that you are a thinking being. Likewise no one has ever told you that you have choices, and since you are so dependent on what you are told to do, you live your life patiently waiting. Not surprisingly, many things pass you by, but sometimes you are much better off for it.

NALITY

● Because your perspectives are so shallow, you easily lose sight of major issues. You are missing that rich inner life that could support you during periods of loneliness and stop you from looking upon your own company with fear.

MALE

Saint

● Your attitude to life is an enthusiastic one. You yearn for your creature comforts and like to over-indulge whenever possible: delicious food can transform you into a galloping gourmet. In your most natural moments you are a confirmed sensualist and a definite supporter of the good life; because of this you are usually a lot of fun to be with.

● Often you enjoy a good degree of success in your job because you are highly intelligent and creative in your approach to most problems and you have the foresight to envisage the personal side of any situation. You will have a highly adapted logical intelligence, combined with the kind of charisma that makes you a person whose popularity would never be in question.

● Because you are so lively, people of all ages and both sexes heartily enjoy your company and put your name at the top of every invitation list. You have the personality of the entertainer and you will never lack an eager audience.

Sinner

● You continue to play the role of playboy even when you reach the age of 80. At this point, behind you lies the legend of love; the truth is that you are in fact the most fickle and inconsistent lover and you care far more about yourself than any other person you could possibly meet. At best you are clever, charismatic, witty – and careful never to get into a compromising position. You are the kind of man who would leave a woman sitting in a train station if you were suddenly assailed by a prettier face. You are shallow, superficial and highly self-serving. The chances are that you would marry a woman for her bone structure and the day after the wedding start having affairs. You are a very busy man when it comes to your romantic activities.

● However, underneath all this cavorting lies a very dependent creature who runs when he has to confront his deeper feelings. Basically you tend to be insecure and depressed, passive and ineffectual, confused and indecisive. You would rather talk for hours about your emotions than let yourself feel them.

● When it comes to living, you are committed to the definitives without any kind of compromise considered, and whoever gets in your way will be coldly disregarded.

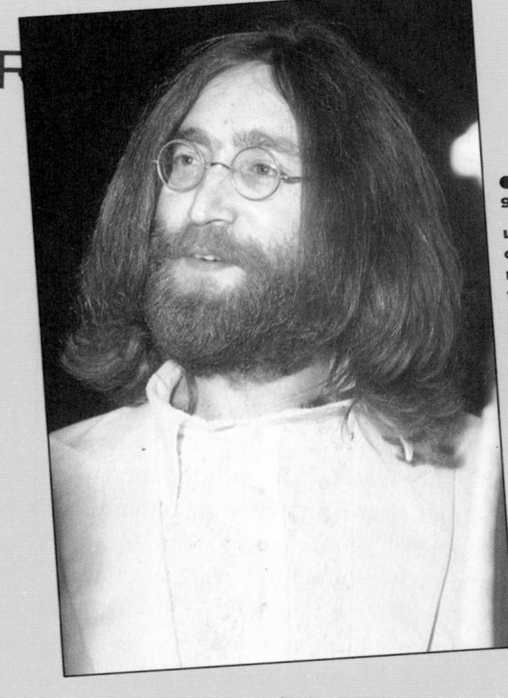

● JOHN LENNON BORN 9 OCTOBER 1940

LIBRA IS THE SIGN OF CO-OPERATION AND PARTNERSHIP, AND WHEN THIS SIGN SUCCEEDS IT IS OFTEN IN CONJUNCTION WITH ANOTHER PERSON – IN THIS CASE PAUL McCARTNEY. FURTHERMORE, LIBRA IS PEACE-LOVING. ALTHOUGH JOHN COULD CERTAINLY KICK OVER THE TRACES, HE WAS GREATLY CONCERNED WITH 'PEACE AND GOODWILL'.

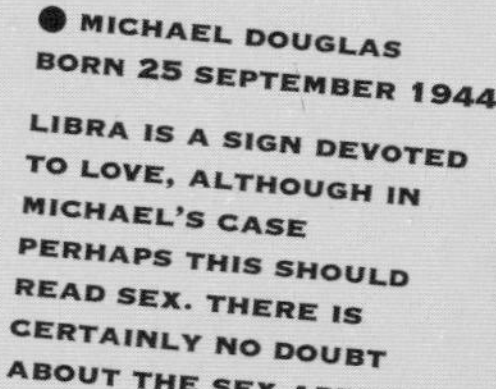

● MICHAEL DOUGLAS BORN 25 SEPTEMBER 1944

LIBRA IS A SIGN DEVOTED TO LOVE, ALTHOUGH IN MICHAEL'S CASE PERHAPS THIS SHOULD READ SEX. THERE IS CERTAINLY NO DOUBT ABOUT THE SEX APPEAL GIVEN TO HIM BY HIS SIGN, RIGHT DOWN TO THE DIMPLE IN HIS CHIN, A CLEAR TOUCH OF HIS RULING PLANET – VENUS. ALL LIBRANS HAVE THEM SOMEWHERE.

● SUSAN TULLY BORN 12 OCTOBER 1967

SUSAN TULLY'S ROLE AS *EASTENDERS'* MICHELLE CERTAINLY SEEMS APT. HER CHARACTER'S LOVE LIFE SEEMS TO BE CONSTANTLY IN A STATE OF CONFUSION OR DEBATE. AS SHE IS RULED BY THE PLANET OF LOVE – VENUS – THIS IS TO BE EXPECTED.

in LIFE

AT WORK

Libra Boss Librans are charming to work for, having a natural courtesy, a diplomatic manner and a genuine desire to please. Further characteristics to recommend them are friendliness, popularity and an easy-going manner. They are the most reasonable of people and possess an ability to see both sides of any question. Because of this, gossips will meet with the scorn they deserve and while Librans will revel in playing Solomon in any dispute, it is advisable to make sure that you are in the right before complaining to them.

Their biggest weakness is a tendency to avoid decisions; they prefer to shelve them and wait and see before acting. It is for this reason that Librans are at their best when working with others and even if the Libran concerned is the employer, they probably work in direct partnership rather than on their own.

Libra Employee Success in life is most likely to occur in partnership with another, but in certain cases, the Libran is equally happy working with a small group of people for independence is not a strong characteristic. When searching for a job, this type will seek out the beautiful, creative or artistic; dirty or hard work is disliked unless the end product is something beautiful, and sometimes even a mildly unsavoury job will be put off for as long as possible.

Although often accused of laziness, Librans are usually fairly eager to get what they want and strong Librans will shine sufficiently to achieve their objectives. They are generally popular in a working environment.

AT PLAY

As you are so lively, people of all ages and both sexes heartily enjoy your company and put your name at the top

FAMILY MATTERS

LIBRA MOTHER For the most part the Libra mother tends to be more of a friend than a parent, usually because she herself has not grown up and is therefore quite happy to clamber about the floor, play with dolls, trainsets or whatever. The only time you assume command is when confronted with bad table manners, and rude behaviour in general. These you will strenuously correct and continue to correct until the message has been received. You are particularly adept at bringing out the artistic side of your children and are delighted when you discover that they are interested in a new musical instrument, painting, and even singing. You are, perhaps, well fitted to bringing up daughters although should a son exist, the Libra mother will do her best to turn him into a real little gentleman.

The Libra mother has good taste and her home is a reflection of this. Fine china and glassware are her pride and joy. She is such a lovable person that as soon as her children are old enough to understand this, they will learn to appreciate all the beautiful things.

LIBRA FATHER It usually takes a Libra man some time to confront the fruit of his loins. Because you are a romantic, you find it difficult to cope with the end product of your courtship. In particular you find young babies rather offputting. However, once the child begins to develop his or her own personality then the Libra father falls in love, stays a constant provider, friend and support for his offspring for the rest of their life. You are particularly well suited to dealing with teenagers. You remember your own pain when a spot appeared in an obvious place on your first date and carry the memory around with you. You therefore find it easy to identify with teenage traumas and cope with them efficiently.

After a slow start, then, the Libran father comes into his own later on.

LIBRA CHILD Dressing up is probably the best-loved game of all Librans and any old clothes should be put aside for this purpose. You should provide a hefty lock for your wardrobes for it is quite likely that your Libran child will decide that old clothes are simply not what he or she had in mind. Music and painting are two other interests that stimulate this type, and tuition in either may well prove to be beneficial and rewarding. Absorption in what is fashionable and what is not may tempt either sex into spending hours in drawing and designing outfits. This in turn may lead to a fascination with sewing, especially if you use a sewing machine.

Bear in mind that this is an air sign and that many of the children born under it are fascinated by aeronautics. This can be developed along many different lines, from reading about the designing of aircraft to modelling. It is up to you to discover which aspect of the hobby is likely to appeal to your own Libran child.

This is not a sporting sign, and the Libran becomes adept at inventing excuses for avoiding netball, football, rugger or any other school game. The fact that the father may be a football fanatic, may amuse the Libran child but it is unlikely to inspire or activate him or her.

of their party list. In general this sign tends to be highly musical – whether or not you play an instrument you could get a lot of pleasure from simply listening to music. An artistic hobby of some description is almost a must.

Sporting endeavours and pursuits which entail getting sweaty and dirty hold little appeal for you. However, you appreciate the multitude of colours that can be found in an English herbaceous border, and use your good taste and care to create some wonderful effects in the garden. Once the hard work is done you stretch out on a sunbed and soak up the warmth, an ice-cold drink in your hand. Such occasions as this really relax the Libran: you will be impossible to shift.

● STING BORN 2 OCTOBER 1950

LIBRA'S PEACE-LOVING INSTINCTS ARE EXPANDED IN STING TO A LOVE OF THE PLANET AND ITS SURVIVAL. HE HAS TRIED TO USE UNIVERSAL MUSIC IN AN EFFORT TO BRING THE REST OF US TOGETHER AND HELP US TO UNDERSTAND OTHER PEOPLE. THE WISH FOR HARMONY IS CERTAINLY STRONG IN HIS LIFE.

MONEY

You are luxury minded and because of this can spend more cash in one day than most people do in the month. You have an eye for the very best, particularly if you are depressed when an expensive bottle of wine or perfume helps to lift your spirits.

You believe in the principle of immediate gratification and that funny little mood can plunder your bank account better than any robber. However, should anybody confront you with the fact that you spend money as if you had your own printing press you would be completely puzzled and surprised. You really aren't at all extravagant you protest! That is because you have forgotten last week's designer suit which you haven't even unwrapped plus the expensive furniture you currently have on order. To your own way of thinking these are all necessities. You secretly believe you lead a very simple and practical life.

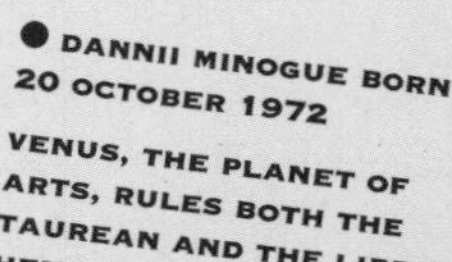

● DANNII MINOGUE BORN 20 OCTOBER 1972

VENUS, THE PLANET OF ARTS, RULES BOTH THE TAUREAN AND THE LIBRAN. HENCE BOTH SIGNS PRODUCE MANY SINGERS. LIBRA IS ALSO THE SIGN OF PARTNERSHIP, THEREFORE IT IS INTERESTING THAT DANNII IS FOLLOWING HOT IN THE FOOTSTEPS OF HER SISTER. IT IS A MOOT POINT WHETHER HER CAREER WOULD HAVE DEVELOPED HAD IT NOT BEEN FOR KYLIE.

In your defence you are capable of keeping to a budget. However, it has to be said that too often that budget of yours has a crafty way of keeping you. Still, you can be rather materialistic. You may not hang on to your possessions with the same firm claw as, say, does Cancer, but you do delight in them and aspire towards having rich and lavish things. Though seldom ostentatious, your taste inclines towards the extravagant, if you can afford it. It is difficult for you to accept austere surroundings. You adore oriental rugs, fine mosaic flooring, velvet sofas on which to cuddle up. And the best curtains you can afford. Neither would you turn your nose up at one or two Impressionist paintings. You have a gift for blending the antique with the modern and secretly wish for a bottomless pocket, in order to fulfil your expensive tastes. A good bottle of wine is another temptation and you'd secretly like your own wine cellar. But, 'I don't want much' you protest – that little bit too loudly to be convincing.

I leave it to you to be honest with yourself. Those who know you well could certainly vouch for your little extravagances. What seem luxuries to them may be mere necessities to you.

● PAUL HOGAN BORN 8 OCTOBER 1939

PAUL HOGAN'S LOVE OF THE OPPOSITE SEX IS MORE RAUNCHY AND CHEEKY THAN THE USUAL VENUS-BORN ROMANTIC LOVER. NEVERTHELESS, PHYSICALLY AND PERHAPS EMOTIONALLY TOO, PAUL IS AN OLD SOFTY. AFTER ALL, IT WAS LOVE – OR WAS IT LUST? – AT FIRST SIGHT WITH HIS SECOND WIFE.

in LOVE

SINGLE

Deep inside you search for romantic bliss but it often appears that you are far more in love with the idea of love than with the actuality. You have a refined idealistic nature and a whole stock of the 'Happy ever after' myth, although this is not to say that two people can't achieve that. However, it always takes at least a little work and many confrontations to come about and, especially in your early years, you cling to the fantasy of being swept away by an uncontrollable force that just accommodates itself to your life. If, from this point, things start to go wrong, you either lose interest or feel hopeless and depressed.

Basically you want to see lights and hear a few bells ringing too. Anyone who can create this situation can occupy a part of your life as long as the bells and the lights last. You are attracted to forceful and strong personalities that reek of stability and charisma. However, when Venus calls you come running and sometimes the situation can be far from ideal. Try to remember that when you put all your energies into one person, you stand to lose a lot if it doesn't work: you tend to get stuck in some painful spaces that only you have created. Until you have learned the lesson of self-reliance the experience of love will be more of a compulsion than a creative emotional situation.

Yes, your main problems lie in your emotions. Whenever they are aroused, you lose your wonderful straight thinking. You become quite silly in a way that is often irresponsible. On these occasions you accept fantasy as truth and are capable of believing anything. As a lover, you are extremely impressionable and tend to see your perfect love in any individual who happens to have one or two of your basic requirements. As a Libra you are prone to early marriage, and probably more than one. And you are sure to become involved in at least one very odd love affair in your life. Sometimes you are parted from the one you believe to be your true love and live the rest of your life in a romantic dream world of hopeful expectation – frequently safer than searching amid the harsh realities of life for someone with whom you can live and love. You would make a great mate if you could persuade yourself to fall for someone with whom you are truly compatible, then let your imagination do the rest. You could then settle down in a successful and workable relationship. Try to stop yourself from constantly comparing that special person to other people.

Another problem you experience is that in romantic affairs you don't like to say 'No'. You are so anxious to please and to avoid unpleasantness that you often take the line of least resistance and suddenly find yourself in an intolerable situation.

MARRIED

For Librans marriage is a must, since you have a deep need for the shared experience. It is not uncommon for this sign to have more than one marriage, because the feelings in the first one mysteriously disappear. However, whether or not any marriage will be lasting really depends on your realistic assessment of your own values.

In addition, many Librans have a severe problem when it comes to give and take. You tend to give far too much or not at all and this imbalance ultimately creates anger on at least one side of any relationship. Deep down you are searching for a soul mate. However, on the quest you often get distracted by superficial qualities which you find terribly attractive and then you abandon your inner need for a mature love to satisfy your outer need for either luxury or physical beauty. Consequently years later you find yourself saddened and lonely.

Your ideal would be never to live your life alone but it is precisely this rigid idea that sometimes makes you desperate, dependent and closed off to a more varied life experience. Libran women usually want to get married at the earliest possible age; Libran men are slightly more cavalier and less overly consumed by the same needs: they can view the field quite happily and make the most of the experiences while they are doing it.

PERFECT PARTNERS

When it comes to finding the ideal mate, the Libran usually becomes happily settled with another air sign, such as Libra, Aquarius or Gemini.

Libra with Libra This relationship promises to be an exhausting one for both partners tend to be bursting with vitality and over-demanding with those they love. Neither will want to spend too much time at home. They need plenty of outside interests to keep them happy – if these are denied them, frustration can set in. Each has a well-developed sense of justice, bringing to their home many fights for their more vulnerable friends and acquaintances. Animals may stray willy-nilly into their house and will always find a welcome. Each understands that partnership needs hard work and understanding and much effort will go into theirs to make it as harmonious as possible. Sexually the attraction between them could be overpowering and each may make a real effort to think of ways of pleasing the other. These two need plenty of excitement and it certainly won't be found lacking in this relationship.

Libra with Aquarius These signs could well meet in the midst of their social whirl and from then on they will have great difficulty in finding any time to be alone together. They are both attracted to activity, excitement and unusual people. Up to this point in life sex may not have meant a great deal to the Aquarian, but Libra is just the sign to change all that. This is because the Libran is an impulsive lover; although amused by this at first, the water bearer will learn to appreciate the value of spontaneity in a partner. The relationship between the two is certainly a stimulating one.

Libra with Gemini A certain novelty and excitement on both sides could be the main factor in bringing these signs together. To begin with they will rush around in a mad circle enjoying themselves and indulging in activities of all kinds. Libra, though, does tend to want to socialize at home on occasions and providing it is made as an attractive proposition, then the Geminian will be happy to go along. Their sex life will certainly be an exciting affair as each knows exactly how to stimulate the other. A third person is unlikely to cause a rift in this relationship as neither will attach undue importance to infidelity. An excellent relationship.

ARE YOU A TYPICAL LIBRA...

Answer honestly the questions below, using YES, NO or SOMETIMES; total up your score, allowing 3 for YES, 2 for SOMETIMES and 1 for NO.

...MAN?

1. Are you interested in women's fashion?
2. Is your wandering eye difficult to control?
3. Are you attracted to glamorous women?
4. Do ugly shows of temperament turn you off?
5. Is your work pattern erratic?
6. Does injustice offend you?
7. Do you think you can enjoy a sex orgy?
8. Are you artistic?
9. Do you fall in love easily?
10. Is it hard for you to say no to those you love?
11. Do you have a complicated life?
12. Do you enjoy playing with children?
13. Are decisions hard for you to make?
14. Have you often thought you were in love with two women at the same time?
15. Is sex a failure for you if the woman is unsatisfied?
16. Do you think you are oversexed?
17. Are you good at expressing inner emotion?
18. Do you think that partnerships are a work of art?
19. Would you repeatedly leave jobs where injustice was condoned?
20. Do you believe in sexual equality?

...WOMAN?

1. Do you find yourself in difficult situations over your own inability to say No?
2. Do you consider yourself a feminist?
3. Do you enjoy seducing your men?
4. Do you find violent men repellent?
5. Do you live for the man in your life?
6. Is it hard for you to exist without love?
7. Do you think it is wrong for a woman to be a careerist?
8. Do you like cats?
9. Do you ever dream or think of being in bed with two of your lovers at the same time?
10. Does beauty thrill you?
11. Do you think a man's body can be beautiful?
12. Do you admire glamorous, famous women?
13. Are you capable of deep hatred for men?
14. Do you wear bright colours?
15. Are you guilty of crazy ideas and schemes?
16. Does the thought of motherhood worry you?
17. Are you musical?
18. Are you hurt when criticized?
19. Do you secretly like possessive men?
20. Do you rebel against injustice?

ARE YOU A TYPICAL LIBRA MAN ?

1–30 You are far too practical, down-to-earth and conservative to be a true Libran. Try reading the chapters on one of the earth signs – Taurus, Virgo or Capricorn, and if you still cannot easily recognize yourself, then Scorpio may be your sign.

31–50 You belong to that 'saintly' group of Librans which is fortunate for you as this is an attractive sign and you are lucky enough to have most of the good points associated with it, and few of the faults. The biggest flaw in your personality could be the reluctance you have to hurt others. You may take this to extremes and this leads to many complex situations.

51–60 This is the score of a 'sinner' Libra and although you may have much of the charm which comes with this sign, you also have more than your fair share of faults. Read the 'sinner' section carefully for it will help you to recognize and overcome your weaknesses.

ARE YOU A TYPICAL LIBRA WOMAN ?

1–30 Your logical answers couldn't be less Libran. You would seem to possess many of the characteristics associated with one of the earth signs. Read the chapters on Virgo, Taurus or Capricorn, for you should recognize yourself more easily as one of these.

31–50 This is the score of 'saintly' Libra which means you possess most of the virtues of this sign and very few of the vices. Indecision could be your greatest fault and one that could bring you much unhappiness if it is not controlled, but apart from this you have an attractive personality and will be very popular.

51–60 Your tendency to over-dramatize your love life and to generally live in a world of fantasy needs to be checked if you are ever to make a success out of a partnership. You should try to view your lot through more realistic eyes, although you are no doubt quite popular due to a lively personality. You may benefit from reading the section on the 'sinner' Libra several times.

CHATTING UP THE ST

Each birth sign has distinct likes and dislikes. Use this basic information to identify someone's birth sign from a distance and then tailor-make your approach for maximum romantic success.

ARIES

HOW TO IDENTIFY Positive, impulsive and forceful, Aries is usually heard before seen. The Aries girl is the one in the corner with the direct honest gaze and exasperated expression, engaged in a boring conversation; the Aries man that one making the peanuts jump every time his fist beats the coffee table. Mental combat stimulates Aries but they need to respect their adversaries. Is there a pinkish glow to the skin and a reddish tinge to the hair? Yes? Then you have identified your Aries. Where do you go from here?

HOW TO CHAT UP *A direct approach is called for. Take a deep breath and introduce yourself. A firm handshake is a must and forget flattery. If you are really interested in this person, be clever. Once he or she is animated, leave for 'some other appointment', adding that you would love to continue the conversation another time . . .*

TAURUS

HOW TO IDENTIFY Taureans have a lazy, sensual walk and an appealing gaze which hints at inner strength. At the party she is the elegant female poised on the sofa successfully juggling drink, napkin and plate. He has the seat near the grub. Both eat their considerable fill before even glancing at the opposite sex.

HOW TO CHAT UP *Remember that the Bull is always irritable when hungry and therefore pile up your Taurean's plate, wait until he or she is satisfied, and then be your natural charming self. This realist hates prigs and posers and is equally comfortable with pop singers and street cleaners. An odd slapstick sense of humour exists. If you can't throw a custard pie relate some amusing stories. Once you have won a smile or laugh, you are home and dry.*

GEMINI

HOW TO IDENTIFY Geminians are restless, talkative and clever. Professional party goers, they can flatter anyone but ask a personal question and you are left with a shrinking violet. Get into an intellectual conversation and you are assaulted with facts about the great philosophers, politicians and poets, or perhaps fascinating trivia. Geminians are usually slender with eyes of twinkling blue or grey. Observe their unexpected agility of movement and speech, and a mischievous delight in shocking.

HOW TO CHAT UP *Stand within earshot and wait. Soon your target will feel irritated and intrigued that you have failed to be impressed. The Geminian is probably an insomniac so rivals will eventually drop by the wayside, leaving the field open to you. Get out the encyclopedia and drink plenty of black coffee – you'll need them.*

CANCER

HOW TO IDENTIFY The Crab can see the ridiculous side of human nature and often reacts with a loud cackle. This sign also has an extremely sweet tooth and a taste for alcohol, especially when depressed. You can bet the girl wading through her third cream puff or the man on his fourth brandy is a Cancerian. The character sitting alone looking resentful is sure to be one too – hurt once, and you ain't going to get the chance to do it again. Cancer has a large bony frame, generous skull, expressive and sensitive eyes and mouth, and an attractive pout.

HOW TO CHAT UP *Wade in gently: this person is shy and fears rejection. Flirt but don't declare your undying love unless sincere or that notorious claw will fasten around your throat and never let go. Ask about the family and discuss cooking, show sentiment, imagination and romantic impulses and once you have been accepted, never forget birthdays or anniversaries – Cancer has a long memory.*

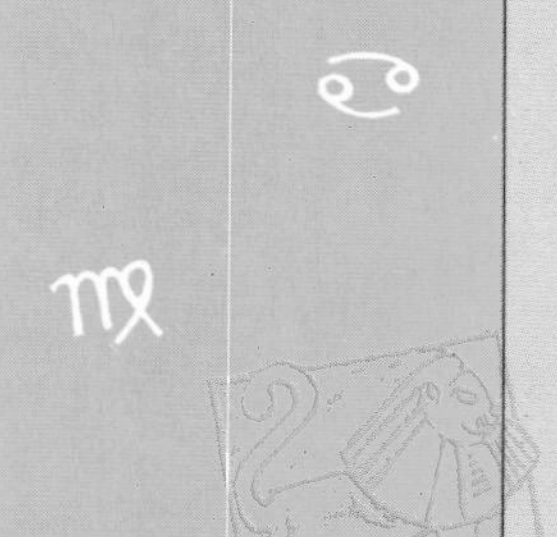

LEO

HOW TO IDENTIFY The Lion stalks into a room. Note the commanding, confident air, the soft yet deliberate voice. He or she rules centre stage, with dramatic movements and statements. In a bad mood the Lion sulks or pouts until someone rushes over to attend to them. Recognize the hair swept back over the face and the eyes which one moment convey gentleness, the next fire and passion. Remember that although the claws may be sheathed, they are willing, waiting and very sharp.

HOW TO CHAT UP *This type likes power so you need confidence, and the ability to lay on flattery really thick. Compliments turn a fierce Lion into an adorable kitten. But be warned, rejection is not easy to spot as Leos can tell people to get lost with charm and style.*

AR SIGNS...

LIBRA

HOW TO IDENTIFY Crowded smoky rooms send Librans cowering into the hallway but at a small gathering, this individual excels. Librans love to play at love and their vital charm, good looks and courtesy ensure them plenty of opportunity. The biggest giveaway is the length of time it takes to reach a decision. Beware of the pained expression when you ask 'Wine or spirits?'

HOW TO CHAT UP *Catch your Libran in a lather of indecision. 'Can I recommend the red wine?' is enough to guarantee a grateful smile. Or gain their attention and respect by rescuing them from an aggressive admirer. This type loves harmony. Arts, cinema and theatre are good topics of conversation.*

VIRGO

HOW TO IDENTIFY Virgos are easily spotted at a party compulsively emptying ashtrays, and inspecting the glasses and cutlery: worry is part of the Virgo persona. Physically this character is slim and well dressed, with bright intelligent eyes. Virgos are capable of being the perfect mates if well matched. They are also capable of being perfect nags.

HOW TO CHAT UP *Check your fingernails, test for bad breath, and then approach with grace and taste. Show your intelligence, sense and reliability, and then suggest you leave together immediately because you hate parties. Your Virgo will be glad to escape. Walk in the rain or feed the local ducks. Once you have passed the test you can trust Virgos with the sexiest friend you have.*

SCORPIO

HOW TO IDENTIFY If the Scorpion is attracted to you, then that's it. You'll feel a pair of hypnotic eyes that will scrutinize you right down to your last eyelash, after which you will be either accepted or rejected. Flirting is useless. Scorpio wants and gives loyalty, devotion and true passion.

HOW TO CHAT UP *Don't bother unless you are fancy free and without a mate. Deception is loathed by Scorpions. Treat this seething volcano with the respect which is expected – and deserved – and you will have a devoted friend and lover for life. Later you may congratulate yourself on landing such a catch, but – poor deluded innocent – it was you who were caught in the first place.*

SAGITTARIUS

HOW TO IDENTIFY The oblivious character in the middle of that embarrassed group is a Sagittarian who has just made a typical blunder. Watch him or her navigating the room. Five seconds elapse and a glass is spilled. Should this disaster area also happen to own a pair of clear blue eyes and an open face then you have identified your Sagittarian.

HOW TO CHAT UP *Very, very carefully, candidly and with an unflagging sense of humour. Sport, the outdoor life and travel are your best bets. Don't be too possessive: those born under this sign possess a strong sense of freedom. The Sagittarian looks for a pal and will regard you as a prospective friend and maybe, if you are lucky, a lover. But never consciously as a husband or wife.*

CAPRICORN

HOW TO IDENTIFY All Goats are ambitious, most are social climbers, and a few are horrendous snobs. Therefore, at a party, locate the smartest, richest or the most successful guests and somewhere in the middle there's your Capricorn. Scrutinize the face: there is a quiet persistence and strength there.

HOW TO CHAT UP *It helps if you happen to be a member of the aristocracy or a self-made success. However, if you haven't made it, a rundown on your hopes and dreams will do nicely. The Goat can forgive failure, but can't understand those who accept it easily or worse still don't even try.*

AQUARIUS

HOW TO IDENTIFY The Aquarian is an eccentric and may turn up in fancy dress at a formal do. When confronted by a policeman or a politician the Water Bearer will demand to know what is going to be done about the homeless and the crime rate. Should the victim be a street cleaner, then what is happening at the local tip will be equally fascinating and important. Aside from honesty, the Water Bearer usually possesses a pair of clear, dreamy eyes and very regular features, but he or she is sometimes lacking in diplomacy. You won't be bored.

HOW TO CHAT UP *Politics, religion and sport are the old favourites. The Aquarian also likes to shock, so why not get in first? Show an interest in whatever is the current fashionable cause of the moment and you can't go wrong.*

PISCES

HOW TO IDENTIFY The Fish is never at home with lots of sweaty bodies around: watch them escape to the garden or the balcony. You can tell a true Piscean by the unworldly but beautiful eyes, soft hair and voice, modesty and ultra masculinity or femininity.

HOW TO CHAT UP *Discuss astronomy, astrology, yoga or meditation. The Fish has vivid dreams and loves to talk about them. By the time you leave, you will have been hooked. Never treat your Fish roughly because his or her scales peel off easily. Be gentle, affectionate, considerate and above all kind.*

SCORPIO

23 OCTOBER – 22 NOVEMBER

IN the typical Scorpion, the need for truth can be seen in the way you are always trying to get to the bottom of situations. You are the instinctive detective of the Zodiac. You don't hold forth with eloquent words, instead you listen. When you have sussed out the situation or the person you are with you can ask the most direct questions without so much as a blink of the eye. Your ability in dealing with downright difficult and offensive people is quite incredible. You loathe affectation and hypocrisy. Anyone with something to hide should certainly avoid meeting up with you. Your understanding of human nature and your intuition are quite phenomenal. You have an unnerving way of asking the right question at the worst possible time.

There is a perversity here, though, for although you are an expert at revealing the secrets in other people's lives, you manage to keep your own affairs very much under wraps. You enjoy secrecy and have been known to deliberately spark the curiosity of others and then block their attempts to find out more. Should anyone try to pry into your affairs or take any liberties with your emotional life, you can get very uppity. It has to be said that it is very unlikely that anyone will ever get close enough to know the real you – that would leave you feeling far too vulnerable.

You are proud but not egotistic, dramatic but never ostentatious. You may appear calm, friendly and relaxed with others, but you are always at the centre of your own existence. Because of this others sometimes think you are a little selfish or self-centred and there is a certain amount of calculation in your character.

You are never lost: you know exactly where you are at any given time. Other people may prefer to reject the real world for a while and be comforted in a sentimental way. Not you. When it comes to the essentials, the last thing you are is romantic. You can't bear to kid yourself. You want the truth, and that is often regardless of how much it can sometimes hurt.

PERSO

FEMALE

Saint

● You are compassionate and kind, and because of this can never say no to a friend who is in trouble. You do like the total truth, though, and with one glance can see everything. You can feel the pain of a laughing stranger and understand the fears behind the smirk of your closest friend.

● You tend to be secretive and somewhat shy, and you guard your privacy because it is one of the things you value most. Because you reveal so little of yourself in any situation, you sometimes gain the reputation of being both aloof and inscrutable. The truth is that you are cautious in all your interactions because you are emotionally vulnerable: you feel so intensely that you place safeguards around yourself to make sure your feelings don't undermine you.

● On a daily basis you battle with the darker side of your character – mood swings seem to engulf you. However, with determination you usually overcome them and do what you have to do – and do it well. Deep inside there is a hunger that has made you search for activities with greater meaning for you are highly intelligent and have a keen memory and a probing mind that demands a broader understanding of the world around you.

● Unlike those with any other sign you express a deep desire to rise above yourself and your limitations. Problems that would make other people fall apart and throw up their hands in horror, you face with calm, poise, dignity and a sense of self-possession. Because your mind is so shrewd and psychic, you never act without having a deep understanding of all possible outcomes. A sincere sense of humility is part of your charm.

Sinner

● Men see you as a kind of witch and you see them as toys to play with at will. As long as they remain within the confines of the structures you have set up they have your stamp of approval, but should they dare to stray from your domain, they might just feel your talons down their faces. In sexual games, you are the cruel elusive gambler who sometimes enjoys the play even more than the prize.

● People, to you, are like actors, so you set the stage, sit back and watch the improvisation. Men can rarely understand you and there are many times when you are not quite sure of yourself. All you are aware of is what you want and where you have to go to get it. It could take you a lifetime to come up with a good reason.

NALITY

● You need a man in your life to make you feel like a woman, but once he is there, your mental acrobatics only multiply. If you hold on to him for sex and emotional security but feel that materially he doesn't suit you, you will do your best to tear him apart. You will never risk involvement with a man of no wealth unless he has some other kind of sensational power.

MALE

Saint

● You are a charming person who knows when to speak and when to stay quiet. You care deeply about others and have a great desire to help them in any way you can. Because you are so kind and compassionate, you continually find yourself listening to lengthy lists of problems.

● You are active and full of life, and never let anything get you down. You can overcome most problems and enjoy the challenge of doing so. You can suffer any degree of pain without burdening other people with it. And you can achieve your ambitions because you have tremendous determination.

● You are rational and passionate, and have a scintillating mind which is interested in probing life's mysteries. Both morally and intellectually you are a perfectionist and demand high standards from those who are closest to you.You have great powers of concentration and a mind that is emotionally aware, intuitive and perceptive. Mentally you are strong, independent, self-reliant and a silent warrior in times of difficulty.

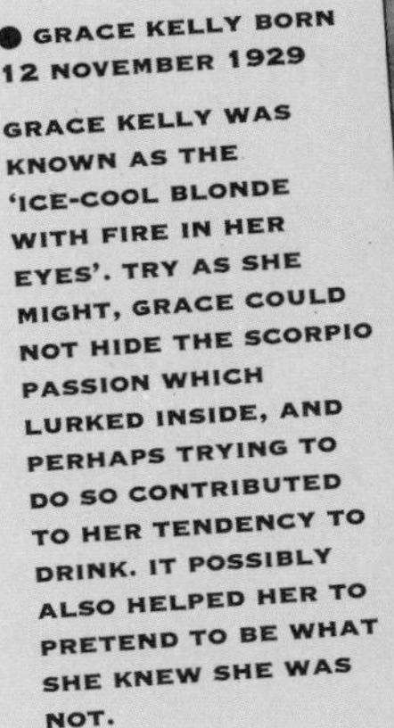

Sinner

● Achieving success is never a problem, since you have very few scruples. You take pride in the power you seem to hold over other people, which is understandable since you have probably poisoned several to get it. You are selfish, sarcastic, and shrewd. Your memory is vaster than a warehouse, your mind is like a laser beam. You have an unnerving habit of unravelling people's minds and motivations while remaining inscrutable yourself.

● You are the greatest of all game players. Whatever the stakes, it is given that you always win. You have more emotional manoeuvres than any fiendish mind could manage to think of and when your mind is intent and highly motivated it is easier to reason with a hired assassin than to talk you down.

● Even in love, you always calculate your options and review your opponent's moves, so that the entire relationship is like a chess game you have already won. The key to your personality is that you are terrified of the intensity of your own emotions and so you either repress or displace them.

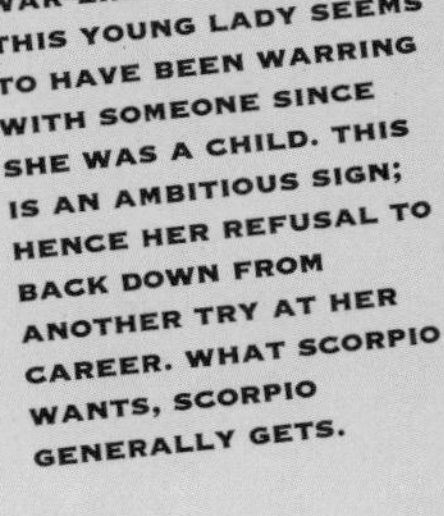

● GRACE KELLY BORN 12 NOVEMBER 1929

GRACE KELLY WAS KNOWN AS THE 'ICE-COOL BLONDE WITH FIRE IN HER EYES'. TRY AS SHE MIGHT, GRACE COULD NOT HIDE THE SCORPIO PASSION WHICH LURKED INSIDE, AND PERHAPS TRYING TO DO SO CONTRIBUTED TO HER TENDENCY TO DRINK. IT POSSIBLY ALSO HELPED HER TO PRETEND TO BE WHAT SHE KNEW SHE WAS NOT.

● BORIS BECKER BORN 22 NOVEMBER 1967

A WAR-LIKE SCORPIO WITH BOUNDLESS AMBITIONS. THIS TENNIS PLAYER'S PHYSICAL STRENGTH AND DRIVE ALL COME FROM HIS RULING PLANET, MARS. BUT ANOTHER INFLUENCE ON HIS CHART SUGGESTS A PRIORITY FOR CHANGING – TEMPORARILY.

● TATUM O'NEAL BORN 5 NOVEMBER 1963

SCORPIO IS RULED BY PLUTO AND MARS, BOTH WAR-LIKE PLANETS, AND THIS YOUNG LADY SEEMS TO HAVE BEEN WARRING WITH SOMEONE SINCE SHE WAS A CHILD. THIS IS AN AMBITIOUS SIGN; HENCE HER REFUSAL TO BACK DOWN FROM ANOTHER TRY AT HER CAREER. WHAT SCORPIO WANTS, SCORPIO GENERALLY GETS.

SCORPIO *in* LIFE

AT WORK

Scorpio Boss A Scorpio boss is not easy to understand and certainly very difficult to work for. If you are wise, you will make sure that there is no possible reason for him or her to be jealous, otherwise life will become unbearable. The Scorpion must be the all-powerful kingpin and when employees fail to respect this they are removed without further ado. The worst thing an employee could do would be to attempt to effect any change in their boss's character: Scorpions must be accepted or rejected as they are, and in most cases it will be impossible to take the middle road anyway. When this boss issues a command, it must be carried out immediately; ten minutes later just won't do. Scorpions always expect reliability and efficiency. This type is manipulative too; he or she likes nothing better than to sit in the background pulling strings.

Scorpio Employee Ambitious and determined to win, when Scorpio employees set their sights on promotion, they will achieve it. Although their methods may be open to question – for they can be quite ruthless if they deem it necessary – Scorpions will always find success and it is impossible for their superiors to overlook them. There is something about them that makes them stand out in an office or a factory full of people. They are not the most popular of employees: those around will either keenly like or dislike them. Many will resent these determined opportunists, whilst others stand back and admire them in spite of themselves. These individuals will resent being given any menial task to fulfil – they have no patience for such things and believe themselves destined for greater things.

There is rarely a happy medium with Scorpio. Whether you are fiercely ambitious, relentlessly chasing what you want, or the sedentary type who sits around thinking ambitious thoughts, you have much to offer those you work for.

FAMILY MATTERS

SCORPIO MOTHER There are plenty of both fors and againsts the Scorpio mother. On the one hand you are 101% devoted to your children and strenuously work hard to supply all their needs. You are quick to defend them no matter what they have done, although you are not so quick to forgive if you secretly know that your offspring were in the wrong. You supply a strong figure that youngsters can rely on. The Scorpio mother is great at creating a secure environment for her children.

Your greatest problems come when the children get older for you are a manipulative woman. However, unless you have been very skilled at the controls it is quite likely that in their teen years your children will discover how they have been coaxed, persuaded or maybe even bullied into doing exactly what you want and then there will be a full-scale rebellion. This side to your character will be greatly softened if you are happily married, for then it will be necessary to divide up that loyal heart of yours and perhaps not focus in so much on every aspect of your children's lives.

Finally, there exists a side to you which your family will need to understand. Since your mood swings sometimes make you want to be alone, occasionally you may retire to the bedroom and take the phone off the hook.

SCORPIO FATHER The Scorpio father can be an intimidating character, sometimes taking discipline to extremes. There is usually no question as to who is boss in your household and your set of principles and morals are flaunted by your offspring at the risk of pain of death. Like the Scorpio mother, you will devote most of your time and energy to raising your children to be productive, useful people. There is a tendency, though, for you to be overly ambitious for them and you may even make the mistake of trying to push them in a direction that they have no wish or desire to follow. Providing this pitfall is avoided the father figure you provide is an excellent one.

Lastly, it is likely that teenage daughters may find themselves on a very short rein with their Scorpio father and you will have to soften up a little bit or face the possibility of losing them.

SCORPIO CHILD Scorpio children are exclusive in friendship as with everything, and they know exactly who they like and dislike and no amount of coaxing or reasoning will change that opinionated mind. They may have one or two devoted friends, but even these will need to tread carefully for as soon as Scorpions decide they have been badly let down – and this can be either real or imaginary – they will not be reconciled. You should attempt to explain the fallibility of the human race: if young Scorpions can be made to understand that none of us is perfect then they may learn to be less intolerant.

Apart from 'playing' secret societies, both sexes are attracted to detectives, cops and robbers, and books, toys and ball games with this theme. Don't make the mistake of assuming that it is the violent aspects that appeal to them – on the contrary, it is the joy of uncovering a mystery. Sherlock Holmes must surely have been born under this sign, for he is a perfect example of the Scorpio in action.

At play

Water relaxes the Scorpion and so you tend to be interested in water sports and fishing which allow peace, isolation and time to unravel your jumbled thoughts. This sign is often muscular and makes tremendously successful sports people, particularly athletes. Endurance is good and many marathon runners are born under this sign. Pottering round in the garden could be fun too: you like to see bulbs thrust out of the dark earth year after year, and are marvellous at creating year-round bulb, corm and tuber gardens, from snowdrops to dahlias.

You are not a great party-goer although you do like your food and drink and sometimes take it to excess. You are picky with your company, though, and very often prefer to entertain at home with a selected few. An interest in wine can lead to a study on the subject: the Scorpion may become something of an expert.

When playing the couch potato, the Scorpion likes nothing better than to unravel a good thriller or detective story.

Money

You believe that money brings power and of course you are generally right. The Scorpion's sense of survival is paramount and you generally know how to make a pound take you as far as a tenner. However, while it is possible for you to exist on next to nothing, this doesn't necessarily mean you enjoy doing so. When financial storms are experienced there is a stern solid side to your character that prevents you from asking for help and you would rather suffer in silence than humble yourself by asking for assistance.

In reality you see the process of gaining money as winning a power struggle in which you have to pit your wits. You heartily enjoy being associated with cash but only because it symbolizes a certain level of success. For you, money has no importance in itself but the pursuit of it is a personal challenge you can't resist. Possession is only a means to an end. What you gain most from having money in the bank, beyond the little luxuries and creature comforts it provides, is a sense of satisfaction from having attained it. To get wealthy is a challenge like chess, but with higher social stakes. The key to success is in staying cool and refusing to allow money to control you.

When it comes to spending, your home often benefits. However, you are traditional, and usually prefer older, more elegant surroundings to the modern styles. Further, you love to spend on entertaining although in this you tend to be fairly formal and sophisticated. You love to splash out on good food and wines but loathe people to drop in uninvited – Scorpio does not like to be taken off guard. Gatecrashers have been warned. But you certainly enjoy letting your hair down at the right time and with the right people.

● WINONA RYDER BORN 29 OCTOBER 1966

SCORPIO IS THE SIGN OF THE MYSTERIOUS, THE UNKNOWN AND ALL THAT IS FANTASTIC AND HARD TO UNDERSTAND. THEREFORE IT IS FITTING THAT WINONA, A SCORPIO ACTRESS, SHOULD FIND SUCCESS IN DRACULA, A CHARACTER WHO EPITOMIZES ALL OF OUR NIGHTMARES AND AT THE SAME TIME NEVER FAILS TO FASCINATE.

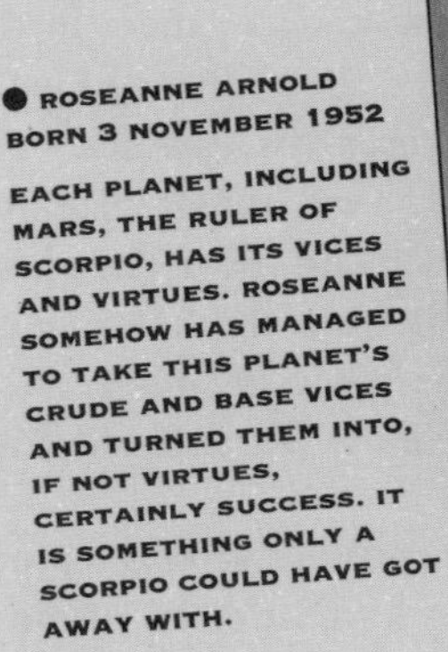

● ROSEANNE ARNOLD BORN 3 NOVEMBER 1952

EACH PLANET, INCLUDING MARS, THE RULER OF SCORPIO, HAS ITS VICES AND VIRTUES. ROSEANNE SOMEHOW HAS MANAGED TO TAKE THIS PLANET'S CRUDE AND BASE VICES AND TURNED THEM INTO, IF NOT VIRTUES, CERTAINLY SUCCESS. IT IS SOMETHING ONLY A SCORPIO COULD HAVE GOT AWAY WITH.

● DEMI MOORE BORN 11 NOVEMBER 1962

SCORPIO HAS A FASCINATION WITH LIFE, DEATH AND REPRODUCTION, THEREFORE IT IS NOT SURPRISING THAT DEMI WANTED THE WORLD TO SEE HER BODY NOT ONLY WHEN IT WAS SLIM AND SEXY BUT ALSO WHEN IT WAS FULL WITH CHILD. THIS IS A SIGN ALWAYS IN AWE OF MOTHER NATURE, SOMETHING SHE ILLUSTRATES BEAUTIFULLY.

SCORPIO *in* LOVE

Single

The Scorpio woman will be more vulnerable than her male counterpart because there is a tendency for him to sublimate his emotions through his career, sexual manipulations and athletic undertakings. Scorpio woman is not generally satisfied with less than an intense, meaningful relationship. Both sexes are loyal and giving. They can appear to be placid even when beneath the surface their emotions are ripping them apart.

As a Scorpio you are reluctant to lose control until you have shrewdly assessed the odds in every romantic situation. Predictably your desires sometimes get the better of you and you may find yourself emotionally tied to an unsatisfactory affair with no clear recollection of how you got there in the first place.

Your sex appeal is quiet and exciting: it is revealed both in your eyes and in the way you walk. Your direct gaze and smile are imbued with a sensuality which can move the opposite sex to lust in less than ten seconds from the first glance. You are sensual and sexually inventive; however, due to your need for control, it may take you years to experience your sexual potential.

Once in love, you tend to be both possessive and jealous and to drown in unresolved emotions long after an affair is over. You often tread a very thin line between love and hate, passion and violence, even when feelings are confined to your private fantasies. At an early age you realize that sex is power and that it will get you wherever you want to go. Your experiences of loving will take you in many emotional directions in one lifetime. Try to bear in mind at each crossroads that you made the decision to be there.

As a lover, you are unsurpassed – you seem to be built to probe the mysteries of sex. Your irrepressible energy is channelled in physical ways, and the result is that you are extremely sensual.

The Scorpio is sexually magnetic and able to give deep satisfaction, but the chances of building a happy, steady relationship are not great. Sexual fulfilment with a mate may be wonderful, but the psychological side may prove more difficult. Scorpio is demanding and fiercely jealous, despite the fact that this sign finds it hard to resist a secret love affair. Your passions can override commonsense and make you give in to a passing fancy, even if you are happily married. Few Scorpios are able to avoid a difficult love life. Those who sublimate their erotic desires in artistic or productive channels have a better chance of making a happy relationship because within their creative activities they find an outlet for those erotic images which haunt this sign. Clearly, great care needs to be taken when making the choice of a partner for life.

Married

On the one hand you may feel that marriage is a necessity; on the other your partner may feel it is a situation which must be escaped from. This is due to your notorious jealousy and possessiveness. After a while that mate of yours may begin to feel like a possession which has to be locked up whenever a threatening presence looms over the horizon.

You use marriage as an emotional base from which you operate all your other activities and it may cause you to choose a partnership you later regret. Although you are shrewd in most areas of life, when it comes to your emotional, sexual and material needs you can easily be overwhelmed.

Although you do not hesitate to be unfaithful when you feel a falling off of the relationship's original intensity and stimulation, deep in your peculiar heart you would most likely prefer to remain a satisfied stay-at-home. This is because, despite your actions, in your mind marriage has a certain sanctity and the violation of it often leaves you more saddened than satisfied.

Perfect Partners

When it comes to finding the perfect mate Scorpio is most likely to discover that special someone under the other water signs, namely, Scorpio, Pisces and Cancer.

Scorpio with Scorpio This attraction could be on impact and the wild infatuation that follows may develop into deep love. Although Scorpios have many virtues their thoughts can be extreme, but if both of them come to realize and accept their weak spots they will avoid unnecessary tension. Suspicion and jealousy are also deeply engraved in subjects of this sign, but their natural loyalty should be able to keep this under control. Career problems could create difficulties for Mr Scorpio who feels he must be the most important influence in this relationship and if he feels his masculinity is threatened, his aggressive side begins to show. Financially no problems should arise, however, as they will see eye to eye on most things.

Their sex life should burn fiercely for a strong physical attraction will exist. Desires and passions are shared and understood and this may prevent their relationship from deteriorating into a war game. Should Mr or Ms Scorpio be of the 'saintly' type they will work at their sex life until they reach the five-star rating.

Scorpio with Pisces The combination of these two signs can make for a dramatic but in general successful relationship for neither party is ruled by commonsense: rather their actions in life are motivated by intense emotion. The Scorpio gift for delving and probing can make it easier for this sign to understand the more secretive side of the Piscean. The Scorpion needs to take control of finances though.

Emotions are dramatized in the bedroom as both soon realize that this can stimulate their sexual appetites and heighten pleasure. The Scorpio jealousy will be calmed by the understanding Piscean. An emotionally charged relationship.

Scorpio with Cancer Because Cancer is also strongly influenced by emotion, this could be the ideal mate for the Scorpion. The sensitivity given to this moon sign allows him or her to appreciate even the slightest variation of the Scorpion's mood. Both parties are concerned about their financial life and are highly organized, therefore debt collectors and bailiffs are unlikely to intrude upon their lifestyle. Neither will their sex life be dull for their physical relationship will rest on emotions which are ever changing and developing together. Mutual desires, passions and needs should find satisfaction in this relationship.

ARE YOU A TYPICAL SCORPIO...

Answer honestly the questions below, using YES, NO or SOMETIMES; total up your score, allowing 3 for YES, 2 for SOMETIMES and 1 for NO.

...MAN?

1. Are you jealous?
2. Do you have fixed opinions?
3. Do you enjoy a drink?
4. Are you stubborn?
5. Do you demand loyalty from your women?
6. Are you offended when rebuffed sexually?
7. Do you bear grudges?
8. Do you use sex as a form of self-expression?
9. Are you capable of using a woman physically if it suits you?
10. Do you always understand your mate's sexual needs?
11. Are you sarcastic?
12. Does sexual perversion interest you?
13. Would you take revenge on an old enemy if the chance presented itself?
14. Can you be violent when deeply stirred?
15. Are you suspicious of strangers without sufficient reason?
16. Do you think a woman's place is in the home?
17. Can you be destructive?
18. Are you proud of your good health?
19. Does laziness irritate you?
20. Is it hard for you to fall in love?

...WOMAN?

1. Is it hard for you to fall in love?
2. Does your intuition reveal the thoughts of others?
3. Are you of a jealous disposition?
4. When desperate for affection will you sleep with almost anyone?
5. Are weak men attracted to you?
6. Do you need a loyal man?
7. Is it hard for you to express your desires in bed?
8. Is it hard for you to forgive and forget?
9. Can you be aggressive in bed?
10. Are you hypersensitive?
11. Is it hard for others to get to know the real you?
12. Do you think teenage brides are making a mistake?
13. Do you become highly nervous when rundown?
14. Do you enjoy a drink?
15. Are you good with finances?
16. Are you reluctant to change your job?
17. Are you a good judge of character?
18. Do you think a regular sex life is important?
19. Is it hard for you to make new friends?
20. Does your imagination do most of the work for you in bed?

ARE YOU A TYPICAL SCORPIO MAN ?

1–30 You may possess one or two of the Scorpio tendencies but in general you are too adaptable and independent for this sign. You should recognize yourself easily under Gemini, Libra or Sagittarius.
31–50 Life can be difficult for a fixed Scorpio but in your case the general characteristics associated with this sign are softened, making you a typical 'saintly' Scorpio. Jealousy could be your weak point and one that will cause you much suffering in life, although this too may soften with maturity.
51–60 This is the score of the 'sinner' Scorpio which is not altogether fortunate for this is never an easy sign to live with. You are critical and your suspicious outlook can make you unpopular and if control is not exercised, you could end up a lonely and bitter man. Do try to make allowances for the weakness of others – after all, none of us is perfect and this certainly includes you.

ARE YOU A TYPICAL SCORPIO WOMAN ?

1–30 Your characteristics seem to be totally opposed to this sign; I would suggest that you search for yourself in the chapters on Libra, Gemini or Sagittarius, for these are the most adaptable signs which could reveal the true you.
31–50 You are the typical, imaginative, emotional and jealous 'saintly' Scorpio. This is not an easy sign to live with for you can feel more deeply than other signs and when hurt you can become confused and highly strung. Try to develop more resilience to the world without growing cynical.
51–60 If young you are probably a popular girl, but the danger in being a 'sinner' Scorpio is that you may grow neurotic, bitter and hard with age, for the Scorpion carries a sting and one that can be turned upon its owner, making her life disruptive. If you can take life a little more lightly then you may avoid this.

TAROT

Astrology is closely tied in with the Tarot, for it is within the cards that astrological features are expressed. Each sign is broken down into three distinct parts and each part represents a card suggesting various characteristics.

ARIES

21 MARCH TO 30 MARCH

The card which represents these Rams is the Emperor.

Positive traits. These Rams are always ready for action, eager to take the lead, and willing to accept responsibility. They are positive, courageous and direct in their approach to life. They are attractive to and attracted by the opposite sex.

Negative traits. They are over-positive and dominating. Their initiative becomes impetuosity, and courageousness deteriorates into recklessness with no regard for the consequences. They start many more things than they can comfortably finish and leave a trail of uncompleted jobs and gestures.

31MARCH TO 10 APRIL

These Rams are allotted the card of the 2 of Wands.

Positive traits. These Rams have strong magnetic charms, personal attraction and others can't resist them. They are energetic, enthusiastic and eager. There is a driving power of great intensity, poise and dignity here.

Negative traits. Dignity and ambition deteriorate into pride and arrogance while that magnetism attracts enemies instead of friends, failure instead of success. There is a streak of cruelty and disregard for other people's feelings here.

11 APRIL TO 19 APRIL

This section of Aries is represented by the 3 of Wands.

Positive traits. There is a logical mind, an active imagination and a leaning towards the orthodox and conventional ways of life here, as well as good judgement, discrimination, and self-reliance. These Rams are versatile.

Negative traits. 'Logical' becomes over-critical and bigoted, shown by a refusal to look beyond the narrow limits of the immediate environment. Neat order turns into uneasiness, breaking down the poise and charm of this personality. There may be nervous instability.

TAURUS

20 APRIL TO 30 APRIL

The card given to this section of Taurus is the Hierophant.

Positive traits. These Bulls possess wit, vigour and an understanding of human needs and wants, together with great staying power. This is the card of the self-starter and self-charger.

Negative traits. Rebellion replaces the desire to improve, and primitive anger is evident. There is a likelihood of disagreement with everybody and the habit of throwing obstacles in others' way.

1 MAY TO 10 MAY

The card given to this section of Taurus is the 5 of Pentacles.

Positive traits. These include personal attraction, showmanship, driving energy and great independence. These people are warm-hearted and always ready to share with other people. They're idealistic and demand perfection in everything.

Negative traits. Pride, indolence and exhibitionism are some of the negative traits. Instability can be present with mood swings from extreme enthusiasm to pessimism, from hope to desire.

11 MAY TO 20 MAY

This section of Taurus is given the 6 of Pentacles.

Positive traits. Varied talents, personal charm, broad vision and a vivid and active imagination are shown in these Bulls. They may be emotional, tending to be interested in spiritual and philosophical matters.

Negative traits. Imagination becomes illusion. There is a tendency to leap to conclusions. Vitality is scattered over a wide front and there is too much wishful thinking and impractical dreams.

GEMINI

21 MAY TO 31MAY

The card that represents this section of Gemini is the Lovers.

Positive traits. These Geminians are thinkers: their minds are analytical, observant and clever. They are great organizers and planners. They have excellent judgement and a gift for accuracy and detail.

Negative traits. They are narrow-minded and over-critical. Rather than risk making a mistake, they avoid action at all and miss out on opportunities; this restricts them.

1 JUNE TO 10 JUNE

The 8 of Swords is given to this section of Gemini.

Positive traits. On the positive side there is much personal force: these people are alert to socializing, are gregarious, generous, hospitable and invariably ready to share what they have with other people. They are lovers of action and their energy is infectious and stimulating.

Negative traits. They are discontented, restless and wander aimlessly. Discrimination evaporates, particularly when it comes to making friends. They are hot-tempered, irritable and nervous.

11 JUNE TO 20 JUNE

The card given to this section of Gemini is the 9 of Swords.

Positive traits. There is power and stability in these Geminians: they are reliable, honest and dependable. There is an innate sense of personal dignity and a love of beauty, a passion for completion and perfection in everything they do.

Negative traits. They are obstinate, following their own will despite everything and everyone. They refuse to adapt themselves to changing conditions, and see danger where none exists. They are also foolhardy and proud.

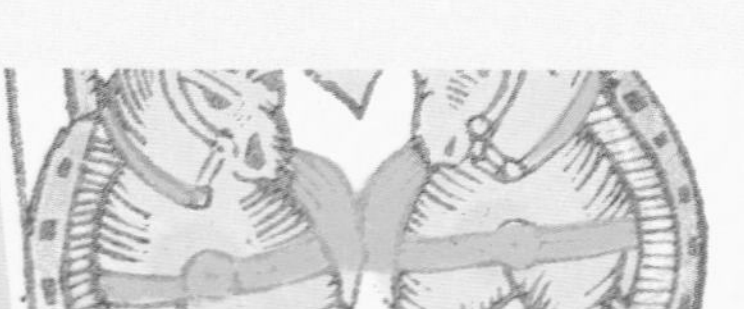

CANCER

21 JUNE TO 1 JULY

The card given to this section of Cancer is the Chariot.

Positive traits. These Cancerians have much charm, flexibility and a delightful personality. They are pleasure-loving, affectionate, generous and happy-go-lucky. There is great intuition.

Negative traits. They are restless, changeable, fickle and discontented. They leap from one activity to another and never get anything completed. They are selfish, sensual and lack discrimination.

2 JULY TO 11 JULY

The card given to this section of Cancer is the 2 of Cups.

Positive traits. These people possess strong intuitive powers and an analytical mind: they feel and think accurately, are dependable and have an instinctive intelligence which functions naturally and easily. They are also by nature pleasure-loving and happy.

Negative traits. They allow their emotions and sympathies to get the upper hand. They are self-indulgent and may debase their intelligence by using it as craft and cunning. There is a good deal of trickery in this nature.

12 JULY TO 21 JULY

The card given to this section is the 3 of Cups.

Positive traits. These Crabs are happy, hopeful, adaptable and poised. Steady workers, they are obedient, disciplined, willing to conform and take life as it comes. They are receptive and sensitive.

Negative traits. These people are far too passive, lazy and dreamy. They are indolent and self-indulgent; they use up energy on unimportant details and cling to forlorn hopes.

LEO

22 JULY TO 1 AUGUST

The card given to this section of Leo is the card of Strength.

Positive traits. This personality is electric with a direct approach, vitality and tireless activity. These Leos are strenuous work-horses, capable of inspiring and directing other people either practically or in their social life.

Negative traits. They are destructive: what they desire is power over others. They are intolerant, arrogant, ruthless and unprincipled, and unable to see other people's points of view.

2 AUGUST TO 11 AUGUST

The card the 5 of Wands represents this section of Leo.

Positive traits. This nature is extraordinarily well balanced: there is a sense of power here, and poise. These people are vital and dynamic. They have a strong sense of justice and their minds are orderly; they are loyal to conventions and traditions.

Negative traits. Intolerant, overbearing and self-centred, there is too much pride, sensitivity to criticism, narrow-mindedness and bigotry here.

12 AUGUST TO 22 AUGUST

This section of Leo is ruled by the 6 of Wands.

Positive traits. There is vitality, acting ability and a love of adventure here. Energetic, enthusiastic and tireless, these Leos are capable of inspiring other people to work for them.

Negative traits. They are defensive, quarrelsome, proud, touchy and obstinate. They lack the ability to co-operate with others: they desire always to dominate and direct.

VIRGO

23 AUGUST TO 1 SEPTEMBER

This section of Virgo has been given the card of the Hermit.

Positive traits. These Virgos are rational, dependable and capable of developing a high degree of skill in any type of work. They are meticulous, logical and constructive thinkers, and have a keen sense of responsibility.

Negative traits. They are over-cautious, narrow-minded, prudish and unwilling to take a step until they have planned for every emergency, and they waste time and energy on small, unimportant things, thus losing their vision.

2 SEPTEMBER TO 11 SEPTEMBER

This section of Virgo is given the 8 of Pentacles.

Positive traits. Creative, imaginative and keenly intuitive, these Virgos have great personal attraction and considerable capacity for physical pleasure. They are highly sensitive and quick to react.

Negative traits. They are lazy, unambitious and self-indulgent. They utilize intuition to jump to conclusions in an effort to avoid real work and they use their understanding of people to get what they want regardless of the consequences.

12 SEPTEMBER TO 22 SEPTEMBER

This section of Virgo is given the 9 of Pentacles.

Positive traits. There is great strength and ability in this personality. They are natural extroverts and think objectively. Their actions are always used positively towards a concrete result or goal. They have analytical minds and are intellectually active.

Negative traits. They are selfish and personal and wrapped up in the materialistic side of life. They see nothing but the single ambition of getting ahead in a practical way and gaining possessions.

LIBRA

23 SEPTEMBER TO 2 OCTOBER

This section of Libra is given the card of Justice.

Positive traits. These Librans are gifted with quick mental reactions, clear vision and an intuitive understanding of people and conditions. They are poised yet flexible and yielding, affectionate and loyal to family ties.

Negative traits. They are unstable, restless and uncertain in their goals. They are blown this way and that by the winds of indecision, unable to make up their minds about anything.

3 OCTOBER TO 12 OCTOBER

This section of Libra has been given the card of the 2 of Swords.

Positive traits. There is great integrity, strength and power here, all combined to give a deep understanding of the human condition. They are enterprising, constructive and tireless workers. They have tremendous vitality and great resistance.

Negative traits. These are fanatics: so very keen on their own particular theories of progress that nobody else can be capable of giving good advice. They are impervious to outside opinion and deaf to suggestions or criticisms. There is a certain destructiveness here too.

13 OCTOBER TO 22 OCTOBER

This section of Libra is given the card of the 3 of Swords.

Positive traits. These Librans are conventional, obedient and traditional. There is a keen appreciation of pleasure and the ability to enjoy life. They have good self-control, a jovial nature and plenty of charm.

Negative traits. They are difficult to please, over-critical, self-indulgent, selfish, proud and sensitive to criticism.

SCORPIO

23 OCTOBER TO 1 NOVEMBER

This section of Scorpio is given the card of the Hanged Man.

Positive traits. There is great charm, affection and high emotions here. These people have great social sense and are true friends. They are generous, hospitable and sympathetic, and tireless at work and at play.

Negative traits. They overdo everything – this is the extremist. They are passionate rather than loving, dominant rather than helpful. They drive themselves and everyone else to exhaustion, and create tension and disorder.

2 NOVEMBER TO 12 NOVEMBER

This section of Scorpio has been given the card of the 5 of Cups.

Positive traits. This denotes a dominant person, having great power and attraction for other people. There is the potential for greater achievements. Leadership comes naturally to this section of Scorpio and they are likely to be highly successful and popular.

Negative traits. These Scorpions are proud, intolerant and self-assertive. They are cruel, inconsiderate, ruthless and have no regard for the feelings and sufferings of other people. Their one desire is to succeed.

13 NOVEMBER TO 22 NOVEMBER

This section of Scorpio has been given the card of the 6 of Cups.

Positive traits. There is an element of greatness in this personality. There are likely to be great achievements covering almost any field of creative endeavour, and a sympathy for suffering and understanding of human desires and emotions.

Negative traits. These Scorpions suffer from illusions: they believe in unrealities. They reject ideas of training and technique, discipline and learning. They are fickle and unstable and are unable to concentrate.

SAGITTARIUS

23 NOVEMBER TO 2 DECEMBER

This section of Sagittarius has been given the card of Temperance.

Positive traits. These Sagittarians are quick-witted, practical and clear-headed. They have dexterity and cleverness, both mentally and physically. They are observant, perceptive and analytical. Everything is approached directly.

Negative traits. They are over-direct, shortsighted, extremely critical, hasty in decision and violent in action. They forget to use their own best quality of analytical discrimination. Recklessness is shown.

3 DECEMBER TO 12 DECEMBER

This section of Sagittarius has been given the card of the 8 of Wands.

Positive traits. There is tremendous vitality, personal power and great resistance here. They are sensitive to impressions and keenly intuitive, knowing what people want and how to give it to them.

Negative traits. Their strength and resistance reverts to unreasonable obstinacy and they go out of their way to be difficult. They follow emotional impulses to the bitter end and take unnecessary punishment.

13 DECEMBER TO 21 DECEMBER

This section of Sagittarius has been given the card of the 9 of Wands.

Positive traits. These Sagittarians are dominant, powerful and constructive. They are prepared for large undertakings and major enterprises as well as heavy responsibilities. They have energy, commonsense, enthusiasm and logic.

Negative traits. They are intolerant, cruel, overbearing, impatient with weakness, unsympathetic with suffering, and tend to dump their responsibilities onto other people.

CAPRICORN

22 DECEMBER TO 30 DECEMBER

This section of Capricorn has been given the card of the Devil.

Positive traits. Most of the agreeable human qualities are found in this personality. These Capricorns are gentle, instinctively courteous and hospitable. They understand other people's emotions and are extremely sympathetic, with a great sense of humour.

Negative traits. They show indecision and uncertainty of purpose. They swing from one side of the question to the other without really knowing their own minds. Natural tact and diplomacy are weakened and they tend to agree with anyone or anything at any time.

31 DECEMBER TO 9 JANUARY

This section of Capricorn has been given the card of the 2 of Pentacles.

Positive traits. There is creative fire in this person and it is controlled and constructive. There is the ability to accomplish anything within reason. They have a gift for accepting limitations and overcoming them at the same time.

Negative traits. They are rebellious, domineering and over-positive. They give full vent to such emotions as jealousy, greed, hatred and anger. They are so determined on their own course that they destroy anything which stands in their way.

10 JANUARY TO 19 JANUARY

This section of Capricorn has been given the 3 of Pentacles.

Positive traits. There is strength of character, farsightedness, and caution here. These Capricorns are constructive, orderly and productive. They are objective thinkers and steady workers and they work towards concrete goals.

Negative traits. Overbearing and dominant: the desire for perfection and justice turn into severity and even cruelty. They have narrow minds, much pride and lack flexibility.

AQUARIUS

20 JANUARY TO 29 JANUARY

This section of Aquarius has been given the card of the Star.

Positive traits. These Aquarians are creative artists. They are emotionally sensitive, hard-working and imaginative. They are constructive in their desires and discriminating thinkers. They have plenty of magnetism for the opposite sex.

Negative traits. These people are highly strung, easily irritated and temperamental. They are over-sensitive to criticism and constantly imagine themselves to be misunderstood, slighted and even persecuted. They are fickle and cool and inconsiderate in their personal relationships.

30 JANUARY TO 8 FEBRUARY

This section of Aquarius has been given the 5 of Swords.

Positive traits. There is a sense of power, a clear, quick mind, and an unshakeable confidence in their own ability here. They have great personal charm, instinctive poise, dignity and self-control.

Negative traits. These Aquarians are dominating, ruthless and lack consideration for other people's ideas, needs and feelings. They can be cold, impersonal and cruel, unforgiving and revengeful.

9 FEBRUARY TO 18 FEBRUARY

This section of Aquarius has been given the card of the 6 of Swords.

Positive traits. These Aquarians have an agreeable charm, a well-equipped personality, and a quick and intuitive intelligence. They are responsive and sympathetic, inspiring and dominating in their relationships with others.

Negative traits. They are fickle, insincere, undependable and self-deceived. They believe in illusions, and take a superficial look at life.

PISCES

19 FEBRUARY TO 28 FEBRUARY

This section of Pisces has been given the card of the Moon.

Positive traits. These characters are persistent, quiet, dependable, trustworthy, sensitive and resourceful. They are fair and just in all their human relationships, be they personal or professional. They are mentally intuitive.

Negative traits. Narrow-minded, intolerant, unfriendly, self-righteous: these people are hypercritical of others' ideas, behaviour and actions, take life far too seriously and tend towards pessimism.

1 MARCH TO 10 MARCH

This section of Pisces has been given the card of the 8 of Cups.

Positive traits. There is in these people an intuitive understanding of changing conditions and human affairs. They are able to apply their theories and knowledge to practical affairs with logical exactness and get great results. They have a good sense of timing, rhythm and are very patient.

Negative traits. They neglect the practical side to life and get themselves into muddles. They suffer from dreams and illusions. They are always waiting for something they feel is going to happen, and live in a world untouched by reality, waiting for the proverbial lucky break.

11 MARCH TO 20 MARCH

This section of Pisces has been given the card of the 9 of Cups.

Positive traits. There is a definite potential for success and achievement in these Pisceans. They are imaginative, creative and intuitive and have a direct approach to life, tempered by sympathy and human understanding. They are energetic and active.

Negative traits. They are impressionable, over-sensitive, self-indulgent and impractical. They follow their personal impulses and desires, obstinately neglecting commonsense and consideration for other people.

SAGITTARIUS

23 NOVEMBER – 21 DECEMBER

YOUR approach to life is daring, different and perhaps even a little mad. There are people who would describe you as keenly ambitious, yet it is not so much the fruits of success you are after – what you want is the thrill of trying, the adventure that could be involved. Other people look for some sort of result. For you it is the quality of life that is important, not the immeasurable quantity.

Others often describe you as restless, impulsive, extravagant, extreme and even reckless. This doesn't faze you a bit – it is the price you are prepared to pay for your own personal freedom. You are optimistic, positive, cheerful and self-reliant. You are also open, truthful and sincere. You have a keen sense of justice, are highly intelligent and are a kind and open-hearted friend. You are something of an attention seeker too. By nature you are expansive, generous and buoyant but you must be wary of the fact that your virtues can become weaknesses through excess.

You love new horizons, change and physical movement. Because of this you are always excited by the possibility of travel. However, you do have one tiny little problem when you are on the move and that is your notorious clumsiness. In your rush, you slip, bump and crash into objects. You are so busy thinking ahead of yourself, you forget what you are doing right now. When you cannot travel physically you enjoy making trips through the pages of books and in your vivid imagination.

You love to be physically active too and Sagittarius is certainly a sporty sign. If you are a true Centaur you are sure to be interested in combative types of games. No sign needs more gentle restraint than you do. Basically you need a dear friend to occasionally slow you down and make you realize what direction you are headed because it could very well be the wrong one.

You are a mobile sign, and need to keep going. The problem is that very often you don't know what your target is. It tends to change fairly regularly.

PERSO

FEMALE

Saint

● You are an intelligent and unforgettable character. You don't demand attention – you just draw it to you unintentionally. Your sense of humour makes you a welcome addition to any social situation and your good nature gives you a following of friends who constantly fight for your company.

● Nevertheless you are independent and do as you please without feeling you have to answer to anybody. You rebel quite strongly against possessive persons and pattern your life according to your own rules and regulations.

● Your interests are so varied and consuming that you really don't have time for idle chatter – in fact you perpetually wonder where the time goes. That is because there are so many things you want to do and so little time in which to do them.

● You believe in self-improvement: you love life, loathe pessimistic people and righteously embrace the optimistic philosophy that 'everything is always for the best in the end'.

● You are optimistic, ever cheerful and staunchly self-sufficient. (If you insist on leaping off in adventurous and exciting new directions without considering the problems which might occur, then you will definitely need these qualities.)

● You are attracted to new environments, change and challenge – they make the blood course through your veins.

● You possess a strong sense of justice, and are guided by a lofty personal ethic.

● You are highly intelligent and an open-hearted friend. What else would we expect of a person whose mission in life is to help others, and one who expects to be accepted, believed and trusted?

Sinner

● There isn't such a thing as a really sinful Sagittarian. Members of this sign all have a lovable side to them. You are devoid of any kind of malice aforethought and the more miserable individuals in life probably mistake you for someone insipid because you smile or laugh all the time.

● Disorganization could be a pitfall, but then again is any real harm done by keeping your income tax receipts in the freezer (especially if you like a tipple from time to time) and who can blame you for putting your plane ticket in your medicine chest? After all, you have got to look at it every time you use your eye drops. The problem with your rather unusual habit of putting important things in so-called safe places is that some of the places are so safe that you never set eyes on those important things again. However, your intentions are always for the best even if your confusion quota sometimes consumes you.

MALE

Saint

● Wherever you go in life you have a robust attitude which makes you friends with the speed of light. Even at the age of 55 you are like a scout who bitterly resents rest periods. You have the enthusiasm of a holy innocent and the wisdom of an ancient statesman. Your simply irresistible sense of humour and intelligence take you far beyond logic. Your motto in this life is expansion and your power is positive thinking.

● You are a freedom-loving person who is highly disinclined to make marital commitments. However, should you find a woman who is far more fun to be with than to be without and who will also pose no threat of confinement, then you might decide that marriage can be far more meaningful than you would ever have thought possible.

● Because you are so impulsive and impressionable, idealistic and spontaneous, you have a high incidence of divorce.

● Your nervous system is highly strung. This shows in your eagerness to be off somewhere, plus your fondness for the great outdoors and complete freedom. You may be impetuous; this is often because you are able to predict the outcome of a situation in a flash.

Sinner

● You are something of a philanderer. You are extremely popular because of your ready laughter and people follow you anywhere but it is only a short time before you can't remember their names. Your attention span is minimal – you are the man who can't sit still because the call of good times is always upon him.

● Your mind wants instant gratification and then it soars off to something else. Meanwhile in the dust behind you there is often a person sunk in emotional pain. You are a taker who doesn't linger long enough to consider what – and who – you are leaving.

● At your most charming you are more like a little boy than a man. In your sad moments you appeal to a woman's mother instinct and know exactly how to manipulate her with a carefully placed head on her breast. You are the playboy of the Western world who seeks the sublime sexual situation. And when you make love, love has nothing to do with it at all.

● BILLY CONNOLLY BORN 24 NOVEMBER 1942

SAGITTARIUS IS ALWAYS CONSIDERED TO BE THE CLOWN OF THE ZODIAC AND BILLY CONNOLLY CERTAINLY FITS THE BILL. THE ARCHER IS ABLE TO MAKE US FACE THE UNPALATABLE TRUTH ABOUT OURSELVES AND SEE THE RIDICULOUS SIDE OF OUR BEHAVIOUR. THIS IS SURELY THE KEY TO BILLY'S HUMOUR.

● TINA TURNER BORN 26 NOVEMBER 1938

SEXUAL INNUENDO IS ALIEN TO SAGITTARIUS. EVERYTHING, INCLUDING SEX, IS BROUGHT OUT INTO THE OPEN, AND THE WORD 'RAUNCHY' IS AN APT DESCRIPTION FOR THE QUEEN OF ROCK, TINA TURNER. A SHRINKING VIOLET SHE DEFINITELY IS NOT.

● KIM BASINGER BORN 8 DECEMBER 1963

A TYPICAL ARCHER DOES NOT SUFFER FROM SHYNESS OR SEXUAL INHIBITION; HENCE KIM WAS ABLE TO CARRY OFF HER ROLE IN *9½ WEEKS* WITHOUT SO MUCH AS A BAT OF AN EYELASH. THE LONG FLOWING LOCKS ARE TYPICAL OF THE EQUINE SIDE OF THIS SIGN.

in LIFE

At work

Sagittarius Boss Sagittarius bosses may overlook many details but their overall sense of planning is admirable. Once trained and disciplined they are capable of a great deal: their mental vigour never tires and their curiosity is never satisfied. Sagittarians are formidable antagonists and foolish suggestions and objections meet with little mercy from them for they have an intuition which allows them to see their adversary's weakest points and act on them.

It is most important to remember when employed by this sign that, above all else, you must be candid and honest. If Sagittarians sense any underhandedness or deceitful action, somebody will be leaving their employ rather quickly.

Sagittarius Employee Sagittarius employees are usually easy to identify: they are generally the lunatics who run around the office enthusiastically enquiring 'Why don't we do this and why don't we do that?'. They are impossible to depress for they abound in enthusiasm and optimism and cannot understand those who sit around feeling sorry for themselves or crying into their beer.

The sinning Sagittarian generally takes these characteristics to extremes and it can only be a matter of time before he or she becomes the office joke. The 'saintly' Sagittarian, too, may find that others patronize him or her when they would be better advised to sit and listen, however crazy the ideas may seem. For, with their luck, Sagittarians can generally succeed where others fail. Attractive colleagues in the vicinity will need to take care though: this sign frequently gets involved with workmates. Lastly, the Sagittarian can reverse chances for success by acting prematurely.

FAMILY MATTERS

SAGITTARIUS MOTHER When considering this sign's penchant for freedom it is a wonder there is such a person – the Sagittarian lady certainly thinks twice before saddling herself with a young family. Chances are that as soon as it is feasible you will be back at work. In many ways this is no bad thing. The children of a Sagittarian mother certainly learn to stand on their own two feet quicker than most. If you are not there to cook for them, they soon learn the machinations of the oven and may even have dinner waiting for you when you get home.

The Sagittarian mother is not really a mother at all: she is more likely to be a chum. Despite your failings as a parent, children flock to you and love to hear the jokes you tell and the outrageous stories you invent.

SAGITTARIUS FATHER Like his female counterpart, parenthood is not something the Sagittarian embarks upon without careful thought. At the beginning you may be horrified by the mess caused by a tiny baby or toddler and you may not even contribute a great deal until the children become older and, in your eyes, more fascinating. As soon as they are mature enough to appreciate your wonderful stories and laugh at your jokes, you discover that you have a couple of playmates waiting for you when you come home.

Overall, however, it is unlikely that the Sagittarius father could ever be called a devoted family man. He has too many irons in the fire to be completely domesticated. He loves his family but often they are squeezed in between his other interests. He rarely feels that his constant presence is necessary; to him it is 'quality time' which counts. Certainly he is generous, kind, and sympathetic to those he lives with or who are dependent on him; however, his warmhearted regard and concern for humanity as a whole gives him a certain elusiveness and detachment. Nevertheless, in emergencies he can be counted on and is rock solid.

This sign does not believe in strict discipline: the Sagittarius father would far rather sit down and hold a sensible discussion as to why a child should or should not do a particular thing. Very often this casual approach pays dividends.

SAGITTARIUS CHILD Young Sagittarians have a booming social life: other children are attracted to this optimistic and mischievous soul and their success in sporting activities often lends weight to their popularity. A lone Sagittarian is hard to imagine. They are natural leaders but at times, especially when their leadership is challenged, there is a great deal of falling out and making up.

You will be unable to keep up with the toing and froing of friendships and perhaps you should not attempt to do so.

Allow him or her to bring friends home whenever possible but do not be surprised if it gradually dawns upon you that in general he or she prefers to be out and about. Sport, sport and more sport, almost to the exclusion of all else, is typical of the Sagittarian and the outdoor life certainly holds strong appeal. Healthy, happy and free just about sums up this little imp.

At play

Life is never at a standstill: whether you are taking off for a weekend at a balloon ranch, planning a hike in the Himalayas, or attending a two-week yoga retreat, you are never bored and consequently never boring. You are always active, intensely alive and ever eager to deal with life head on. You like to travel, play around at sport, and pursue a path to greater growth and development. Even when you are at home, you find it impossible to sit still and if you have a garden, as soon as the sun shines there you are, asking friends round for barbecues.

Trees have a special fascination for you. You may collect them from all kinds of exotic climes – perhaps places you have visited on holiday. You also enjoy woodland and are frequently a keen hiker or rambler. Although you are invited to as many parties as you can comfortably fit in, you are not really one for smoky environments. You will go for the company but escape as soon as everything becomes a little bit too overpowering.

Money

When it comes to this side of life, you are pretty hopeless. You are a wastrel who simply doesn't know when to stop. Your generous nature means that you give lavish presents to friends and loved ones. In addition to this, your voice is always foremost when it comes to picking up the bill at the pub, club or restaurant. You never let money control you but at the same time, you need to have enough to be able to feel free.

When it comes to your spending habits, you are more likely to buy a private aeroplane than a Rolls-Royce. You make sure you get the maximum amount of pleasure out of anything you buy. One morning you may wake up to a mysteriously empty bank account, having withdrawn a large sum the day before. However, you do have a lot of fun when you are spending. You are one of the few people who knows how to translate money into living and every experience that comes your way is sure to be fantastic.

Surprisingly for an undomesticated type, you love to spend on your home – it is the place you return to after your adventures, isn't it? You like your base to be spacious, hating to be cooped up. Because you delight in sharing things with others, you entertain whenever possible, sometimes giving large parties and sometimes relaxed soirées. You love giving parties and don't consider the expense – you loathe restriction in any guise and want to provide the best in the way of food and drink. You would rather empty your bank account for one exciting night than try to survive by counting the pennies. You are the type who lives for the present and will take a chance on tomorrow. Your confidence in yourself often astounds those who know you well.

● STEPHEN SPIELBERG BORN 18 DECEMBER 1947

LIKE SAGITTARIUS'S OPPOSITE SIGN, GEMINI, THE ARCHER RETAINS A CHILD-LIKE QUALITY AND IMAGINATION THROUGHOUT LIFE. STEPHEN'S *E.T.* IS A WONDERFUL EXAMPLE, AS IS HIS ABILITY TO CREATE NEW PROJECTS JUST WHEN THE PUBLIC THINK SURELY HE MUST SOON DRY UP.

● PAMELA STEPHENSON BORN 4 DECEMBER 1951

LIKE HER MATE BILLY CONNOLLY, PAMELA LOVES TO ACT THE CLOWN AND TO COCK A SNOOK AT HUMBUG AND THE 'ESTABLISHMENT' AT EVERY OPPORTUNITY. THE FEMALE ARCHER IS OFTEN A TOMBOY AND THIS CERTAINLY APPLIES IN THIS PARTICULAR CASE.

● JEFF BRIDGES BORN 4 DECEMBER 1949

JEFF BRIDGES IS, LIKE OTHERS OF HIS SIGN, ATHLETIC, ADVENTUROUS, ENTHUSIASTIC AND VERY PHYSICAL. THESE TRAITS ARE GIVEN TO HIM BY THE ELEMENT WHICH RULES THIS SIGN, NAMELY FIRE. NOT FOR HIM ROLES OF POIGNANT ROMANCE. THEY BELONG TO THE ELEMENT OF WATER.

SAGITTARIUS *in* LOVE

SINGLE

You are independent, liberty loving and forever looking for a challenge. Your romantic dream is far more a trip into the exotic than an earthbound evening of champagne and roses. You would rather share a camel across the Sahara than confine yourself to a candlelit restaurant with a piano player. Because you are so impulsive and restless, you are looking for the wildest kind of excitement and this does not make loving you easy.

If you are male you loathe making a commitment: a freedom fanatic, you run, rather than walk, into the lives of a crowd of women. There are some who might accuse you of being averse to love. However, this really isn't true. The fact is that you tend to be too insensitive to even think about being considerate. You live for what you can gain in a moment rather than for what you can give, and see love as a floorshow that comes straight to you.

If you are female you are less consumed by the chase and more by the quality of the experience. You too are impulsive, independent and a lover of adventure, but you are more capable of making a commitment should the right man come along. You want an exciting man who respects your independence and sparks your interests with his enthusiasm. It is not necessary for him to have a private aeroplane; a strong sense of humour and an assertive nature will do very nicely thank you.

Sexually, you have a highly developed body consciousness and are rarely coarse. You display the fineness of a thoroughbred racehorse, and possess a lusty sexual openness and candour. You don't focus in on sex, nor are you preoccupied or obsessed by it. Sex has its place in your life, as it does for all of us, and you express yourself with swiftness, enthusiasm, vigour and a strong sense of freedom. You are uncomfortable with heavy love scenes or emotional outbursts. To you physical love is a great game for two, and sometimes more, played each time with refreshing newness and constant action. Sex can never make you happy when it becomes a duty or, worse still, a habit. Frequently you get carried away by the excitement of the moment, and are likely then to promise the world – you spend a good deal of time later dodging those to whom you made rash promises.

In romance, you have a problem, then. It is essential that you pick a compatible mate. Avoid at all costs getting tied down to anyone on the basis of a superficial, physical attraction. Frequently, you marry more than once, and it's difficult for you to avoid disappointment in romantic matters. Your emotions, which seem stable one day, are likely to go completely overboard the next. Recognize the fact that your judgement is poor. It is important that you find someone who can accept and understand your need for freedom.

MARRIED

When it comes to marriage, you may have more than just the one. Your freedom-loving philosophy takes you through many places and many people and you usually see marriage as the most primitive kind of trap. However, after a period of almost too many experiences, you can concede to possessing a persistent hunk for a soul mate. In marriage you need a clever, fun-loving companion far more than a breathless lover. You see a successful marital union rooted in a strong friendship that is both dynamic and non-confining. You need to be able to take an impulsive jaunt to the health club without having to face a jealous mate on your return, and you need to have the knowledge that your mate wants to share the experience with you rather than rid you of it.

Unfortunately if you start to feel the progressive lack of illumination, your mind and your body may begin to wander, especially if you are the male of the species.

PERFECT PARTNERS

When looking for an ideal mate, the Sagittarian frequently finds it among the fire signs: Sagittarius, Aries and Leo.

Sagittarius with Sagittarius These two could be brought together by their common tendency to treat relationships in a light-hearted manner. Each respects the other's driving need for personal freedom, and it is possible that for the first time in their lives they will feel totally free to go their own way and at the same time retain a good relationship with one particular member of the opposite sex. Their social life will be hectic, for Sagittarius attracts other people. This will suit both of them, but they may come to realize their moments alone are few.

Sexually this is a versatile combination, both minds are open to experiment – anyone for an orgy? Providing they are able to make one another feel important and do not ruin the other's ego through playing it too cool, this could be a fitting relationship for both of them.

Sagittarius with Aries Before Sagittarians get into this relationship, they need to make up their mind whether they can accept the fiery emotions of Aries. However, when it comes to their notice that apart from the passion, they share many good ideas and a sense of adventure, then it is likely these two can get seriously involved. Finances could be difficult though: the Aries finds it hard to plan for the future sensibly, although in this relationship he or she may very well take over the reins of control because Sagittarius is completely hopeless.

Sex should work out fine providing they are able to find the time to get to bed in the first place: with so many outside activities it will be difficult. Nevertheless when they finally do get together aren't the sparks going to fly!

Sagittarius with Leo When Leo makes a move in on Sagittarius the latter will wonder what hit them. What Leos want they invariably get. Whereas with a different character this could cause rebellion, Sagittarians find the Lion hard to resist. They soon learn that by applying a little bit of well-aimed flattery it is relatively easy to wrap the Lion around their little finger. Once caught and trapped, of course, the Lion becomes the proverbial pussy cat, willing to do anything to please the object of its affections.

Sagittarians can be fairly animalistic in bed; teamed with Leo their sexual appetites are very well developed and they will spend a lot of time happily engaged in physical activity. Provided the Archer can control that wandering eye and, on occasion, hands, all will be well. If not, then they are about to find out that they certainly met their match when it comes to the arena of conflict.

ARE YOU A TYPICAL SAGITTARIUS...

Answer honestly the questions below, using YES, NO or SOMETIMES; total up your score, allowing 3 for YES, 2 for SOMETIMES and 1 for NO.

...MAN?

1. Is it hard for you to relinquish your personal freedom?
2. Is fidelity difficult for you to achieve?
3. Do you take part in some sport?
4. Do you chase get-rich-quick schemes?
5. Does jealousy in others bore you?
6. Are you lucky?
7. Is it hard for you to budget?
8. Do you think it is perfectly natural to try all sexual experiences?
9. Would you drop your girl if she became possessive?
10. Does the thought of staying in the same job for 20 years depress you?
11. Are you free from inhibitions?
12. Do you speak rapidly?
13. Are you clumsy?
14. Do you think marriage is old-fashioned?
15. Can you indulge in three or four affairs at the same time without feeling guilty?
16. Do small-minded people annoy you?
17. Does routine bore you?
18. Are children excluded from your life plan?
19. Is it hard for you to remember birthdays?
20. Are you attracted to married women?

...WOMAN?

1. Do you think you will ever surrender your personal freedom?
2. Does jealousy kill love for you?
3. Do married or attached men attract you?
4. Would you do anything a man wanted in bed?
5. Do you enjoy some outdoor activities?
6. Are you a restless person?
7. Do you need a target in life?
8. Does fidelity come hard to you?
9. Could you sleep with a friend's husband or lover without feeling guilty?
10. Are your physical movements quick?
11. Do crazy and unorthodox ideas appeal to you?
12. Can you get out of one man's bed and then leap into another's half an hour later?
13. Do you support women's lib?
14. Is your friendly approach to everyone misconstrued by men?
15. Do you have a hectic social life?
16. Do you live in the present for the present?
17. Are you drawn to a man who does not appear to fancy you?
18. Do you hate formal occasions?
19. Are you lucky?
20. Is it hard for you to form a deep and lasting relationship?

ARE YOU A TYPICAL SAGITTARIUS MAN ?

1–30 You are much too fixed and sensible to be a true Sagittarian: your outlook on life and moral behaviour would seem to fit in more with the steadier signs. You may recognize yourself more readily under Taurus, Aquarius, Leo or Scorpio.

31–50 Sagittarians have the kind of personality that can draw others to them and you are of the 'saintly' type, meaning that you possess more of the good points of this sign than the bad. However, a sense of loyalty is still likely to be absent from your mental makeup and this is the weak point you should work at improving.

51–60 This score belongs to the 'sinner' Sagittarian, a charming, bright person, but a disaster area as far as other people are concerned. Your insistence on personal freedom and your total lack of financial ability can make it hard for those who come into contact with you. Read the section devoted to the 'sinner', for it may help you to overcome these weaknesses.

ARE YOU A TYPICAL SAGITTARIUS WOMAN ?

1–30 Your personality is far deeper than the average Sagittarian, although one or two characteristics may apply. You may find yourself under Aquarius, Scorpio, Leo or Taurus. Read these chapters but make no attempt to make them fit. Your sign should be obvious.

31–50 You are the true 'saintly' Sagittarian, possessing most of the gifts endowed by this sign yet you have somehow avoided the more unpleasant tendencies that generally go hand in hand with the former. Your biggest fault could be one of insecurity and you should do your utmost to put this right.

51–60 Although you are similar to your sister above, you do in fact belong to the 'sinner' Sagittarius group for you have many of the faults outlined in that section. Read and think about it with your usual open mind and it may be possible for you to accept and overcome some of your weaknesses.

WHAT MAKES YOU

ARIES

Members of this sign are usually happy when beginning anything new – a job, a car or a fresh writing pad. They enjoy purchasing a new status symbol or winning a game – be it tennis, Trivial Pursuits or tiddlywinks – although in actual fact there is no such thing as a game to them, it is a life or death struggle each time.

Arians are content being waited upon either at home or outside, whether returning a faulty purchase or reprimanding an inefficient public servant. Above all, Arians are happiest when they know they are the most important person in someone else's life.

TAURUS

Taureans are happy when experimenting in the kitchen, or when they are asked to dine with friends and find that the cook happens to possess a Cordon Bleu diploma. They are delighted when their opinion regarding the wine is eagerly sought, and when someone else agrees they are right.

Taureans are in seventh heaven when some kind person brings them breakfast in bed. They are also delighted when the greenfly have been vanquished, when their nostrils are assailed by an exotic bloom or expensive perfume, or when they discover that last year's swimming costume still fits.

GEMINI

Geminians need the constant mental activity of stimulating company. Being madly in love helps and they lap it up when sexual advances are made at parties. They are delighted when they discover a new interest, or when they are doing almost nothing in the sunshine (a Geminian never does absolutely nothing).

Being happy also means getting a good night's sleep, learning from someone who is considered much brighter, or finding that one of their myriad ideas successfully takes off.

They love it when remarks are made about their youthful faces or figures and rejoice when their child does better at school than expected. They like change and solving problems. Playing with their children's toys at Christmas brings great pleasure, but mostly Geminians are happiest when there are not enough hours in the day.

LIBRA

Happiness is being in the throes of a heavy romance, when a lover brings some flowers, champagne or at least dedicates a song to them. Librans are also content when acting as mediators, or when righting any kind of wrong.

They enjoy picking out a new outfit for something special, or discovering a new restaurant. Librans are delighted when the owner of a familiar haunt greets them by name and when their first love re-enters their life and still appears to be carrying the torch.

They are thrilled when they have successfully lost all their winter fat and when their children show an appreciation of beauty. Provided life is peaceful, beautiful and harmonious, then the Libran is happy. It is hardly surprising, then, that they can be quite depressed at times.

SCORPIO

Loyalty, a mystery to be unravelled or praise for sexual prowess could all be guaranteed to make Scorpions smile.

They revel in the respect of loved ones who can be trusted, and in their own ability to get the better of others professionally. They appreciate someone who is willing to listen to their opinions, especially when they need an audience to applaud their successes.

Scorpions are delighted when other people keep their promises or when a child admits a misdemeanour. They love planning a surprise party for loved ones, sitting around a blazing fire with the family, or trying exotic foods.

SAGITTARIUS

Fresh air, open spaces and outdoor activities make Sagittarians happy, and a straightforward approach to both professional and personal life. They are competitive individuals who live to win. They love to do things their way, no matter how offbeat this may seem to others.

They are happy being with eccentric but brilliant people. They also love throwing impromptu parties and going away for Christmas. Anything which panders to their sense of freedom will make them happy.

HAPPY?

The answer clearly varies from person to person, although our astrological signs frequently give us a clue . . .

CANCER

Cancerians are happy when surrounded by their family, when others express their love, or when they are given a box of their favourite sweets. They are delighted to be near the sea, or in the bath – especially if they can sing a favourite song at the top of their voices.

They are ecstatic when they finally get a sun-tan and when there is a present to unwrap.

They love carols, gently falling snow, and romantic music. For some Cancerians, happiness can mean a Barry Manilow record, while for others, happiness is when their marrows or sprouts win first prize at the vegetable show. They are exceptionally pleased when someone asks them for their favourite recipes or when other people tell them silly – but certainly not blue – jokes.

LEO

Leos are delirious when they are flattered, no matter how corny the line. They enjoy spoiling someone they love or respect, and winning an argument or a gamble.

They like to treat themselves to luxuries and are happy when they have thrown a successful party or get-together.

Leos are smug when they are warm and comfortable or when invited to a swish social occasion: they love titles. They glow when they are praised for their good taste and become hysterical with delight when they do better than their friends. Since they love being in the limelight and in positions of power, you should watch out if your local traffic warden happens to be born under this sign.

VIRGO

Virgos are happy when life goes according to plan, or when those around them put away their belongings. Fresh flowers in the office or clean sheets on the bed make them brighten visibly.

They really enjoy it when others abide by their hygiene rules and if friends and acquaintances notice when they are ill. They are delighted to know that they can actually afford the holiday they are enjoying, and when they can hold their own in the company of cleverer and more interesting people.

What could very well send them into seventh heaven is to discover after a party that not a single glass has been broken, nor is there one cigarette burn on the new carpet – but then who would dare?

CAPRICORN

Goats are traditionalists who love thatched cottages and old hunting lodges, a royal wedding, births or family celebrations. Nothing is too good for their loved ones, although they will be tickled pink if they can get a special present and a good discount.

They are delighted to be invited to grand social occasions, especially if these necessitate dressing up to the nines, and they love mixing with successful or well-bred people. Happiness also comes when the bank balance finally goes into the black and they can afford an occasional luxury. Happy to be lavish on special occasions, Capricorns are unhappy to be parted from their cash on a day-to-day basis.

AQUARIUS

Political meetings, demonstrations against any kind of tyranny, good companionship and the truth, no matter how painful – all these bring happiness to the Aquarian. They also love to celebrate their birthday and to travel, especially if it is in order to discover what can be done to help their fellow man.

Aquarians adore their friends. They are happy to do things spontaneously and like to wear comfortable clothes.

They enjoy disregarding convention and wear jeans for formal occasions, splash in puddles and play snowballs – being as outrageous as possible is the Aquarian's idea of fun!

PISCES

It is the gentler side to life that keeps Pisceans happy – tending a bird with a broken leg, nursing a sick goldfish, or watching a beautiful sunset. It doesn't take much except the most difficult thing in the world – finding the right person with whom to share all this. Pisceans are delighted with the look on a child's face when opening a present, while an old movie can reduce them to tears of happiness. They are givers – even if it is only a matchbox with an 'I love you' note written inside, they give as much as they can.

Nature is a constant source of pleasure and a delight to them – from assisting as midwife to the family pet cat, to the wonders of a perfect rosebud. In many ways Pisces is the luckiest sign of the Zodiac: happiness comes to the Fish through things that the rest of us either fail to notice or else take for granted.

CAPRICORN

22 DECEMBER – 20 JANUARY

IT is never easy being born under the sign of the Goat. No one in the Zodiac is more cut off from their fellows: it is almost impossible for you to communicate the depth of your feelings in the usual way. You desperately need to be understood but few people ever come to terms with your extreme sensitivity. They get the wrong impression because you seem so self-assured, unflappable, confident and detached – in fact an enviable loner. Few realize that inside you are craving attention, affection, recognition, appreciation and most important of all, love.

On the surface you seem a little too stiff with others, cautious, reserved, aloof and sometimes a little bit too brisk. Those who would normally reach out to you on the first meeting are often deterred by your coolness and what seems to be your lack of response. It is not your fault. The peculiarity of the makeup of your sign, suggests you can't help building up a wall around yourself in order to protect that extreme vulnerability: although you may be fearless in a worldly way, you are terrified of being hurt emotionally. Others rarely guess that under that self-control is a gentle anxious person wanting to emerge but terrified to do so.

All Capricorns can be surprisingly impulsive at times. This is a contradiction in your nature: usually you are the epitome of discipline. At times you are likely to do the rashest of things without warning. These inexplicable impulses land you in some awful trouble because the formal Capricorn nature is not equipped to handle spontaneous or unreasonable behaviour. When it occurs you are shattered and secretly ashamed because usually you like to analyse and use careful judgement. You are right to try and avoid acting on the spur of the moment because this is when you make some of the biggest mistakes in your life. Nevertheless once you have found someone to truly trust then it is important that you allow that vulnerable being within out into the open.

PERSO

FEMALE

Saint

● There are times when you seem remote and cool, however that is only to protect the softer you. Your feelings are deep, vulnerable, sensitive and strong – and so is your sense of duty.

● You have little time for endless chatter or frivolity. You are highly organized and ambitious; idleness is never thought about in your book. Continual activity keeps you going. You push ahead through illness, physical disability and depression. In brief you are a hopeless workaholic who thinks of a holiday as a different kind of work.

● Because of your fierce ambition, you usually get wherever you want to go and that is usually directly to the top. However, your modesty and your self-criticism mean that when you do, you can barely believe it yourself.

● On a more personal level, you are kind, responsible and faithful and have the sort of integrity which makes people want to stay in your life. You are usually a friend of long standing and help others in their needy and painful moments.

● You need a strong man to share your life with you, preferably one with a sense of humour who is free with his feelings, rather than confined by the fear of them.

Sinner

● You are critical and cranky and consumed by superficial manoeuvres. Your emotions are tainted with a kind of intolerance that leaves little room for basic human understanding. You are niggardly in your sympathies, narrow-minded, and unwilling to look at an issue from anything but an impersonal perspective. You are very cold and care very little for other people's feelings. When you do help them out it is only with ulterior motives in mind.

● Because you are so status conscious, you will go after what you want and you frequently pretend to be something you are not.

● You work very hard and make a point of always knowing 'the right people'. When they cease to be useful any more you toss them aside without a second thought as though they were used tissues.

● In terms of the opposite sex you are only interested in those who have 'made it'. You are the type who would treat a husband like a bank account that is collecting interest. Because you go to ridiculous lengths for appearance's sake, you probably won't even let him sit on the furniture because it might make the place look untidy. He is quite likely to find himself a nice tidy chair next to the cat's bed in the kitchen.

Male

Saint

● You have authority, strength and ambition and this, together with endurance, makes you a formidable person. Once you have decided what you want, you go wholeheartedly after it and seldom falter. You love to take charge as you make your way forward towards the top. There are times when you can drive yourself past the average person's limits; with a will of iron, you move ever onward towards success, regardless of the hardships you may have to endure to get there.

● Emotionally you are intense, and yet, to all appearances, stiff and cool. Basically you are shy, romantically reserved and insecure. Until you are sure of someone your approach is often guarded and rarely flowery. Your presence may loom large where work matters are concerned but in the romantic situation you are often self-effacing. Your personality is suited to serious relationships, and you are more comfortable in marriage than those born under any other sign.

Sinner

● Your basic interest in life seems to be controlling others; you suffer terrible discontent if forced to play second fiddle.

● Your immense ego problems mean you always need to be on top. One of your favourite pastimes is telling other people what to do. You are arrogant, patronizing, commanding and careless about the feelings of others. You are a snob who is constantly demeaning yourself to superiors, but abrupt or barely civil to those in the lower echelons of life.

● Your maddening personality could force a saint to contemplate murder. After a period of listening to what you say people will do anything to shut you up. You never give up trying to convince the world that you are something you are not.

● Your basic attitude to women is that they are meant to serve and should be sensible enough to keep their mouths shut and listen and, last but not least, be content to take as many orders as you issue. Because a woman is something you regard like a new pair of shoes, it is important that you get the kind that looks great but costs little. If it dawns on you that the object of your desire is not interested, you become hostile and defensive. After all, it is only your feelings that really count; in your book she really doesn't have the right to have any.

● You are particularly apt to use pressure and when you bring it into play you have a way of obliterating resistance and reducing people to mewling, sweating creatures begging for peace. However, peace is not your style. All you care about is power, the kind that carries enough propaganda to prepare the unenlightened for your second coming.

● ANNIE LENNOX BORN 25 DECEMBER 1955

ANNIE IS A STRONG, DETERMINED LADY AND A GREAT FIGHTER. LIFE IS NEVER EASY FOR THE GOAT AND IT HAS BEEN AN UPHILL STRUGGLE FOR HER ON OCCASIONS. HOWEVER, HER CAPRICORN DETERMINATION NEVER FLAGS, AND SHE WILL ALWAYS TRIUMPH OVER DIFFICULTIES.

● ROWAN ATKINSON BORN 6 JANUARY 1955

WHILST ON THE SURFACE CAPRICORN CAN BE CONSERVATIVE, NEVERTHELESS, THERE ARE OCCASIONS WHEN THIS SIGN IS HAPPY TO PLAY THE GIDDY GOAT. THIS ACTS AS A RELEASE. ROWAN HAS DISCOVERED THAT HE CAN MAKE IT PAY, AND MONEY FOR CAPRICORN IS A GREAT MOTIVATION.

● HUMPHREY BOGART BORN 25 DECEMBER 1899

HUMPHREY BOGART HAD ALL THE TOUGHNESS AND GRIT ASSOCIATED WITH HIS EARTHY SIGN. PERSONAL HAPPINESS IS OFTEN EITHER DENIED THE GOAT OR COMES LATE IN LIFE. HE MARRIED FOUR TIMES BEFORE HE FOUND HIS IDEAL MATE, LAUREN BACALL, WHO WAS ASTROLOGICALLY PERFECT.

CAPRICORN *in* LIFE

At work

Capricorn Boss In many respects this is the sign of the self-made person for despite any drawbacks in their background, Capricorns will succeed in life once they have made up their mind to do so, through hard work and sheer determination. If this is the case they could be difficult people to work for as they will expect much from other people. Once they have arrived, they will be strongly attracted to big ambitious projects but feel fully obligated to any contract and usually fulfil their responsibilities despite all odds. They expect a lot from their employees (loyalty and hard and long work are well appreciated) but they have little time for shirkers. Because of their ambitious and fighting spirit Capricorns will be quick to recognize this quality in others and while, of course, they will respect such an employee, the latter would be well advised not to make the Capricorn feel threatened.

Capricorn Employee The Goat is very happy when working on a lower level but the weak or perverted Goat will be constantly pining and expressing heavy moroseness. A cold or distant nature may mean that they can carry despondency and gloom, painful not only for themselves, but also for those connected with them. Strong Capricorns are capable of attaining a great height as they possess ambition and endurance and with their meticulous attention to detail and thrifty and acquisitive manner, they can build while others are still dreaming.

These individuals will make the most of all opportunities open to them and being self-reliant, can accomplish their objectives. Basically Goats know they are going places and while this is mostly achieved through their own efforts and personal merit, influential friends will sometimes alter the course of their lives. Lastly, Capricorn represents fame, honour, positions of authority, prestige and professional standing – to sum up, you want it all.

FAMILY MATTERS

CAPRICORN MOTHER For you motherhood is simply another duty you knew would be forthcoming at some point. Naturally you ensure that your children's basic needs are provided for. However, it has to be said that you can be a rather cool, sometimes strict mother figure. To your children you seem remote, preoccupied with helping your husband and making the right impression; they think twice before bringing their little problems to you. It is important to remember to let loose with those little people in your life and show them the more gentle side to your character. It certainly is there. It is simply that your life is so crowded that you frequently forget to give your children that little extra hug and kiss when it is most needed. See what you can do to soften up a bit. Play the giddy Goat occasionally. Get your reward from the happy laughter that this will generate.

CAPRICORN FATHER The Capricorn father is very similar to the mother. You spend so much time and energy trying to get on in the world in order to provide for your family that you tend to forget that there are other needs apart from material ones. You are ambitious for your children too, and read their school reports in great detail, always concerned when grades are dropping or your offspring have got themselves into trouble. You really need to try to respond to your children from the heart more often: not all problems can be sorted out by writing a cheque or a stiff talking to. There is a soft gentle man inside and it is important that children are allowed to see this person.When they do, Capricorn man will realize that they will do their best to please him simply because they love him and not because he provides for them.

CAPRICORN CHILD The Capricorn child may be extremely antisocial on occasions, apparently in no need for companionship. Capricorns really do enjoy their own company. They are also rather suspicious individuals and it takes time for someone to win their trust and approval. Therefore don't expect a continual stream of pals. One or two are basically all they need to keep them happy. Don't worry about the love of solitude too much – the young Capricorn will emerge from it when he or she is good and ready.

The little Goat tends towards traditional games rather than modern: tales of yore at bedtime will enthrall, where science fiction and adventure will bore. Later on the volumes of Charles Dickens may prove to be a much-loved possession. The Goat is fascinated – even obsessed – by the past and this will be reflected in the choice of television viewing, play acting and reading materials. Should such a preoccupation be combined with a love of bargain hunting, then you have a child who will be in his or her element at jumble sales, markets or junkyards. A browse around an ancient dusty bookshop will delight them, while metal detecting on the sites of past battles will keep the small Goat absorbed for hours, especially if this activity can be shared with the family.

A party-goer the Goat is not: sticky buns and wobbly jellies do not set pulses racing, and jolly party games are viewed with scorn. This is due to a basic shyness and pressure should not be exerted or suffering can result.

At play

Because of Capricorns' workaholic tendencies, coupled with their need for solitude and the ability to endure, Goats are often attracted to mountaineering or treks across the desert, anywhere they can find a challenge and solitude. On the sporting front this is no flash-in-the-pan character and it is sports that require tremendous endurance – cross-country running, weight lifting and body building – which appeal.

Capricorns are also at one with nature: you like to ramble across the countryside, taking in the sights and smells; this allows that busy brain of yours to cool down and let go. Capricorns don't need a fancy hotel on these occasions: youth hostels or camping are perfectly acceptable.

When at home solitude is often sought in the garden. You are extremely good at pot, tub and patio gardening and love to blend plants with architecture, but have little patience for lawn mowing or digging up weeds.

The Goat naturally likes its food – therefore eating out in sumptuous restaurants is something that is keenly looked forward to.

Money

You are so shrewd with money that you could be a tycoon. You are the type that knows how to make it, keep it and multiply it.

When it comes to finance you are hard-headed, willing to work and realistic. Regardless of the size of your income you always manage to have some savings. You tend to be very frugal and others often accuse you of being stingy or even cheap. However, there are some luxury-minded Goats who spend a small fortune in an hour on a shopping spree. This is because they appreciate beautiful things – the Goat seldom spends aimlessly. Each purchase, regardless of its price tag, will bring a lot of pleasure for a long time to come.

This is certainly a sign that will never starve. Goats are much too smart for that and usually too successful. However, because you tend to worry you will probably not believe this. What the Capricorn regards as a small amount of money a Sagittarian, for example, will probably consider a small fortune. The important thing, though, is to remember not to be so engrossed in figures that you forget how to live your life.

Lastly, it has to be said that you love bargains and can be found hunting them at sales, fairs, car boot sales and jumble sales. You may fall in love with something but have sufficient patience to hang around for months until it is entered into a sale. Some call this meanness, but to the Goat it makes perfect sense. After all, you work hard for your money. Special occasions are the only times when you are happy to splurge.

● MARLENE DIETRICH BORN 27 DECEMBER 1904

SATURN IS THE RULER OF CAPRICORN AND IT GIVES GREAT STAYING POWER AND OFTEN LONG LIFE. MARLENE MAY HAVE BEEN BLONDE BUT THAT EARTHY TOUGHNESS WAS ALWAYS THERE. SHE KNEW WHAT SHE HAD TO DO TO GET WHAT SHE WANTED – FEW DARED STAND AGAINST HER WISHES. A DUMB BLONDE SHE WAS NOT.

● NIGEL KENNEDY BORN 28 DECEMBER 1956

NIGEL MAY BE A BRILLIANT MUSICIAN AND A HIGHLY AMBITIOUS ONE, LIKE MOST CAPRICORNS, BUT HE ALSO POSSESSES A TENDENCY TO PLAY THE GIDDY GOAT AND TO GO OUT OF HIS WAY TO SHOCK. HOWEVER, IT IS LIKELY THAT WITH AGE HE WILL BECOME *ALMOST* AS SOBER AS OTHERS IN THE PROFESSION.

● JOAN OF ARC BORN 6 JANUARY 1412

THIS SIGN FREQUENTLY WILLINGLY SACRIFICES ITS OWN WANTS AND NEEDS FOR OTHERS OR FOR A CAUSE. IT IS ALSO PERHAPS THE STRONGEST AND MOST DETERMINED SIGN IN THE ZODIAC. THEREFORE, IT IS NOT SURPRISING THAT THE MAID OF ORLEANS WAS CONTENT TO DIE FOR HER BELIEFS.

CAPRICORN *in* LOVE

Single

You may be a big wheel in the business world, but you are vulnerable and shy when it comes to loving. This is due to a sense of insecurity and because of this you feel that the love situation is often more painful than pleasurable.

You have a remarkable sense of realism in all areas but in matters of romance it is not unusual for you to go through several relationships with the wrong people. This is because you tend to get sidetracked by glamorous surface qualities and this means you can set yourself up for being badly hurt. You are not the most resilient of human beings either so emotional pain can hang on long after an affair is over. It is quite likely that you will go through many difficult situations before you come to the conclusion that this side to life is all-important. A less than total love may be great for a freedom-loving Aquarian but the compromise of a partial love for you with the satisfactions it may bring in the beginning will, in the long run, only make you sad. When you fall in love you are serious and in turn need to be taken seriously. You find games loathsome and immature behaviour turns you completely off.

You need desperately to be understood, but few recognize your extreme sensitivity. You seem so confident, unflappable, and competent. They don't realize that inside you are longing for attention, affection and love, which would give you that warm glow of emotional security and acceptance. It's hard for you to ask; you feel loved ones should know.

A warm, stable affectionate person is your best choice for a happy relationship.

Married

You are definitely the marrying kind, but often don't do so until your mature years. Ideally you need a partner who represents a bastion of security and stability. While some Goats have been known to marry for money, the vast majority seek a kind of emotional nurturing and caring. Although you are undeniably self-reliant, you also need some support to boost your feelings of self-worth.

When married, you are capable of total loyalty and expect the same. You are a person who trusts, and one who, in turn, can be deeply trusted. Once you have made a commitment, you are responsible and determined to make the relationship work. What you need most in a partner is someone whose feet are on the ground and whose head is in the air, someone who sparks your enthusiasm, adds a little laughter to your life and can make you smile. A rich marital relationship can serve as an important foundation for your other activities.

Perfect Partners

When it comes to finding the perfect partner, Capricorns invariably find themselves amongst the other earth signs of Capricorn, Taurus and Virgo.

Capricorn with Capricorn This relationship could well spring from a mutual outlook on life, for both take life seriously and it may be a relief to find another person who approaches every day in a realistic fashion. Each believes that hard work is the only possible way to success and although they are ambitious, this could lead to problems. Finances are unlikely to create problems as each is careful with money.

The Capricorn's sexual appetite is well developed, and these two normally rather serious people are able to play the giddy Goat with one another and this helps to arouse sexual interest in the relationship. Life will be well organized. When it is time to work, they slog themselves to death and support one another and share one another's problems. However, they also realize when it is time to let go and have a bit of fun. Inside all Goats there is a soft core which is only shown to those who are truly trusted. And who but another Capricorn will realize what is going on deep inside that mate and will find ways of bringing it to the surface? Once these two get together they may conquer the world but they are also likely to have a rich inner life too.

Capricorn with Taurus The physical attraction is unmistakable between these two earth subjects, so that the differences between their personalities are sure to be minimized. Although in general not an artistic person, the Goat may become so when observing a Bull's interest in this direction. Likewise, the Taurean's interest in food can rub off on Capricorn and the two of them could very well develop epicurean habits, trotting along to a wine tasting or experimenting at new restaurants. The need for a domestic background is shared and they will put much energy into it, drawing strength from each other's interest. The mutual horror of debt will eliminate the possibility of financial difficulties which undermines some relationships. They may collect antiques, for both will be interested in the past in some form or another. Their need to get back to nature is also strong and may show in a love of gardening or camping holidays.

Sexually this is probably the best relationship for them as they can awaken much passion in each other where others may fail, and there is a strong possibility that their interest in each other will not weaken as the years pass.

Capricorn with Virgo Love could spring up pretty quickly between these two characters, for they will have an immediate respect for each other's outlook on life. Affection can be hard for them to express with other people, but together the inhibitions should soon melt away. Capricorn is often accused of cold behaviour and while this may still apply at times, for the most part the Goat will be at its warmest with Virgo. Complete agreement is achieved over finances as both are interested in money and in saving for the future. Their social life is unlikely to be sophisticated because they share an interest in the outdoors and some healthy activity or sport will usually take preference over a dinner party.

The home is important to both and each will contribute to its comfort and beauty. There will be a mutual understanding of each other's need to escape at times and separate weekends may occasionally be enjoyed. However, these are unlikely to include a third party. This relationship is likely to rest on compatibility and mutual interest, rather than on consuming passion.

The sexual appetites are about equal but are never allowed to dominate their life. This is a happy combination of personalities and they should be able to live happily ever after.

ARE YOU A TYPICAL CAPRICORN...

Answer honestly the questions below, using YES, NO or SOMETIMES; total up your score, allowing 3 for YES, 2 for SOMETIMES and 1 for NO.

...MAN?

1. Are you a pessimist?
2. Would it be difficult for you to function properly without your career?
3. Is deep depression part of your personality?
4. Are you a snob?
5. Does your sex life go to extremes?
6. Do you hide money in odd places?
7. Does the feminine touch around the house irritate you?
8. Are you attracted to older women?
9. Are you strictly straightforward in your sexual desires?
10. Do you often flirt when an attractive girl enters the room?
11. Are you accused of meanness?
12. Does the thought of paying for sex offend you?
13. Do you take off for periods of time on your own?
14. Do you think success will come late in life for you?
15. Are you interested in history in any shape or form?
16. Do you have an aptitude for study?
17. Do you think you were a late starter in sex?
18. Do you need to be at least fond of a woman before you can sleep with her?
19. Is your taste in clothes plain and simple?
20. Do you sometimes feel that your life is restricted by some inexplicable force?

...WOMAN?

1. Do you experience depression that can last for days?
2. Are you a small eater?
3. Do women who spend hours in front of the mirror irritate you?
4. Do you save secretly?
5. Do you like to be subjugated in sex?
6. Do you think you were born into the wrong time?
7. Do you think you were a late starter sex-wise?
8. Do you spend much time on your own?
9. Does study come easily to you?
10. Do tradition and history interest you?
11. Do you tackle things slowly but carefully?
12. Does the future of the world worry you?
13. Has your father influenced you strongly for good or bad?
14. Will you make a strict mother?
15. Are you attracted to older men?
16. Do you think you would break it off quickly if you discovered that a boyfriend was married?
17. Rightly or wrongly do you prefer to go your own way, no matter what?
18. Do you take sexual affairs seriously?
19. Are you a snob?
20. Do you feel restricted by some influence you cannot explain?

ARE YOU A TYPICAL CAPRICORN MAN ?

1–30 It just isn't possible for a Capricorn to answer these questions in the way you have: you are much too extrovert. If you turn to the chapters on Gemini or Sagittarius you may find your true self, but don't attempt to make the characteristics fit you. You should be able to recognize yourself easily.

31–50 This is the score of a saintly Capricorn which means you inherit most of the nicer qualities associated with this sign without the more unpleasant characteristics. However, you do tend to be a little serious and reserved. You should try to relax more and enjoy yourself – it will be good for you and for those you love.

51–60 Such a high score could only have been achieved by a 'sinner' Capricorn meaning that the faults associated with this sign will be very much to the fore of your personality. Your melancholic character can have a depressing effect on those around you and you should try to control it. Read the section dedicated to you and try to learn something from it.

ARE YOU A TYPICAL CAPRICORN WOMAN ?

1–30 You just could not possibly be a Capricorn, your answers are too extrovert and open-minded. You are far more likely to find yourself under Gemini, Sagittarius or possibly Pisces. Read these chapters without trying to make yourself fit them for your sign should be obvious to you.

31–50 This is the score one would expect a 'saintly' Capricorn to achieve. You are lucky enough to have inherited most of the better qualities associated with this sign without necessarily also possessing the more unpleasant traits. However, you do tend to take life a little too seriously; you and those around you could benefit from more relaxation on your part.

51–60 You are quite obviously a 'sinner' Capricorn and you may be a very melancholic personality who usually looks on the gloomier side of life. When these moods threaten, try to keep busy and forget your problems for you could be a dampening influence on your loved ones. Also read the 'sinner' section aimed at you and try to learn something about yourself.

YOUR MAGICAL NUMBER

To find your Magical Number for any year, follow these instructions. If you were born on 20 September then write down 9 (birth month), 20 (birth date) and, for example, 1999 = 1 + 9 + 9 + 9 = 28. Add all the numbers together, namely 9 + 2 + 0 + 2 + 8 = 21. Then add 2 + 1 = 3. Now you have your Magical Number for that year – 1999. The same procedure is used for any year.

1

In general A time to be self-sufficient, put the past behind you and prepare to start again. There will be many new experiences and chances for you. If you are born under the sign of Leo or Aries, or on the 1st, 10th, 19th or 28th, this should be an all-important time. You will be laying down a blueprint and will be reaping the benefits over the next nine years.

Love Again there is a theme of change. There is an important new relationship here, perhaps with somebody a good deal younger than yourself. If you are in a steady relationship then you will be making a fresh start. People born under Leo, Aries and Aquarius will be especially important to you, and you are likely to meet them during January, May, July and October.

Career Here again important changes are suggested. Your drive, decisiveness, talents and aggression will certainly be making a big impression on those who count and they will be ready and willing to give their help to you. If you are looking for a job or making any sort of career change, Monday and Tuesday will be the important times.

2

In general You need to be helpful, diplomatic and considerate. Plans you made last year are beginning to show signs of life. Changes take place on the domestic level and you may move house. There is more movement than usual in the family circle and also in your relationships with the opposite sex. This is a great year for getting others to support you, but avoid being too pushy. If you are born under the sign of Cancer or Taurus or if your birthday falls on the 2nd, 11th, 20th or 29th of the month, the year ahead will be an important one.

Love Friendship, romance and all relationships are a great need for you. The opposite sex holds greater sway over your life than usual. Major milestones – pregnancies, marriages or engagements – are likely for you or those close to you. The caring side of your nature will be much in evidence. You will be extra-sensitive to others. Those born under Cancer, Taurus and Libra will be especially important and April, June and September are your peak periods.

Career There is change and upheaval within your work: maybe your company is moving. Extra responsibility is also likely. If you are looking for a job, arrange events for Monday and Friday.

4

In general It is important to begin this year with a clear idea of what you want from life. At times you will feel others expect too much of you; then you will feel overloaded. Recognize and accept your limitations. If you are an Aquarian, Leo or a Geminian or born on the 4th, 13th, 22nd or 31st, this year will be extremely important.

Love People generally thought to be unusual and even eccentric will join your friendship circle. Someone from your past may reappear. You can be drawn to those from a different age group or from outside your ethnic or social background. Geminians, Leos and Aquarians are likely to be best for you this year; your lucky months are February, April, July and November.

Career This is a year of extremes for your career: you may be out of work when an unexpected opportunity comes along; if so, grab it immediately. But sudden developments may be bad ones. This Magical Number tends to bring strange events, but also added responsibilities. Don't avoid extra burdens – they can pay off in the end. Leave anything world-shattering to do with work to Monday or Wednesday. January, February, October and November are times when you must be ready for opportunities.

5

In general You may get a chance now to pick up from where you left off some time ago. You will begin to feel more optimistic and will find it easier to accept change. You are likely to be doing a considerable amount of growing up. If you are a Geminian or a Virgo or born on the 5th, 14th or 23rd of the month, this will be a particularly important time for you.

Love The magic of number 5 is often found in its sexual attraction, and even without making any kind of change your sexual magnetism will be pulling people into your circle. You may become involved with those younger than yourself. People born under Taurus, Gemini, Virgo and Libra will be especially important to you.

Career This is an extremely good year for improving your job and career prospects. You will be able to sell yourself or your talents with great conviction and success. Others will be aware of your talents and what you have to offer. Wednesday and Friday are the best days for looking for jobs and going to meetings. The best months for opportunities are March, May, September, October and December.

In general A good year for those who are creative, promising a lively social life. A time for growth – you may take up a new interest or go in for self-improvement. An especially good year if you work with the public. You may take up something artistic, which will add depths to your life. Something you began two years ago is likely to be bringing results. An extremely important year for you if you are born under the sign of Pisces or Sagittarius or your birthday falls on the 3rd, 21st or 30th of the month.

Love Romance looks lighthearted and flirty: you are constantly chasing passing fancies. You may find relationships with those a good deal younger than yourself developing. Those particularly fortunate for you are people born under Pisces and Sagittarius and others born on dates that add up to 3, 6 or 9. The best time for emotional decisions is March, May and December.

Career Because of recent events, you are likely to have grown quite considerably and your work outlook is bright. Stay optimistic and pursue your ambitions. If you have a responsible position, be sure to fulfil your duties well. If you are seeking self-advancement, pick Thursday and Friday for meetings and interviews.

In general Most of the year's important events will centre around your domestic and emotional life. Upheavals within the home are likely; possibly you are moving. A great year for generally improving yourself. Social life will be hectic; you will be spoiled for choice. Business will be more mixed with pleasure than usual. If you are born on the 6th, 15th or 24th of the month, or your sign is Taurus, Libra or Cancer, this is an extremely important year.

Love A mega-important year where emotional matters are concerned: a time for major events – engagement, marriage or divorce, pregnancy, changes in existing relationships. Those born under Taurus, Cancer and Libra are sure to have a major role in your life and your outstanding months will be February, May, September and November.

Career Of all the numbers this is the one which is likely to bring great success: your praises will be sung. This will help to swell your flagging bank account. If you are out of work, or want to form your own company or interest others in your talents, then your best days are Monday, Thursday and Friday. Opportunities will be coming to you in February, April, August, September and November.

In general A year for making a big impression, especially if you are born on the 8th, 17th or 26th or under Capricorn. You will be developing a greater sense of yourself and your worth, and a good deal of growing up is likely. You will feel capable of reaching out for opportunities that arise. Where cash is concerned, you may have to deal with something from the past. Think big during this particular year.

Love Magical Number 8 is strongly mingled with marriage, divorce and pregnancy. Those who are a good deal more experienced than yourself or are in positions of power and wealth will have a special attraction. An old love may pop up unexpectedly, as could people from your childhood. There will be no emotional problems if you are a Capricorn or a Libran. Romance is likely during March, July, September and December.

Career A great year for success, bringing reward for past efforts. Keep a high profile and put your talents on display; it is not a time for self-effacement. Set ambitions and objectives: you will be succeeding in the greater portion of them. To tackle anything important use Thursday, Friday and Saturday. Watch out for chances during February, June, July, September and November.

In general A year with the emphasis on your personal life. You will go over the past more than usual. At times you will need space to think through what you are striving for, life; if you work out exactly what you are striving for, you should be able to succeed. This is a year when other people's secrets may surface. If you are born under Pisces or Cancer or on the 7th, 16th or 25th of the month, this year will be especially important.

Love You are advised to be flirty and not take things too seriously. A new relationship that starts may be less permanent than you would like. The worst thing to do now is go out looking for that special someone. Those born under Cancer and Pisces could be important. Romantic opportunities come during January, April, August and October.

Career Some of you may be retiring, some reassessing what you want from life; this can involve travel. A hidden talent may suddenly surface. This is a year for probing within yourself and your opportunities. Monday and Friday are possibly the best days if looking for a job; the important months are January, March, July, August, October and December. Snap up all the opportunities that arise then.

In general This is perhaps the best year you could possibly have. You seem more confident and will find it easier to sweep aside all that may have been holding you back. Your nurturing side is strong; be more prepared to give time and energy to others without looking for a pat on the back. If you are an Aries or a Scorpio or born on the 9th, 18th or 27th, this will be a magical year.

Love Magical Number 9 gives an unorthodox approach to love and emotion, and you could become involved with those from completely different backgrounds or countries. Aries, Leo and Scorpio people are likely to hold sway over family matters. February, June, August and November will be especially lively for emotional and romantic life.

Career A time when you will get your just deserts: something you have been pushing for some time will suddenly be accepted as sheer genius. Conversely this number can suggest retirement or job loss. Despite this you will come out on top. Success can come through a change of direction. Those working in harness with others will find enhanced opportunities. Tuesday and Thursday are your best days for anything important. Changes are most likely in January, May, June, August and October.

AQUARIUS

21 JANUARY – 19 FEBRUARY

UNLIKE other flashy signs, you rarely show off or go out of your way to prove how clever you are. You are what you are, you wear what you wear, offbeat or otherwise, because it is you and you are different. You couldn't care less what other people think. More eccentrics are born under this particular sign than any other but always bear in mind that there is not a great deal of difference between genius and eccentricity.

You are generally thoughtful, sympathetic and peaceful. Of course you have your weaknesses, but for the most part you express moderation in all aspects of your personality. You don't go looking for trouble, you are not excessively ambitious and you don't consider cash important.

There is a natural, rather charming, tendency in you to see the good in everything and everyone. You are a dreamer and an idealist but are clever enough to know what is attainable and what is not. You often have a dreamy look in your eye. You are always looking forward to tomorrow and back to yesterday, seldom to now.

Your optimism is not the kind that imagines things are going to be better, only that things are going to change, and to your way of thinking this is improvement enough.

You never cease probing and sounding with well-placed questions, helped by your intuition. Everybody you come across without exception goes under your microscope. On a good day you are tactful and subtle, on a bad, insensitive and, let's face it, embarrassing. You have a way of penetrating to the very core of people's private feelings and this will make them feel uncomfortable. It has to be said, too, that you quickly lose interest in individuals once you understand them and that back in your past there is generally a whole stream of people who are both puzzled and confused by your behaviour and the way you lead your life. Never mind, you enjoy being different and true to yourself. In your book that is all that counts.

PERSO

FEMALE

Saint

● You skip through life making friends with all sorts in all spheres. You bombard other people with questions because you are the most curious female in the Zodiac. The more weird things are, the better: the eccentric and unusual bring a gleam to your eyes.

● The more bizarre the incidents in your life the more you like it. One of your favourite things is to stay up all night analysing and speculating. Totally incongruous situations stir you up and make your blood boil over.

● You are definitely the unforgettable type that scares some people but delights others. Sometimes you ask so many questions that people think you are taking a survey. You have a great time, too, listening to gossip – the stranger, the better. You are perhaps the best listener in the Zodiac and thrive on helping other people, getting them out of trouble and learning the latest scandal. The chances are you know the details of everybody's business.

● Basically you are the friendly sort who needs constant stimulation and excitement, but what you call excitement might make the next person a little wary: magic, mind controls, high mathematics, numerology, palmistry and astrology are all likely to attract you at some point. You have a brilliant, original, far-seeing mind that dares to look at the world differently.

Sinner

● Although there are Aquarian females who are militants, the vast majority are not even tempted. On the contrary you tend towards conformity because it is more comfortable. The chances are, your ego is as fragile as an egg. You are terribly insecure, shy and sure that you are not going to get what you want, so sometimes you don't bother asking in the first place. You would like to like people, but you have a hard time trusting them. Therefore you can be aloof and wary of spontaneous friendly entanglements.

● You often need to submerge your individuality in whoever seems to be a stronger influence at that moment. In the event, there is frequently no stronger influence. Your attitudes are wishy-washy and your mind embedded in both sides of the question; your intelligence is superficial and your ideas scattered. Your greatest desire is to marry and to move to a security zone where domestic trinkets and treasures will surround you. You are more likely to marry a man for his money, his last name or his credit cards than you are for his smile, his personality or his soul.

Male

Saint

● You have the mind of the mad inventor: a brilliant mathematician or scientist who can never find his glasses because they happen to be hanging around his neck. As a general rule, people are timid when it comes to the new, but this is the realm in life that you prefer to live in. Your mind is so forward-thinking that from the time you were about 3, you considered becoming the first astronaut to visit Venus. Now you daydream about building a summer home on Pluto. When other precocious children played with microscopes you were busy inventing one that magnified to a higher power.

● You are scientific, individualistic and eccentric. You love new ideas, new games, new concepts and new areas of knowledge.

● On a personal level, you are idealistic, honest, dispassionate and very human. Outwardly your disposition is serene; inwardly you pass through more emotional spaces than most people are aware of, but because you possess a certain amount of objectivity towards yourself, you don't dwell on your emotions long enough to allow them to drag you down. The first stab of pain or sadness is always replaced by a thought that tells you that it is really not important in the long run. Yes, you are a positive thinker.

Sinner

● Your personality is anxiety producing to other people and erratic. Working for you is like signing your soul over to a psychopath. Being married to you is less satisfying than curling up next to a fire which has definitely gone out. Being your friend is like creating a playground for the criminally insane.

● You live your life in a state of emotional uninvolvement, camouflaged by the fact that you are almost constantly in a frenzy. Sometimes you have a nervous tic which makes it seem that you are grinning. You are so anxiety-ridden that one has to look twice to be able to distinguish a smile from a spasm. You want to be out in front, even if you have to mangle a few minds to get there. Mind games are your forte and you play them like a jaded gambler who no longer needs to look for the secrets of the casino. Watch out – in the end your mind games imprison you and make you grow old and sad. Only those who have suffered through you know for sure that your body is at the mercy of a malevolent mind.

● JAMES DEAN BORN 8 FEBRUARY 1931

REBELS, INNOVATORS, AND HUMANITARIANS ARE ALL ASSOCIATED WITH AQUARIUS. TRUE TO FORM, DEAN KICKED OVER THE TRACES AND THUMBED HIS NOSE AT ALL AUTHORITY FIGURES. IN DOING SO HE INSPIRED A WHOLE GENERATION TO DO THE SAME. HAD HE LIVED, HE WOULD STILL BE DOING THE SAME THING.

● OPRAH WINFREY BORN 29 JANUARY 1954

OPRAH IS A DEEPLY CARING PERSON AND ABOUT AS HUMANE AND AQUARIAN AS IT IS POSSIBLE TO BE. WHILE THIS HAS LED TO GREAT SUCCESS, IT IS QUITE OBVIOUS THAT SHE IS SPURRED ON BY HER NEED TO RIGHT WRONGS AND HELP THE UNDERPRIVILEGED.

● MIA FARROW BORN 9 FEBRUARY 1945

THE RULING PLANET OF AQUARIUS IS URANUS, AND IT ENDOWS HIS SUBJECTS WITH A CERTAIN ECCENTRICITY, INDEPENDENCE AND OFTEN A CHANGEABLE LIFE. THERE IS LITTLE OR NOTHING ABOUT MIA'S LIFE THAT COULD BE DESCRIBED AS CONVENTIONAL. SHE DOES AS SHE PLEASES, REGARDLESS OF THE CONSEQUENCES.

AQUARIUS in LIFE

AT WORK

Aquarius Boss Many who work for Aquarians will come to respect their aggressive attitude and original and fertile mind, but the Aquarius detachment could prevent them from forming any close ties with members of staff. For the Aquarian is not concerned with what other people think and will often simply not bother to form any opinions of their behaviour. Not that Aquarians lack imagination; their thinking is often ahead of their time and is clear-cut, clinical in style, rational and intelligent. But because they do not bother to find out what other people really think, these individuals usually let others' opinions pass. This can make Aquarians frustrating people to work for, as any suggestions put forward for approval will usually be disregarded. Aquarians generally prefer to trust their own evaluation and ideas.

Aquarius Employee The Aquarius employee's greatest gift is breadth of vision, closely followed by his or her unbiased and open mind, free from superstition or prejudice of any description. Authority, however, generally leaves them unmoved and when faced with it they will regard it with serenity or a degree of friendship or interest. No amount of courtesy extended can prevent them from turning the spotlight of truth on the body concerned. Because of this, the Aquarius employee will be wise to try and locate a boss that can be generally respected and admired, otherwise it will not be very long before they will be at odds with one another. Once suitably placed Aquarians rarely stay in the background for any length of time for they need progress. They will probably decide they can do the boss's job just as well and possibly better, and they are probably right. More eccentrics are born under Aquarius than any other sign. There isn't much difference between genius and eccentricity – often only the time it takes posterity, or the boss, to make a judgement.

FAMILY MATTERS

AQUARIUS MOTHER In the main it is fair comment to say that you are more concerned with your children's mental and spiritual development rather than the physical. This isn't to say that you would ever neglect them – in this direction they are usually fine. However, you do spend an inordinate amount of time in finding out what they are interested in and if that doesn't include what is happening in the big wide world you will be very quick to enlighten them. However, it may not be a good idea to explain the wickedness of man to a sensitive 3-year-old. It may give the child not only nightmares but also precious little reason to want to grow up in this rather frightening place we call Earth.

You will teach your children how to ask questions and that is good, but you won't teach them when to do so. Tact is not the Aquarian mother's strong point, neither is punctuality, and both faults can easily be handed down to offspring. Nevertheless this lady certainly means well.

AQUARIUS FATHER The Aquarius father is interested in politics and sciences and it may be unfortunate if one of your offspring is an artistic or sentimental character. Instead of a bedtime story, you are most likely to want to talk about the latest space shot or nuclear physics. In short, the Aquarius father treats his children as if they were already grown up. This puts old heads on young shoulders and whilst some people may feel this is a good thing, it is a great pity for any child to miss out on childhood. After all, it is perhaps the only time when they can feel 100% secure and free to daydream and grow in their own time. They really do not need the healthy shoves into reality the Aquarius father is likely to provide. Still at least offspring will not be bored. They will meet all kinds of interesting people since this character will probably bring home more sleep-in guests than a hotel keeper.

AQUARIUS CHILD The Aquarius child may conform to the various stages of development, but this is the only concession he or she will make to convention. They see no reason why Christmas cannot be celebrated in June or why they can't have their birthday parties in December, despite the fact they were born in February. Not surprisingly other children are attracted in droves to such an eccentric character. The Aquarius tendency to experiment continually with life is also appealing to young children. What interests the Aquarian? Anything. There is nothing which, at some time or other, will not come under scrutiny in a bid to uncover the truth.

A good deal of the Aquarian's time is spent doing favours for friends – rescuing a pal from a soaking in a pond, bringing him home to dry off, placing the wet clothes in the cooker. And discovering later on that the garments have been burnt to a crisp.

Aquarius children are quite likely to arrive home with their best overcoat wrapped around a sick shivering bundle which turns out to be a flea-infested stray dog. On such occasions parents will not know whether to laugh or be angry. But you had better make up your mind – and quickly. This situation will occur with alarming regularity.

At play

Fun and relaxation to the Aquarian mean meeting new people – the more unusual they are the better. It also means visiting odd locations where other people would not dream of being caught dead. Visits to the Science Museum appeal: you will collar some unsuspecting official and cross-question them for a couple of hours or so. Anything to do with aviation is another favourite pastime and many Aquarians make model aeroplanes and visit airports. On the sporting front, hang gliding, flying, even parachuting, make your heart beat faster. Club activities also feature prominently in the social round, providing an opportunity for meeting new people.

Expect changes in your friendship circle: once someone has been investigated you get bored rather quickly and look around for a fresh subject to turn the searchlight of truth onto.

Some Aquarians enjoy pottering in the garden and are wonderful at bringing out the best in flowering shrubs, creating year-long colour in the garden with precious little work. Don't ask me how you do it, it is just a touch of magic you have! You also like to visit exotic restaurants: the more unusual the surroundings the better. You may only peck at the food itself, but it is the experience that you are drinking in.

Solitude and mother nature also appeal and pony trekking is a pastime which you may enjoy. It affords you an opportunity to blow away the cobwebs and to get life back into perspective, and at the same time observe the wonderful scenery.

Money

The Aquarian does not value money for itself; however, it does help you to do the impromptu things that pop into your head in those hours of insomnia. You are not the type to save lump sums in a biscuit tin, but you count every now and then. At the same time, you do have the ability to think ahead which means you will have the spending money needed for your first trip in space.

You appreciate the finer things in life and have a level of practicality that people who love you are constantly surprised at. How can someone who is so up in the air be so firmly on the ground when it comes to anything as mundane as cash? There is no doubt about it, you are full of surprises.

In general you are as generous as Father Christmas: when the restaurant bill comes, you grab it as your best friend is travelling towards the bathroom. In fact the only value you find in money is giving it away. You will hand out your next to last pound to someone who has only 50p, and thereby come out with less money than the loser.

Money could never control you. Whatever you decide to do with it, you make sure that you enjoy it, even if that means just getting rid of it.

● PHIL COLLINS BORN 30 JANUARY 1951

ALTHOUGH AN ACTOR, PHIL IS ALSO FAMED AS A ROCK 'N' ROLLER, BUT IN TYPICAL REBELLIOUS AND PERVERSE FASHION, HE DOES NOT WEAR THE UNIFORM OF A ROCK SINGER. HE PREFERS TO PROJECT THE IMAGE OF A BUSINESS MAN AND OF COURSE DRAWS ATTENTION TO HIMSELF AMONGST THE LEATHER-CLAD, LONG-HAIRED BRIGADE.

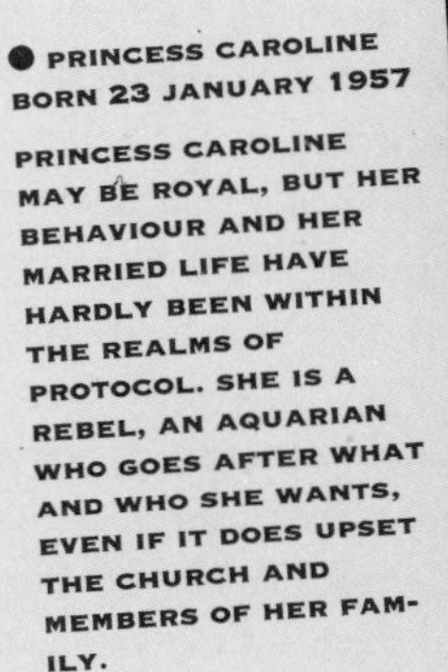

● PRINCESS CAROLINE BORN 23 JANUARY 1957

PRINCESS CAROLINE MAY BE ROYAL, BUT HER BEHAVIOUR AND HER MARRIED LIFE HAVE HARDLY BEEN WITHIN THE REALMS OF PROTOCOL. SHE IS A REBEL, AN AQUARIAN WHO GOES AFTER WHAT AND WHO SHE WANTS, EVEN IF IT DOES UPSET THE CHURCH AND MEMBERS OF HER FAMILY.

● TOM SELLECK BORN 28 JANUARY 1946

TOM SELLECK MAY BE A HEART-THROB BUT HE HARDLY TAKES THE ROLE SERIOUSLY. WHENEVER POSSIBLE, HE TRIES TO BRING HIS QUIRKY SENSE OF HUMOUR TO BEAR ON HIS WORK. LIKE FELLOW AQUARIAN PAUL NEWMAN, HE HAS THE AQUARIAN BLUE EYES, BUT BEHIND HIS LIE A CLOWN AND NOT A FILM IDOL.

in LOVE

Single

You are truly independent, a person who creates a comfortable space and stays at a safe distance. Therefore your attitude towards love is just like you, unconventional.

Soft lights and music don't move you half as much as somebody intelligent to talk to. The more interests they have the better, since you are looking for mental stimulation that arises from a vital and inquisitive mind. Basically you are looking for someone to share your passion for photography, body painting, nuclear physics, or, best of all, you would like someone who also has as many passions to share as you do. Falling in love for you means having a mind so stimulated that the body is sometimes forgotten.

Even in love you are freedom-loving and detached, which may madden and confuse a possessive lover. You probably see your lover as your best friend and might find flowery language and overt romanticism embarrassing. Basically you discover so much drama and excitement in the details of daily life that you don't feel the need to impose weepy movie standards on your love relationship.

Because you are an idealist in your own strange way you are also romantic. However, most people neither see this nor understand. When you do love, you embrace all the person's faults and virtues without illusion and without the compulsion for reform. Your attitude is that the greatest gift you can give a human being is respect for individual freedom. In other words you accept other people and how they are. In fact there is a reluctance to exaggerate personal feeling in any relationship, and because of this you often project your emotions onto unattainable people. You seem to put the object of your affections out of reach, and are capable of harbouring a secret unrequited love for many years. You will marry; however, no one can ever live up to that wonderful 'ideal love' you carry with you all through your life. Sometimes that person is your first love or a parent.

Married

Because you are so action-packed and freedom-loving, marriage is certainly not the be-all and end-all of your existence. Many born under this sign marry late, some not at all. However, those who do, settle into the state of matrimony happily and it usually lasts.

You need absolute freedom to come and go as you please and to have a solitary space set aside for pursuing your own interests. Therefore, possessive or jealous partners who follow you around make you anxiety-ridden and suffocate you.

What you most need out of marriage is solid companionship based on communication. However, you don't want it badly enough to pay the price of heavy restrictions. You are a people person who can never get enough new faces. It doesn't mean you are looking to fall in love with them but the fascination you hold for other people can be downright threatening to any insecure marriage partners.

Although you could probably live your life alone and like it, provided your social calendar were filled, marriage can also provide satisfactions if you find the right person. In a situation based on a sharing of interests, ideals and attitudes, you could find a lot of stimulation, happiness and personal pleasure. Ultimately the freer you feel in marriage, the more faithful you will be. When you are caged, you slowly lose consideration for any marital commitment.

Perfect Partners

When it comes to finding the ideal mate, he or she is usually located amongst the air signs: Aquarius, Gemini and Libra.

Aquarius with Aquarius Mental compatibility could be the reason for this attraction. Friends and their problems will be brought home and shared and each will be constantly involved in one kind of reform or another. A detached façade may lead others to believe there is a lack of warmth, but it may be possible for the partners to drop their images with each other. An Aquarian relationship will grow and develop and both should find this satisfying. She is capable of changing her direction or train of thought just as quickly as he is and life will be a challenge as they will constantly be attempting to keep up with one another. It seems unlikely that sex will play a major role in their partnership for their concerns can easily be charmed away from the bedroom by outside interests. So even if unsuited physically it may either not be discovered at all or not be considered sufficient reason for a serious rift. In general however, a certain chemistry will exist between them and such trouble may not arise.

Aquarius with Gemini The Geminian's versatility and need to communicate could strongly attract the Aquarian: both love to debate and discuss every subject under the Sun. They become totally absorbed in each other's interests, appreciating the fact that this stimulates their minds and fulfils their needs to learn and expand. They will have a lot of fun together, whether this relationship lasts for six weeks or ends in marriage.

The sexual attraction between them is likely to be intense: Geminians will be able to take the Aquarian's cool façade and fill him or her with burning passion, as easily as they are able to supply the mental stimulation. There can be little fear of routine spoiling their sex life. Both can be impulsive and will seldom wait for nightfall.

Aquarius and Libra The Aquarian is strongly attracted to the Libran's energetic search for harmony, charm and apparent aptitude for enjoyment. The Aquarian's independence, active mind and need for other people can lead a Libran to give hot pursuit. Both are determined to remain individuals and stay involved in the world around them and both are extremely sociable. Provided each can hold their own against competition, life will run smoothly enough. Both partners' emotions can be superficial at times and with a more sensitive partner this could cause hurt, but the resilience of these two can cope with this.

Both subjects are born of the air element and their feelings and desires are normally very much on the surface, but combined together a strong passion may be aroused, stimulated mostly by the mind. Sex is likely to be an impromptu affair, very much influenced by the mood of the moment, with versatility, novelty and experiment all playing an important part. A good relationship.

ARE YOU A TYPICAL AQUARIUS...

Answer honestly the questions below, using YES, NO or SOMETIMES; total up your score, allowing 3 for YES, 2 for SOMETIMES and 1 for NO.

...MAN?

1. Do you expect friendship from your lovers?
2. Do you think you could throw up a job if it offered you insufficient scope?
3. Do you really need to believe in the work you do?
4. Can you abstain from sex for more than a week without noticing it?
5. Do you sidestep unpleasantness?
6. Would you get up in the middle of the night to help a friend?
7. Are you a positive thinker?
8. Would you chase a woman who seemed uninterested in the hopes of changing her mind?
9. Are you accused of being detached?
10. Do you make friends with people because of their usefulness?
11. Do you think that to worry about money is a waste of energy?
12. Are you stimulated by good conversation?
13. Can you make love to any woman when desperate?
14. Are you impressed by wealth?
15. Do you insist on the truth at all costs?
16. Are you politically minded?
17. Are you accused of being unimaginative in bed?
18. Do you take part in protests of any description?
19. Do you think you could take a girlfriend back if she had been to bed with a close friend?
20. Are you unpunctual?

...WOMAN?

1. Does the Women's Movement interest you?
2. Can you separate love from sex?
3. Do you prefer good conversation to poor sex even when frustrated?
4. Do you think jealousy is a waste of energy?
5. Are you a truthful person?
6. Does the state of the world concern you?
7. Can you go for long periods without sex?
8. Are you an optimist?
9. Is it hard for you to change your opinion?
10. Can you make love coldly and clinically?
11. Are you an opportunist?
12. Do you find it hard to find a man you really like?
13. Do you feel that your maternal instinct is undeveloped?
14. Is it impossible for you to live a purely domesticated role without going mad?
15. Does blue suit you?
16. Are your thoughts with the future, rather than in the past?
17. Does housework get neglected at the first possible excuse?
18. Are you attracted to a married man's mind rather than his body?
19. Are you a secret snob?
20. Are you a positive thinker?

ARE YOU A TYPICAL AQUARIUS MAN ?

1–30 This score shows that you are not a true Aquarian – you are too emotional and sensitive. You may find yourself under Pisces, Scorpio or Libra, but don't try to make the sign fit, it should be obvious.
31–50 You are a true, 'saintly' Aquarian which means the qualities listed here will apply to you and although you may also have one or two rather more unpleasant traits written about under the 'sinner' Aquarian, in general this section will not apply. Too much cool could be a flaw in your personality, a characteristic which others may describe as coldness.
51–60 This is the score a 'sinner' Aquarian can be expected to reach. You have most of the faults associated with this sign, but fortunately even a bad Aquarian isn't that awful, although you could learn something about your weaknesses by reading the 'sinner' section carefully.

ARE YOU A TYPICAL AQUARIUS WOMAN ?

1–30 You are far too sensitive, home-loving and emotional to be a true Aquarian subject. You are more likely to recognize yourself under Pisces, Scorpio or Taurus. Read those chapters objectively without trying to make them fit: it should be obvious which one you are.
31–50 You are a true reforming 'saintly' Aquarian and have more of the virtues than the vices of this sign. You could, however, be accused of detached and, in some cases, cold behaviour. Read the 'saint' section and try to be a bit more human.
51–60 This score belongs to the 'sinner' Aquarian which means you have more of the vices than the virtues connected with this sign. Do read the 'sinner' section carefully for it may help you to overcome your weaknesses, although no Aquarian can be all bad.

PISCES

20 FEBRUARY – 20 MARCH

SOMETIMES you get the feeling that you are not of this world but then you are not quite sure where you belong. You have difficulty in coping with everyday life and there are occasions when you are not quite sure which is the most real, the substance of your everyday living or the very strong fantasy life created by your imagination.

If *you* are confused, imagine how those closest to you feel trying to understand you. You are certainly a hard person to follow, even on one of your better days. Still at least you are good-hearted, sympathetic, helpful, kind, pleasant to meet and at the same time, inconsistent, emotional, sentimental and contradictory. Watching you flit from one mood to another is like watching a chameleon change colour and being the kind of person you are, it is likely that many will give up on you throughout your life, but those who do occupy an important part of it are rewarded with devotion, dignity and compassion.

It has to be said that there is a lot in you which can be infuriating and perverse, usually caused because you don't understand yourself. Trying to have the best of both worlds simply isn't realistic. You can only live in one world – the other has to live within you. And when you confuse them, you fail to cope with either and begin to lose your grip on reality. Which world? This is the Pisces question.

The Pisces persona is represented by the ancient symbol of your sign: two fishes tied together by a single ribbon, one swimming downstream the other swimming upstream. This symbolism is also representative of your notorious indecision. You are so anxious to see both sides of the question, to do the right thing, that you hesitate at making any move whatsoever and when you do finally make a move you are never sure whether it is the right one.

You have some brilliant and original ideas, as well as some pretty crazy ones. In fact, ideas are what you trade in.

PERSO

FEMALE

Saint

● The inner you has a need to be needed and cared for, if only to compensate for your feelings of vulnerability. You may look tough on the surface; underneath you are the classic romantic. The problem is you keep on waiting for your knight in shining armour, but he is usually that modern version – a playboy.

● It seems to you that everybody else is at the ball when all you do is stand in front of the mirror. If, as time goes by, you find no answers, then you know your life has to be in for some profound changes to make things happen for you.

● Essentially you want to be superwoman but if someone should give you a gold pin, you would be the first person to think it was all a mistake. Your self-image is not only hazy, it is hazardous; and although you are devoted to the act of self-improvement, you are the last one to see where and how you have improved. However, you do have a beguiling personality and a sense of humour that can be seductive. During relaxed moments, you are a dreamy-eyed sensualist.

● You are an intense, vital human being with the captivating charisma of a sex siren and the emotional purity of a virgin love goddess. Despite what many at times feel, you are not at all weak, but deeply feeling and afraid of your own emotions. You have the soul of an artist and your vision is one that could resurrect the conscience of the world.

Sinner

● You are a woman who never tires of high drama: friends become exhausted with the repetition of your problems.

● You keep making the same old mistakes and never seem to learn from them. You like to go off into a corner and lick your wounds, hoping that someone is looking. However, since this is not the most effective attention-getting mechanism, you usually end up sitting by yourself feeling slighted and abandoned. You have a special talent for bringing on those experiences that you need most of all to avoid. That is because you are a slave to your self-destructive tendencies and find a subtle sensationalism in sadness.

● You often fall in love with the wrong people. Your men are usually married, sedentary or ne'er-do-wells, suave playboy types, macho hit men, or men who simply prefer their mothers. This really doesn't matter to you because you can create what you want with your mind and never listen to anyone anyway. The sanity factor is so strong in your personality that sometimes you don't need a man – a mere mind trip will suit you just as well.

NALITY

MALE

Saint

● Because of your lively imagination and sense of humour, you are a delight to spend time with. However, regardless of your crowd of admirers, there is a mysterious side to your personality. At times you play the gregarious *bon vivant* and at others seek serious moments in solitude. You tend to be private and secretive, but, unpredictably, you can also be open and indiscreet.

● At the highest level you have an illuminating intelligence and a personality that is self-sacrificing and self-effacing. Your mind is receptive, thoughtful and meditative. Underneath is that penetrating shyness and extreme sensitivity which prevents you from speaking openly on occasions. When the shyness seeps through, your personality appears diffident and unassuming. You may retreat within yourself – you are the most inaccessible of people at times. However, you are romantic in the deepest sense of the word and can get carried away by nature's springtime music and, of course, scintillating women.

Sinner

● You languish in fantasies and hunger after forbidden delights. You live according to a kind of primitive pleasure principle and will embrace anything which brings you pleasure, no matter what the pain.

● You adore being dominated by strong, sharp-tongued women who sport a streak of cruelty; it helps if they are beautiful. The key to your personality is that you always want what you cannot have, therefore you are often enslaved by the memory of faded love affairs and beautiful faces who have come close enough to get your attention but stay far enough away to hold it. You are a fervent excitement-seeker who is easily bored, highly critical, perpetually discontented and forever searching for the sublime. Because of the duality in your nature, you need two kinds of women: one to alleviate your loneliness, and one to give your life a romantic lustre. Inner conflicts which can arise from such a situation mean that you are the kind of coward who can cut someone so deeply that years later the damage still remains.

● At your lowest point you become a cripple searching for a cocoon. However, all that exists is the self-created bedlam that emotionally beguiles you. Loneliness, alienation and fear force their way into a far-reaching fermentation that starts in the mind and ends up by incapacitating the body. Life continues, and there is no sanctum that is long lasting. In moments of solitude, sorrow submerges the mind and truths are avoided at all costs. Self-pity, then, is very common.

● ELIZABETH TAYLOR BORN 27 FEBRUARY 1932

THE PLANET OF NEPTUNE RULES PISCES AND IT BRINGS MYSTERY, ROMANCE AND SOMETIMES SCANDAL INTO THE LIVES OF THE FISH. LIZ IS A TRUE ROMANTIC AND DESPITE HER DISAPPOINTMENTS SHE REMAINS UNDAUNTED, A FERVENT BELIEVER IN TRUE LOVE. HER MANY FANS LOVE HER FOR IT.

● RICK ASTLEY BORN 26 FEBRUARY 1966

PISCEAN CHANGEABILITY IS STRONG IN THIS POPULAR SINGER. HE BEGAN HIS CAREER CONVENTIONALLY DRESSED, SINGING LOVE SONGS. HE THEN HAD A CHANGE OF IMAGE AND OF SONG, AND IS NOW WORKING BEHIND THE SCENES – PERHAPS WHERE HE REALLY BELONGS, AS MANY FISH PREFER TO KEEP A LOW PROFILE.

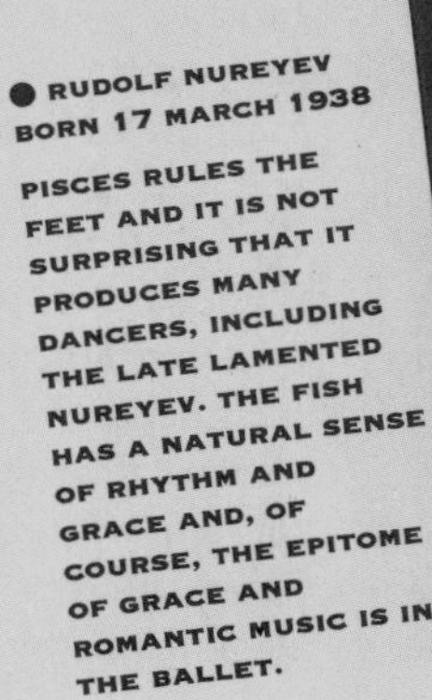

● RUDOLF NUREYEV BORN 17 MARCH 1938

PISCES RULES THE FEET AND IT IS NOT SURPRISING THAT IT PRODUCES MANY DANCERS, INCLUDING THE LATE LAMENTED NUREYEV. THE FISH HAS A NATURAL SENSE OF RHYTHM AND GRACE AND, OF COURSE, THE EPITOME OF GRACE AND ROMANTIC MUSIC IS IN THE BALLET.

PISCES **PISCES** PISCES ♓ PISCES ♓ PISCES

in LIFE

AT WORK

Pisces Boss The Piscean is not really suited to the role of employer but this does not mean that you cannot locate several Pisceans in high positions, rather that they will not be typical of their sign. Whatever the other influences, however, the Piscean is sure to be lurking beneath the surface somewhere.

Usually you will find two clear factions amongst the staff working for this individual – those clearly for and those positively against. Some will describe their Pisces boss as a wonderful human being who is always ready to help them whenever they are overloaded with problems; others will claim that their employer is neurotic, confused and muddle headed. This type, however, can achieve much more by kindliness than the majority of others will by cracking the whip.

Pisces Employee Pisceans need to hero worship. While this may seem childish and stupid to more practical types, it is an important part of their life if they are to progress. They need to identify very strongly; they need a source of inspiration – their own particular god, as it were. Because of this Pisceans should be sure to work for someone they can respect. Generally Pisceans are popular in any company or factory; their gentleness, sympathy and compassion do not appear to threaten the more ambitious types, while others are naturally drawn to such sensitivity. Nevertheless, although Pisceans do not seek recognition, it is often thrust upon them for if they are involved in the artistic field in any connection they are often quite brilliant. While they may not progress through devious moves and ruthlessness, their genius is sure to be recognized eventually. They may wonder whether the work struggle is worth it since all their efforts will disappear in the end, but for the artist this is not necessarily true.

FAMILY MATTERS

PISCES MOTHER The Pisces mother has much going for her. You are usually artistic and sentimental as well as possessing a great love for music, and you generally try to encourage these interests in your offspring. You worry and fret about your children, sometimes unnecessarily so, and they are touched by your devotion. There is literally nothing you will not do for your children, but your one weak point is that you find it extremely difficult to discipline them in any way. To raise your voice brings tears to your eyes and often your children are rather confused until they grow older, when they recognize that big gentle heart and respond to it.

One of the problems with a Pisces mother is that you find it extremely difficult to say no to your children and as a result they can become unruly and inconsiderate. If you can learn to be firm and gentle at the same time, then you are on the way to winning the Mum of the Year award.

However, there can also be problems, for the Pisces mother can, at this stage in her children's lives, be very demanding. Usually she loves her home and is passionately proud of her family, but she does need to be constantly praised and made to feel important and appreciated. In return, she will do anything for her children, and is prepared to spoil and indulge them to great lengths. She can rarely be given enough consideration or affection, and without it she may feel neglected and even betrayed.

PISCES FATHER The Pisces father certainly shines. You are unusually sensitive to the moods, wants and needs of your children and ever anxious to fulfil them, no matter what they may be. Your soft and gentle ways earn your children's undying love, although as teenagers they may just take advantage of this fact. You will teach them to appreciate music and the arts, if they are open minded to this; if not you will not attempt to stamp your own personality on the young for you truly believe in other people being allowed their own individuality. Despite this you will secretly plant ideas in the imagination of your offspring and leave them to mature. At a later date they will come to you with what they imagine to be an original idea and you will smile that secret smile when you recognize that the seed you planted has now reached fruition. Manipulation, yes, but all in a good cause.

PISCES CHILD The Pisces child is shy and nervous when confronted with strangers. Nevertheless, other children are attracted to this type: they sense a natural Pisces gentleness and kindness. Friends are therefore made slowly and invariably for life. Pisceans need to be free to grow and develop and express themselves in their own way and this is often through the arts. They generally love to paint, dance, write poetry or play an instrument, and this is important for both their emotional and mental development. Discover which applies and encourage it, perhaps arranging specialized tuition where necessary.

The Piscean also needs a pet; it may only be a goldfish, but it will be the best kept and most loved fish for miles around. The more love objects in this little person's life the better.

At play

The Fish likes peace and quiet and therefore solitary pursuits such as rambling, hiking and walking generally appeal. Water sports are also popular, as water has a calming effect on you. Deep sea diving and fishing, all provide that exhilaration and solitude that is a prerequisite of Pisceans. When married there is nothing you like better than to entertain but it is only close friends who are invited back to meet your family. Acquaintances are left on hold until you have had a chance to find out what they are really all about. Photography is another pursuit which often appeals, as is birdwatching. You also occasionally enjoy pottering around in the garden and certainly excel at growing water plants; you will love wading among your favourite flower, the water lily. You are also good with primulas and irises.

● LIZA MINNELLI BORN 12 MARCH 1946

SHYNESS IS HARDLY A WORD TO FIT LIZA – OR IS IT? THOSE WHO ARE INSECURE AND NERVOUS MAY OVERCOMPENSATE BY BEING TOTALLY OVER THE TOP. CERTAINLY THE PISCES VERSATILITY IS PRESENT HERE AS IS THE ROMANTIC; FEW CAN PUT OVER A LOVE SONG AS POIGNANTLY AS SHE.

Money

Money slips through your fingers like water and you generally have absolutely no idea where it has gone. This sign especially loves to spend on dreary days in order to boost the ego or the spirits: luxury gives a plethora of pleasure. Champagne can help you through the night, along with silk sheets and, of course, an elegant body to keep you company. You really don't require a country estate with a team of servants! However, what you do crave is comfort and sometimes your version of it can be quite costly. Other signs will be thrilled with the prospect of living in a barn because it has that adventurous out-of-doors feel; you need those final little touches that can easily take you into debt if you don't watch out.

On the other hand, the spiritual side of you can make a home out of a blanket and refer to the sky as a roof. On this level, the only interest you might have in money will be in giving it away. However, it is likely that you have a long way to go before you get that far. Therefore in the meantime when it comes to spending, try to consider your priorities. Unless you can afford to pay for a merry-go-round of pleasure, try to challenge yourself to try and find happiness with a little bit less.

Remember too that when you find yourself in a tight corner financially, often your impulsiveness has put you there – you are so impressionable that you tend to react to situations without thought. A pull at your emotions can set you on a disastrous course before you realize. You are a soft target for phonies and those with a hard-luck story because you accept people at face value. You only need to be told of someone's problems or so-called 'good idea' and you go charging in waving your cheque book. Once that powerful imagination of yours has been aroused it may be good news for some, but bring tears to the eyes of your bank manager.

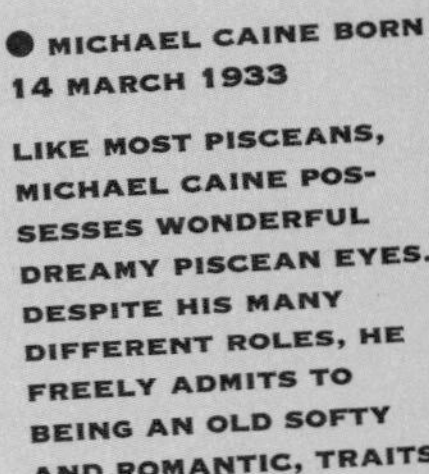

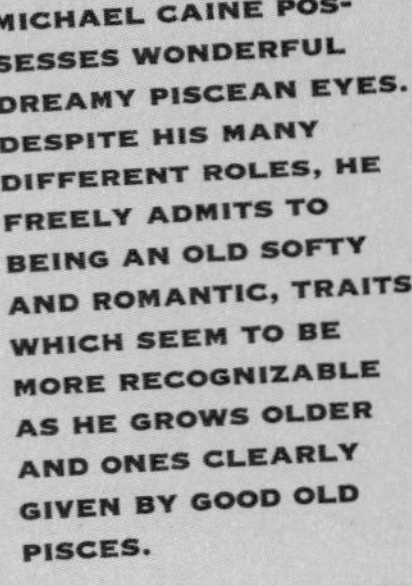

● MICHAEL CAINE BORN 14 MARCH 1933

LIKE MOST PISCEANS, MICHAEL CAINE POSSESSES WONDERFUL DREAMY PISCEAN EYES. DESPITE HIS MANY DIFFERENT ROLES, HE FREELY ADMITS TO BEING AN OLD SOFTY AND ROMANTIC, TRAITS WHICH SEEM TO BE MORE RECOGNIZABLE AS HE GROWS OLDER AND ONES CLEARLY GIVEN BY GOOD OLD PISCES.

● JULIE WALTERS BORN 22 FEBRUARY 1950

JULIE IS STRONGLY ATTRACTED TO THE WEIRD AND THE COMIC, DESPITE HER ABILITY TO COME OVER AS A SERIOUS ACTRESS WHEN THE RIGHT PISCEAN MOOD DESCENDS. THE VERSATILITY OF THIS SIGN IS OBVIOUS IN HER AND IT IS UNLIKELY THAT SHE WILL EVER ALLOW HERSELF TO BE PIGEON-HOLED.

in LOVE

SINGLE

Although you often loathe your sensitivity, you are a wild romantic, longing for emotional intensity. You experience a desire to be swept away by nothing less than a grand passion. However, in such situations you often let your emotions get the better of you. You are an emotionally detached lover living in a dream of how exquisite life could be if only – needless to say you are an idealist who is both devoted and dreamy-eyed to the act of loving. The problem is that too often you become enslaved by negative situations and hang on to the past like a drowning swimmer. When you really want someone you will sit back and wait, feeling that time will be able to change people and conditions that you can't.

When your romantic life is really bad, you feel lonely, unloved and alienated. The next step is to escape through drink, drugs, sleep, food, promiscuity or workaholism.

On your bad days you want to be alone. One of your favourite retreats is to crawl underneath the covers and curl into a ball, feeling sorry for yourself and withdrawing from the world, wishing it would go away. However, when the time comes when you feel like a bitter, jaded, loveless victim, remember that it was you who made all the choices.

The Pisces man is often an aloof lover. He possesses an indefinable detachment and may appear passionate enough, but some women feel he is holding back. This is because he is searching for the perfect mate, but the chances of finding perfection are slim. Generally he has many affairs, for his physical and emotional aloofness presents something of a challenge. Pisces love is often universal, not purely physical or individual.

MARRIED

Because you have a roving eye and a sharp tongue, marriage is not always your best bet.

You think in terms of beginnings instead of endings, and so you are loath to contemplate the termination of an affair. You prefer that all your lovers remain friends for ever. A civilized amount of distance, combined with a number of friendly visits, would suit you nicely and leave you enough room to roam. However, at one time or another you usually sell out on your visions of romantic spender for marital security and here is where the fun either ends or begins, depending on the direction you want to go in. Married life could be ideally lived in a Zulu colony where polygamy is not considered a perversity. Monogamy can be a problem, especially if you choose a mate who might murder you in a moment of sweet revenge. You often choose the very individual route of infidelity, especially when you see someone attractive to make your eyes bulge, or you get so drunk that everyone starts looking good.

Deep inside you are searching for a drug-like attraction that makes you feel like you are once again 17 and heartbroken. By about the 50th time around, it is surprising how that pain starts to feel familiar and kind of cosy. There is a kind of poetry in motion of which marriages never seem to be made.

On the other hand, marriage has the security of knowing that somebody close loves you even if your cheekbones start to sink and you develop five double chins. Some Pisceans remain faithful once they have made a commitment and it is true to say that it is the Pisces man who is more prone to wandering around in search of sensational thrills.

PERFECT PARTNERS

When tracking down the perfect partner, he or she can often be found among the signs of the same element, in this case water – namely Cancer, Scorpio and Pisces.

Pisces with Pisces These two should be able to appreciate the sensitivity of the other, but although this may seem to make for harmony it could be that they will know exactly how to hurt each other with a word or a glance. Mentally, emotionally and physically they could appear so attuned as to make separation impossible. These mutual characteristics can, on occasions, lead to conflict for at times each will be trying too hard to please the other, and at others the incommunicative side of their natures will clash and silence will descend. However, it is likely that the good will outweigh the bad.

Although both parties here are free to follow their own careers, it can happen that each becomes so totally involved that they forget the needs of their partner.

The sexual chemistry between these two will be extremely strong and their determination to keep romance alive, together with their active imaginations, could result in a great physical side. Because of this the whole relationship may well be based on sex which will consequently help to overcome other problems on those dreary days. This can be a perfect relationship – all it needs is a little bit of determination.

Pisces with Cancer Depth of feeling, sensitivity and understanding of romance are common to both these characters and could provide a good basis on which to build a close relationship. Both need a happy domestic life and much time will go into improving the home's appearance and making it more comfortable. Fantasy may bring them closer together for they will be able to share in each other's hopes and dreams. Each is so concerned about the other's comfort and wellbeing that they could well place rather too much emphasis on small matters, but with all the other things going for the two of them, this won't be a major problem.

Their sex life should be filled with tender-loving and gentle emotion and romance is likely to be a stimulating force rather than a more brutal passion. This couple's chances of success are really great.

Pisces with Scorpio Although Scorpio can be a difficult person to be with, this sign is at its best when combined with the Piscean. The Fish is able to make Scorpions feel supported, boosts their morale and helps them to unburden themselves and be a little bit more open. Regardless of which sign 'she' is, she will be so happy with this relationship that her need for a career is minimized. She is going to be far too busy looking after her mate and will be totally fulfilled in doing so.

Their sex life should be a constant expression of deep emotion: all kinds of feelings and sensations will be experienced and shared. Passion, tenderness and even lust are given full rein and their sexual relations will be totally uninhibited. It is probably impossible for anyone or anything to come between them.

ARE YOU A TYPICAL PISCES...

Answer honestly the questions below, using YES, NO or SOMETIMES; total up your score, allowing 3 for YES, 2 for SOMETIMES and 1 for NO.

...MAN?

1. Do you enjoy a pint?
2. Are you secretive?
3. Can you suffer from short but deep depression?
4. Does pornography turn you on?
5. Can you be cowardly when faced with unpleasantness?
6. Is your appetite for food small?
7. Are you unlucky?
8. Does it stimulate you to think that your woman may be thinking of someone else while you are making love to her?
9. Are you a romantic?
10. Are you torn in two directions when needing to make a decision?
11. Do you enjoy the company of your own sex?
12. Can you be violent when under stress?
13. Do you have hypochondriacal traits?
14. Are you fond of animals?
15. Do you prefer to sort out your problems on your own?
16. Do you suffer from bouts of cynicism?
17. Do you believe that marriage is here to stay?
18. Do you think we should all be limited to having two children?
19. Do you enjoy sex when your lover takes the lead?
20. Do you over-indulge in any form of escapism?

...WOMAN?

1. Are your eyes expressive?
2. Are you a feminine romantic and proud of it?
3. Do men always want to protect you?
4. Are you secretive?
5. Do you retire into your own world to sort out your problems?
6. Are sex and love inseparable to you?
7. Would it upset you if you were incapable of having children?
8. Are you shocked at your thoughts while making love?
9. Do mysteries intrigue you?
10. Do you over-indulge in alcohol?
11. Are you a nervous chatterer?
12. Can you be violent when annoyed or under stress?
13. Does the idea of having a cottage in the country appeal to you?
14. Do you like the feel of fur on your body?
15. Are you jealous?
16. Do you loathe masculine women?
17. Are you easily persuaded into sexual activity that doesn't really appeal?
18. Do you change your mind at least half a dozen times before making a firm decision?
19. Do you need a man before you can function properly emotionally?
20. Is depression a part of your personality?

ARE YOU A TYPICAL PISCES MAN ?

1–30 Your logical, practical and down-to-earth qualities do not belong to a Piscean. You may find yourself under one of the three earth signs, Virgo, Taurus or Capricorn. Read those chapters without attempting to make them fit, for it should be easy to recognize yourself.

31–50 You have answered your questions as a true Piscean would. Fortunately you belong to the 'saintly' side of your sign and are therefore not quite so neurotic as the 'sinner' type would be. Although you can still be too sensitive at times, and need a partner or lover, you can understand this side of your character.

51–60 This score belongs to the 'sinner' side of your sign. Read that section and try to improve on your faults. Your vivid imagination could lead to many kinds of sexual perversion and your hypersensitivity to suffering.

ARE YOU A TYPICAL PISCES WOMAN ?

1–30 You possess too much commonsense, logic and realism to be a true Piscean. Your characteristics would seem to belong to one of the earth signs, Taurus, Virgo or Capricorn. Read those chapters without attempting to make them fit you for you should recognize yourself easily.

31–50 Your score would suggest a typical 'saintly' Piscean which means you have most of the virtues, but not necessarily many of the vices, associated with this sign. You could, however, be too easily influenced by others which could cause you many problems.

51–60 This is the score of the 'sinner' Piscean which makes you very sensitive and possibly a weak individual. Read the section which applies to you and try to overcome the faults written there – you are adaptable and could do this if you desired.

Published by Longmeadow Press,
201 High Ridge Road, Stamford, CT 06904.

Cover design by Cooper Wilson Design
Interior design by Peter Dolton
ISBN: 0-681-00688-9
Printed in Slovak Republic
First Longmeadow Press Edition
0 9 8 7 6 5 4 3 2 1